An Introductory Reader
in the Philosophy of Religion

An Introductory Reader
in the Philosophy of Religion

EDITED BY
James Churchill and David V. Jones

LONDON
SPCK

First published 1979
SPCK
Holy Trinity Church
Marylebone Road
London NW1 4DU

Editorial sections and selection © James Churchill and David V. Jones 1979

For copyright reasons, this edition
is not for sale in the U.S.A.

Printed and bound in Great Britain at
The Camelot Press Ltd, Southampton

ISBN 0 281 03603 9

*To the guinea-pigs
Andrew, Chris, Robert
and Nigel*

Contents

Numbers in brackets indicate sources: see Bibliography, pp. 229–30.

Preface	xi
Acknowledgements	xiii

1 RELIGIOUS LANGUAGE

Introduction	1
JOHN M. HULL, Nonsense: Meaning: God (16)	3
A. FLEW, Theology and Falsification (11)	8
J. H. HICK, The Doctrine of Analogy (Aquinas) (15)	9
G. F. WOODS, The Idea of the Transcendent (32)	11
J. H. HICK, Religious Statements as Symbolic (Tillich) (15)	13
PETER DONOVAN, Ian Ramsey on Religious Language (8)	15
JOHN M. HULL, Some More Replies (16)	19
JOHN M. HULL, The Uses of Language (16)	23
R. B. BRAITHWAITE, An Empiricist's View of the Nature of Religious Belief (25)	25
PETER DONOVAN, The Bible as Authoritative Religious Language (8)	28
PETER DONOVAN, Getting at the Truth in Religion (8)	31
PETER DONOVAN, On Not Having the Last Word (8)	32
BASIL MITCHELL, The Stranger (11)	33
J. H. HICK, The Road (15)	34
Study Topics	35
Bibliography	36
Further Reading	36

2 REVELATION

Introduction	38
ORIGEN, *from* De Principiis (18)	39
ST CYRIL OF JERUSALEM, *from* Catechetical Lectures (18)	40
COLIN BROWN, Natural Theology (5)	40
D. M. BAILLIE, The Good News (1)	44

D. M. BAILLIE, The Mighty Acts of God—Event and
  Interpretation (1)   45
KARL BARTH, The Christian Understanding of Revelation (4)   47
WILLIAM JAMES, Mysticism (17)   54
A. FLEW, Religious Experience (10)   55
COLIN BROWN, Revelation and History (5)   63
J. H. HICK, The Propositional View of Revelation and Faith (15)   67
J. H. HICK, A 'Non-Propositional' View of Revelation and
  Faith (15)   69
J. H. HICK, A Corresponding View of the Bible and Theological
  Thinking (15)   71
JOHN MACQUARRIE, A General Description of Revelation (23)   73
JOHN MACQUARRIE, Revelation and the Modes of Thinking
  and Knowing (23)   76
JOHN MACQUARRIE, A Further Scrutiny of Revelation (23)   80
Study Topics   82
Bibliography   82
Further Reading   82

3 THE PROBLEM OF EVIL

Introduction   84
DAVID HUME, *from* Dialogues Concerning Natural Religion (33)   85
BERTRAND RUSSELL, Has Religion Made Useful Contributions
  to Civilisation? (28)   86
H. D. LEWIS, *from* Teach Yourself the Philosophy of Religion (21)   86
J. H. HICK, Grounds for Disbelief in God (15)   87
A. FLEW, Theology and Falsification: from the University
  Discussion (11)   90
H. K. SCHILLING, *from* The New Consciousness in Science and
  Religion (29)   91
NINIAN SMART, F. R. Tennant and the Problem of Evil (30)   93
J. L. MACKIE, Evil and Omnipotence (22)   95
J. H. HICK, *from* Evil and the God of Love (14)   95
JOHN MACQUARRIE, *from* Principles of Christian
  Theology (23)   97
BRIAN HEBBLETHWAITE, Coping with Evil and Explaining
  Evil (13)   99
BRIAN HEBBLETHWAITE, Heaven and Hell (13)   100
Study Topics   102
Bibliography   102
Further Reading   102

Contents

4 MIRACLES
Introduction	104
PATRICK NOWELL-SMITH, Miracles (11)	106
DAVID HUME, *from* An Enquiry Concerning Human Understanding (33)	109
NINIAN SMART, *from* Philosophers and Religious Truth (30)	112
THOMAS McPHERSON, *from* Philosophy and Religious Belief (24)	121
H. D. LEWIS, Some Outstanding Problems (21)	125
H. H. FARMER, The World and God (9)	128
JOHN MACQUARRIE, Miracles (23)	131
C. S. LEWIS, Miracles (20)	135
E. and M-L. KELLER, Miracles in Reality (19)	136
Study Topics	137
Bibliography	138
Further Reading	138

5 SCIENTIFIC PRESUPPOSITIONS
Introduction	140
C. A. COULSON, Scientific Method (6)	141
IAN G. BARBOUR, *from* Issues in Science and Religion (2)	146
A. R. PEACOCKE, Truth for the Scientist (Broadcast talk)	148
A. R. PEACOCKE, *from* Science and the Christian Experiment (27)	149
Study Topics	152
Bibliography	152
Further Reading	153

6 THE QUESTION OF ORIGINS
Introduction	154
J. HABGOOD, Nothing but Apes (12)	156
L. GILKEY, What the Idea of Creation is About (3)	163
IAN G. BARBOUR, Theological Issues in Evolution (2)	169
Study Topics	178
Bibliography	178
Further Reading	178

7 MODERN BIOLOGY AND THEOLOGY
Introduction	180
G. R. TAYLOR, Where are the Biologists taking us? (31)	181

Contents

    G. R. TAYLOR, The Biological Break-through (31)   183
    G. R. TAYLOR, Who am I? (31)   186
    G. R. TAYLOR, Life and Death (31)   189
    IAN G. BARBOUR, Conclusions: On Man and Nature (2)   192
    T. DOBZHANSKY, Self-Awareness and Death-Awareness (7)   198
    HUGH MONTEFIORE, Medical Engineering (26)   201
    Study Topics   205
    Bibliography   206
    Further Reading   206

8   MODERN PHYSICS AND THEOLOGY
    Introduction   207
    IAN G. BARBOUR, Three Ways of Isolating Science and Religion (3)   209
    H. K. SCHILLING, Directionality of Total Process (29)   215
    H. K. SCHILLING, Time's Relational Character (29)   216
    H. K. SCHILLING, The Physical Content of Time (29)   218
    H. K. SCHILLING, Awareness of the 'Nature' of Physical Reality (29)   219
    H. K. SCHILLING, Nature as a Source of Insight for Faith (29)   222
    IAN G. BARBOUR, The Heisenberg Principle and the Wave-Particle Dualism (2)   224
    IAN G. BARBOUR, The Principle of Complementarity (2)   224
    IAN G. BARBOUR, Conclusions: On Implications of Physics (2)   225
    Study Topics   227
    Bibliography   227
    Further Reading   228

Bibliography of Sources   229

Index of Authors   231

Preface

The idea of compiling this book arose from our experiences of trying to teach the new Joint Matriculation Board A Level, Philosophy of Religion course. Many of the recommended books were too advanced (and too expensive) for our students. What was required was a book which brought together in concise form a variety of opinions on certain specific topics. It was also felt that such a book could be usefully employed in College of Education courses. The end product, after much pruning, is an attempt to ease the beginner in gently by greatly simplifying the issues and breaking the whole area of philosophy of religion up into reasonably manageable pieces.

Each chapter of the book is complete in itself and can be read in isolation from the others although, of course, there are cross-references to other chapters where areas of study overlap. The introduction to each chapter sketches out the problems and indicates what answers have been suggested. The selections which follow are not exhaustive but attempt to convey the general argument of the author. At the end of each chapter is a bibliography which gives a representative selection of books at the time of going to press. The study topics are some of the issues which the material in the preceding chapter has thrown up which may be of use in a study group.

The book is a tool and is intended to be only an introduction to the areas studied. The reader must go beyond this volume to fill out the bare outline contained in each chapter. Philosophers and theologians are notoriously long-winded, and in trying to condense their arguments some unevenness of style inevitably occurs in spite of our efforts to keep this to a minimum. We have tried to do justice to the authors whose deliberations we have so drastically reduced, but the limitations of space and money leave no room for fuller treatment. However, *pace* our victims, we hope that one result of reading this book will be to stimulate the reader to go back to the original 'unabridged' sources and so be able to judge the arguments for himself.

Preface

It is in the nature of a Reader, especially an introductory Reader, that it is felt to be incomplete and unsatisfactory. We acknowledge the limitations of this book but we feel that there is a need for it. We can only say that if, after having read this book, the student goes on to gain fuller understanding through further reading, then it will have performed the task for which it was written.

Acknowledgements

In addition to all the authors whose works we have so shamelessly plundered, we would like to express our thanks to Mr David Craig and Miss Lesley Riddle of SPCK, without whose encouragement and assistance the manuscript would never have been produced. We are also indebted to the pupils of Hutton Grammar School, and to the Headmaster, Mr J. Nelson, whose interest in, and support for, Religious Education at A Level was responsible for the origin of the whole undertaking. In addition there are many people who assisted and encouraged us along the way, too numerous to mention here, but to whom our thanks are also due.

Finally, we are deeply indebted to Miss Diana Churchill and Mrs Margaret Jones, who helped to type the vast amount of material from which our final selections were made, and Mrs M. E. Wood for her invaluable assistance in the final stages of the preparation of the manuscript.

WJCC
DVJ

Thanks are due to the following for permission to quote from copyright sources:

George Allen & Unwin Ltd: *Why I am not a Christian* by Bertrand Russell

Basil Blackwell & Mott Ltd: 'Evil and Omnipotence' by J. L. Mackie, in *Mind*, April 1955

Cambridge University Press: *An Empiricist's View of the Nature of Religious Belief* by R. B. Braithwaite (by permission also of the author), and 'The Idea of the Transcendent', from *Soundings*, edited by A. R. Vidler

William Collins Sons & Co. Ltd: *Miracles* by C. S. Lewis, and *Can Man Survive?* by Hugh Montefiore

Columbia University Press: *The Idea of Revelation in Recent Thought* by D. M. Baillie

Doubleday & Co. Inc.: Selection from *Maker of Heaven and Earth* by Langdon Gilkey. Copyright © 1959 by Langdon Gilkey. Reprinted by permission of the publishers.

Acknowledgements

Hodder & Stoughton Ltd: *Religion and Science* by J. Habgood, and *Teach Yourself the Philosophy of Religion* by H. D. Lewis

Hutchinson Publishing Group Ltd: *God and Philosophy* by A. G. N. Flew, and *Philosophy and Religious Belief* by Thomas McPherson

Inter-Varsity Press: *Philosophy and the Christian Faith* by Colin Brown

The Liturgical Press: *The Faith of the Early Fathers* by W. A. Jurgens, published by the Liturgical Press, copyrighted by the Order of St Benedict, Inc., Collegeville, Minnesota

Macmillan, London and Basingstoke: *Evil and the God of Love* by John H. Hick

James Nisbet & Co. Ltd: *The World and God* by H. H. Farmer

Oxford University Press: *Science and Christian Belief* by C. A. Coulson, and *Science and the Christian Experiment* by A. R. Peacocke

A. R. Peacocke: 'Truth for the Scientist' by A. R. Peacocke, a BBC broadcast talk in the series Religion in its contemporary context, 1971

Prentice-Hall Inc.: *Philosophy of Religion* by John H. Hick, 2nd edn © 1973

Rapp & Whiting Ltd: *The Biology of Ultimate Concern* by T. Dobzhansky. Copyright © 1967 by Theodosius Dobzhansky. (By arrangement also with the New American Library, Inc., New York, N.Y.)

Sheldon Press: *Religious Language* by Peter Donovan and *Evil, Suffering and Religion* by Brian Hebblethwaite

SCM Press Ltd: *Issues in Science and Religion* By Ian G. Barbour, © 1966 (reprinted by permission also of Prentice-Hall, Inc.); *Science and Religion*, edited by Ian G. Barbour (by permission also of Harper & Row, Inc.); *Against the Stream* by Karl Barth; *New Essays in Philosophical Theology*, edited by A. G. N. Flew and A. MacIntyre; *Sense and Nonsense about God* by John M. Hull; *Miracles in Dispute* by E. and M.-L. Keller; *Principles of Christian Theology* by John Macquarrie (with the permission also of Charles Scribner's Sons, copyright © 1966, 1977 John Macquarrie); *The New Consciousness in Science and Religion* by Harold K. Schilling (published in New York by the Pilgrim Press, 1973, copyright © 1973 United Church Press. Used by permission also of the United Church Press); *Philosophers and Religious Truth* by Ninian Smart

Thames & Hudson Ltd: *The Biological Time-Bomb* by G. Rattray Taylor

1
Religious Language

INTRODUCTION

Any cursory look at religious language (RL) reveals that words used in RL are being used in an unusual and special way. Clearly language is being stretched beyond its normal everyday use when Christians talk of God as 'Three in one and one in three'. To talk of God as 'Father' to a child might prompt questions like 'who are his children?' or 'what does he look like?' or 'who is his wife?' The answers to these questions would soon lead the child to conclude that God was not a father like other human fathers and that his family was no ordinary human family. It would not be an unreasonable question to ask, 'What does "father" mean when it is applied to God?'

This confusion, or lack of precision, is the characteristic problem of RL. As long ago as the thirteenth century St Thomas Aquinas was aware of the peculiar nature of RL and he tried to solve the problem by explaining RL in terms of analogy. Analogy is the attempt to explain the nature of some unknown thing in terms of something familiar (e.g. trying to explain to an American the function of the Prime Minister as 'a sort of President'.) Recently RL has been criticized by a group of linguistic philosophers (known as logical positivists) who held that RL was, in a strict sense, meaningless. The first extract from John Hull's *Sense and Nonsense* sets out in simple terms the arguments of the linguistic philosophers. The corollary to logical positivism is empiricism, and Antony Flew puts the empiricist's viewpoint forcibly.

There are basically two reactions to the criticisms of the logical positivists. The first is to accept their assessment of RL as being basically meaningless but yet to maintain that RL can have a useful function in spite of that. Some theologians tried to carry on a discourse in which terms like 'God', 'soul', 'heaven' had no place (on this see especially the 'God is Dead' school of thought), whilst others saw RL as moral language. The chief exponent of this last type is R. B. Braithwaite, who sees RL as a way of expressing an intention to live and act in a particular way. P. Tillich tried to maintain that RL was essentially symbolic, but unfortunately some of his ideas were not fully worked out and it is sometimes difficult (especially in the original) to be quite clear what he is saying.

The second reaction to the criticisms of the logical positivists is an attempt to refute their arguments by showing that their own analysis of language is incomplete and by demonstrating that RL can be meaningful. Ian T. Ramsey tried to show that RL is meaningful by claiming that it is empirical language used in a particular way. This idea of RL using 'models and qualifiers' is a kind of modern analogical theory of RL. Donovan gives an interpretative role for RL and directs our attention not only to RL as such but also to the experiences which produce religious statements and commitment.

Finally there are two short parables, by Hick and Mitchell. These are stories indicating how our attitudes to the same human experiences can be diametrically opposed. The world of experience is ambiguous, and our attempts to 'make sense of it all' lead us to varying conclusions. J. Wisdom's parable of 'The Garden' (referred to in the extract by A. Flew) is told in such a way that the differences between the believer and the sceptic are thrown into sharp relief. The thrust of the story seems to show the believer as an obstinate man whilst the sceptic deals only with the facts. In contrast, in these two parables of 'the Stranger' and 'the Road' the characters are different in that they are both committed to something (or someone). This commitment influences their interpretation of subsequent events, and the evidence appears to be much more evenly balanced than in 'the Garden'. Wisdom is not a Christian, whilst Hick and Mitchell are, which accounts for the different emphasis in the stories. Yet it is important to remember that in all three stories there is no argument over the basic evidence (i.e. human experience), only over the validity of the interpretation of that evidence. Both Hick and Mitchell point to some future time at which all ambiguity will be swept away – a reflection of their Christian hope – whilst Wisdom does not concern himself with such things, which is indicative of the gap between them.

Religious Language

John M. Hull, *Sense and Nonsense about God,* pp. 1ff

PART ONE   *Nonsense*

1.1   The curtain goes up, the orchestra plays, and on come the Diddy People. They open their diddy mouths and out comes their diddy song, 'Nick nocky nick nack nicky nocky noo.' People laugh and clap. But nobody turns to his neighbour and says 'Do you agree?' or 'I'm not going to clap that, it just is not true!'

1.2   The diddy song cannot be true or false because it does not say anything capable of truth or falsehood. It makes no assertion. So here we have the first way to recognize nonsense.

Nonsense is incapable of being true or false because it does not say anything which could be true or false.

1.3   Nonsense need not take the form of nonsensical words like 'nocky'. Normal words, the meaning of which everyone knows, may be arranged in ungrammatical form so as to produce nonsense, e.g. 'sat cat on the the . . .'. Nonsensical statements are incapable of contradiction. They cannot conflict with anything since they assert nothing.

1.4   Can normal English words be used in a grammatically correct way and still produce nonsense? Suppose I ask you, 'Don't you think this coffee tastes too red?', you could answer neither yes nor no. You could only ask me what on earth I meant. You would seek clarification, because although the words of my question were arranged in a normal manner with the verbs and adjectives and nouns in the normal places (unlike the cat example), I would be using one of these words in a very unusual way. I was asking for a judgement about the flavour of the coffee in terms of a word which could only refer to the colour. Ordinary words used in the wrong sense or in the wrong context may produce nonsense.

. . . . . .

SUMMING UP

We have found three kinds of nonsense.

1. Nonsense which depends upon the use of words which have no recognizable meaning. Nicky nocky (paragraphs 1.1 and 1.2).

2. Nonsense which depends upon words which have a recognizable meaning but are used in ungrammatical contexts. Lamb Mary had little a (paragraph 1.3).

3. Nonsense which uses words with recognizable meanings in grammatically correct contexts, but in such a manner that the normal meaning of the word seems not to apply. 'Does gravity run faster than virtue?' Sometimes the meanings of the words will actually conflict. 'Draw me a straight curved line' (paragraph 1.4).

In every case, the test is not, 'Does it sound funny?' (it might contain unfamiliar vocabulary, or be in Japanese) but 'Is it capable of being true or false?' If it is not even capable of falsehood, it cannot be a wrong statement, but mere nonsense.

. . . . . .

PART TWO *Meaning*

2.1 Nonsense is the absence of meaning. Let us now look at the positive side of the problem. Where do we find meaning? Individual words, in strict isolation, have little or no meaning. Even a very concrete noun, such as 'dog' has little meaning out of context and in isolation. If I came up to you in the street and muttered in your ear 'Dog' you would wonder what I meant. Was I trying to say 'Look out for the dog' or 'There is a dog' or what? You would assume there was some kind of link in my mind between the sound I had uttered and the particular class of creatures called dogs, so what I had said would give you some information about my mind at that moment. But this would be *psychological* information about me; what I had said could not take on *logical* significance (as distinct from psychological) until I used the word to assert something . . . e.g. 'There is a dog'; 'I want you to look'.

2.2 *Meanings depend upon assertions*. Meaning is usually located not so much in isolated words as in sentences telling how the words are being used. If this is true of nouns like dog, man and planet, it is even more true of words like but, or and however; for such words derive all their significance from the sentence they are in. The same applies to abstract words such as home, relationship and contradictory.

2.3 We have already seen . . . that not all apparent assertions are meaningful. Is there a further test by which we may know that 'He is a teenage werewolf?' is a meaningful assertion but 'He is a ruppilty-bloop' is not? For both sentences have the grammatical form of assertions. But in the case of the former assertion, one can think of a variety of tests which could be carried out on the unfortunate subject. One could look at his birth certificate to see if he is indeed of teenage. One could call in medical and zoological experts to determine any

Religious Language

lupine characteristics. But how could one carry out tests for the ruppilty-bloop assertion? Not knowing what could characterize such a creature, there would be no way of telling what could count for the assertion and what would count against it. It would, therefore, be revealed as a meaningless assertion. This brings us to a most important principle – *The meaning of any statement is determined by the steps by which one could verify it.* This is sometimes called 'the Verification Principle'. Statements which can be verified, in fact or in theory, are meaningful. Statements which cannot be verified, because you would not even know what to look for, are meaningless.

2.4 It is sufficient to guarantee the meaning of a statement if the steps by which it could be verified are determinable in principle, even although it may be impossible to carry them out in practice. For example, the statement 'There is life on Mars' cannot be verified in practice at the time of writing but it is easy to think of many ways in which it could be verified. The problem is technical, not logical.

2.5 Note that the statement 'The moon is made of cheese' is not nonsense in the logical sense in which we are using the word. For although you might reply 'That's nonsense!' if someone asserted that the moon was cheese, you would mean that the evidence against the proposition is so overwhelmingly strong that only a fool could continue to hold it. And yet, the very fact that it is possible to accumulate evidence against the proposition shows that it is not logically nonsense. . . . So it may be silly, or against common sense, to say the earth is flat, but it is not logical nonsense. We know what would count for or against it.

2.6 Let us suppose someone says to you 'There is an elephant under the desk.' However unlikely this may seem, we can think of various factors which would count for and against it, and it is not, therefore, nonsensical. You might say 'An elephant wouldn't fit under the desk' and the answer might be that it was a special type of little elephant. But suppose you then stooped down and had a look and you were then told 'Oh, you won't see it. The breeding process which produces these tiny elephants also makes them invisible.' You might gingerly stretch out your hand and feel nothing and if your friend then said 'And I don't think you will feel him – these elephants have the quality of yielding like air to any attempt to touch them,' In exasperation you would enquire by what steps the existence of the elephant could be decided one way or the other. If your friend replied that it could not be proved, there was nothing which could count one way or the other, even in principle, but that it was a matter of faith, you would be quite correct if you then dismissed his claim as mere nonsense. For if the meaning of a statement is to be found in the steps by which it might be verified and if the statement about the elephant will allow no such steps to be even imaginable, the statement has no meaning. One might just as well say that there was a ruppilty-bloop under the desk or that there was a ruppilty-bloop mider the bigrust.

. . . . . .

PART THREE   *God*

3.1   Bearing in mind what has been said about the verification principle, let us consider what kinds of proposition can be tested or verified. The first type of proposition consists of statements about simple matters of particular fact, i.e. empirical statements (which means ones which can be tested by reference to the experience of the senses). If it is claimed that rain is falling, I test the meaning (as well as the truth) of this by sticking my head outside. . . .

3.2   The second kind of testable sentence is one dealing with statements of general fact such as scientific theories. These may often be highly abstract and may not be testable by direct sense experience. This would be the case if a theory postulated some new sub-atomic particle which could not itself be seen, touched, heard etc. However, no matter how abstract and general it may be, the scientist will be able to state some conditions which support his proposition and will name others which if they occurred would count against his theory. . .

3.3   The third kind of statement consists of the statements of basic principles of maths and logic which are true by definition and may be tested simply by looking up in a dictionary to see what the words mean. This kind of statement is called *analytic* because it consists of an analysis or redefinition of a word. Sentences such as 'All bachelors are unmarried males' or 'The sum of 2 + 2 is 4' tell us something about the way we use such words as 'bachelor' and 'four'. You will notice that these statements do not tell us anything new about states of affairs. They convey no actual information. They only tell us what words mean. . . .

3.4   Analytic propositions have another interesting feature. Just as they tell us nothing about the actual world of experience, so they cannot be refuted by anything which might occur in the world of experience. If I came to you and said, 'What do you think, I've just been talking to Mr Jones, who turns out to be married and yet is certainly a single male. He must be an exception to the rule', you would understand that I did not know the correct use of the words 'married' and 'single'. These terms are mutually exclusive, so that the expression 'a married single man' is nonsense, like 'a round square'. No, the truth that bachelors are single males is not derived from examination of actual single males but from a definition. It is impossible therefore that any actual fact can count against an analytic statement. They are immune from danger of falsification. But they win their immunity at the high price of saying nothing about anything apart from themselves.

3.5 Into which of these three classes does the proposition 'God exists' fall? If we say it is an analytic statement, that is, God exists by definition, then we are merely saying something about the way we use the word 'God'. We might in the same way say 'God is love' is true by definition, since (we might argue) the word God means the same as the word love. But we must remember that analytic statements do not tell us about the world beyond themselves and yet when a religious person says he believes that there is a God, or that God is love, he surely intends to be saying something about his view of reality. He thinks he is talking about a state of affairs outside himself, and not merely acting as a sort of religious word book.

3.6 If such propositions are not analytic, then they must fall into the other classes discussed in paras 3.1 and 3.2. These are called *synthetic* statements because they synthesize or put together two or more different aspects of reality so as to yield new information, e.g. the apple is ripe. The relationship between the two terms is not a necessary one, as it is with analytic statements, but an observed one. And we have seen that although synthetic statements have the obvious advantage of telling us something meaningful about the world, they have to face the risk of being wrong. The apple may not, after all, be ripe. Now if the believer claims that his statements about God are synthetic statements, he falls into a number of difficulties.

3.7 The first one is that religious believers usually claim to know with absolute certainty.... But the only kind of statement about which absolute certainty is possible is the analytic statement which the believer denies he is making. All synthetic statements, because they are in principle open to falsification, must fall below the level of absolute certainty. . . . Could the believer claim that belief in God was a kind of intuition or a self evident truth? Some truths are so highly probable that we rarely if ever doubt them – the sun rises each day – but will the believer be satisfied by a probability, however high? Perhaps the believer could reply that what he claims is not certainty but certitude. The difference is that the former is objective, and the latter subjective. The believer claims to experience complete inner security or a feeling of absolute certitude. Is he compelled to claim also that his inner certitude must correspond to a state of affairs outside himself, e.g. the reality of God? In other words can he be content with certitude and admit he has no absolute objective certainty?

3.8   There are other more serious difficulties. Is saying 'I believe in God' like saying 'I believe that man is my father'? Religious people sometimes say that their belief is a simple matter of fact confirmed by experience as immediate as that which leads us to believe in the reality of our parents. But what the religious person usually means is that he has had certain kinds of inner emotional, mystical, perhaps moral experiences and that from these he concludes that there is a God.

A. Flew, 'Theology and Falsification' from *New Essays in Philosophical Theology*, p. 96

Let us begin with a parable. It is a parable developed from a tale told by John Wisdom in his haunting and revelatory article 'Gods'. Once upon a time two explorers came upon a clearing in the jungle. In the clearing were growing many flowers and many weeds. One explorer says, 'Some gardener must tend this plot.' The other disagrees, 'There is no gardener.' So they pitch their tents and set a watch. No gardener is ever seen. 'But perhaps he is an invisible gardener.' So they set up a barbed-wire fence. They electrify it. They patrol with bloodhounds. (For they remember how H. G. Wells's The Invisible Man could be both smelt and touched though he could not be seen.) But no shrieks ever suggest that some intruder has received a shock. No movements of the wire ever betray an invisible climber. The bloodhounds never give cry. Yet still the Believer is not convinced. 'But there is a gardener, invisible, intangible, insensible to electric shocks, a gardener who has no scent and makes no sound, a gardener who comes secretly to look after the garden which he loves.' At last the Sceptic despairs, 'But what remains of your original assertion? Just how does what you call an invisible, intangible, eternally elusive gardener differ from an imaginary gardener or even from no gardener at all?'

In this parable we can see how what starts as an assertion, that something exists or that there is some analogy between certain complexes of phenomena, may be reduced step by step to an altogether different status, to an expression perhaps of a 'picture preference'. . . . Someone may dissipate his assertion completely without noticing that he has done so. A fine brash hypothesis may thus be killed by inches, the death by a thousand qualifications. . . . And in this, it seems to me, lies the peculiar danger, the endemic evil, of theological utterance. . .

When the Sceptic in the parable asked the Believer, 'Just how does what you call an invisible, intangible, eternally elusive gardener differ from an imaginary gardener or even from no gardener at all?' he was suggesting that the Believer's earlier statement had been so eroded by qualification that it was no longer an assertion at all.

J. H. Hick, 'The Doctrine of Analogy' (Aquinas 1224–1274) from *Philosophy of Religion*,* p. 69

The great Scholastic thinkers were well aware of the problem and developed the idea of analogy to meet it. The doctrine of 'analogical predication' as it occurs in Aquinas and his commentator Cajetan and as it has been further elaborated and variously criticized in modern times, is too complex a subject to be discussed in detail within the plan of this book. However, Aquinas' basic and central idea is not difficult to grasp. He teaches that when a word such as 'good' is applied both to a created being and to God it is not being used *univocally* (i.e. with exactly the same meaning in the two cases). God is not good, for example, in identically the sense in which human beings may be good. Nor, on the other hand, do we apply the epithet 'good' to God and man *equivocally* (i.e. with completely different and unrelated meanings) as when the word 'bat' is used to refer both to the flying animal and to the instrument used in baseball. There is a definite connection between God's goodness and man's reflecting the fact that God has created man. According to Aquinas, then, 'good' is applied to creator and creature neither univocally nor equivocally but *analogically*. What this means will

* 2nd edn, © 1973. Reprinted by permission of Prentice-Hall, Inc., Englewood Cliffs, N. J.

appear if we consider first an analogy 'downwards' from man to a lower form of life. We sometimes say of a pet dog that it is faithful, and we may also describe a man as faithful. We use the same word in each case because of a similarity between a certain quality exhibited in the behaviour of the dog and the steadfast voluntary adherence to a person or cause that we call faithfulness in a human being. Because of this similarity we are not using the word 'faithful' equivocally (with totally different senses). But, on the other hand, there is an immense difference in quality between a dog's attitudes and a man's. The one is definitely superior to the other in respect of responsible, selfconscious deliberation and the relating of attitudes to moral purposes and ends. Because of this difference we are not using 'faithful' univocally (in exactly the same sense). We are using it analogically, to indicate that at the level of the dog's consciousness there is a quality that *corresponds* to what at the human level we call faithfulness. There is a recognizable likeness in structure of attitudes or patterns of behaviour that causes us to use the same word for both animal and man. Nevertheless, human faithfulness differs from canine faithfulness to all the wide extent that a man differs from a dog. There is thus both similarity within difference and difference within similarity of the kind that led Aquinas to speak of the *analogical* use of the same term in two very different contexts.

In the case of our analogy 'downwards' true or normative faithfulness is that which we know directly in ourselves, and the dim and imperfect faithfulness of the dog is known only by analogy. But in the case of the analogy 'upwards' from man to God the situation is reversed. It is our own directly known goodness, love, wisdom etc. which are the thin shadows and remote approximations, and the perfect qualities of the God-head that are known to us only by analogy. Thus, when we say that God is good, we are saying that there is a quality of the infinitely perfect Being that corresponds to what at our own human level we call goodness, both to man and (on the basis of revelation) to God....

Analogy is not an instrument for exploring and mapping the infinite divine nature; it is an account of the way in which terms are used of the Deity whose existence is, at this point, being presupposed. The doctrine of analogy provides a framework for certain limited statements about God, without infringing upon the agnosticism, and the sense of the mystery of the divine being, which have always characterized Christian and Jewish thought at their best.

G. F. Woods, 'The Idea of the Transcendent' from *Soundings*, ed. A. R. Vidler, pp. 50 f.

When the transcendent is defined as what our minds cannot surmount, it is not surprising that all explanation of the transcendent, including analogical explanation, is dismissed as futile. In an act of analogical explanation we seek to make one thing plain by the use of another. We try to explain what is obscure by reference to what we find less obscure. We use it both to make matters plainer in our own minds and in conversation with others. The conditions of a successful act of analogical explanation are extremely complex. There is, however, one condition which is of outstanding importance. No one can explain something to himself or to some one else if there is nothing which in his own or in their common experience is sufficiently plainer than what is being explained to be used as an analogy. There must be something which is sufficiently plain to be employed as the analogical instrument. For example, I may wish to explain to an American what it means to be Prime Minister in England. I shall probably try to explain the office of the Prime Minister in terms of the office of American President. I may say that each is the head of the government in his own country. I may say that each is democratically appointed. But I shall immediately begin to make many qualifications in what I have said. I shall refer to the position of the monarchy in England. I shall point out that the method of democratic appointment is very dissimilar. I shall remark that the powers associated with the two offices are very different. The question will begin to press upon me whether I can say that the two offices are really alike. I begin to see that they are not really alike either in general or in a number of particular points of exact likeness. The whole comparison, in general and in particular, is not an exact likeness but an analogous likeness. There is an analogy between the two offices but never precise similarity. At some points the analogy is closer than at others but at no point is exact similarity to be found. In fact, if this were found we should not need to use analogy at all to explain such a point. It would be a mere replica or repetition of what the American already knew. Analogies cease to be when they attain perfect similarity with what is being explained by them. Wholly successful analogies like good teachers render themselves dispensable.

. . . . . .

The curious and fascinating point about genuine analogies is that they are not at any point exactly like what they are supposed to explain. And yet they do work. They do help to explain what is obscure. How can this happen? No theory can be adequate which concludes that what happens cannot take place. What is the central characteristic of what analogies do? Somehow, they express sameness in difference and difference in sameness. There is a sudden and exciting recognition of an analogical likeness between entities or situations which are strictly speaking not alike. This is a mysterious capacity. It resists clear and distinct understanding. There is no logical room for an analogical likeness which is somewhere between strict likeness and unlikeness. It is like the strict line between partiality and impartiality which an Irish Chairman is said to have pursued. Formal reasoning has a proper abhorrence of such notions. To the mathematical mind, they are detestable. Our capacity to explain analogically is more than an ability to exploit the mobility of our mental standpoint in order to gain more advantageous standpoints from which we can discern exact similarities. A blind man does not improve his view of a royal procession by gaining permission to stand on a balcony. Nor is our use of analogies just a matter of making an ingenious employment of the limited number at our disposal. It is more than a skilful use of the limited number of tools provided with our mental car. We are, somehow, able to apprehend what is novel and unusual, and in this act of expanding apprehension we perpetually make use of explanatory analogies. We invent them. We modify them. We discard them. We use them. Our power to invent, modify, discard and use them is not identical with the analogies which we invent, modify, discard and use. It is this creative power which is the secret of analogical explanation. It seems to be endless. It can notice analogical likenesses which have hitherto been overlooked. It can express these mysterious likenesses between things which are strictly unlike in all kinds of analogical models, frameworks, structures and constructions. Analogical thinking may be the source of the universals, such as 'man' and 'stone' which we use in our thought and speech. It is by no means obvious that all legitimate understandings of the transcendent must fall outside the range of all analogical explanation.

. . . . . .

But even the genuine use of analogical explanation has certain limitations which are not defects. This is true of any kind of instrument which through the very fact of being utilizable in certain circumstances is incapable of being useful in other circumstances. For example, a good spoon is not good as a thermometer. The most obvious limitation of analogical explanation has already been mentioned. It can never, so long as it remains an analogy, become exactly similar to what is being explained. Even the best analogy is not as good as the genuine article. Like an understudy, it is never quite the same as the principal. It follows that no analogy is perfect. There is a ceaseless oscillation between confidence and diffidence about the usefulness of analogical explanation. The debate about the utility of analogy becomes more fruitful when it becomes less abstract. The value of particular analogies can be very usefully discussed. Each one can be examined on its merits. Some are better than others. It is not unlike the situation in which, having been told that there is no substitute for *The Times* newspaper, we may still have legitimate preferences between the newspapers which are in fact available. Some may still give accounts of the events of the day which are better than others. But the possibility that we may be able to give an analogical explanation of what the transcendent is like does not show that we can experience it or prove that it exists.

J. H. Hick, 'Religious Statements as Symbolic (Paul Tillich)' from *Philosophy of Religion*,* pp. 71ff

An important element in the thought of Paul Tillich is his doctrine of the 'symbolic' nature of religious language. Tillich distinguishes between a sign and a symbol. Both point to something else beyond themselves. But a sign signifies that to which it points by arbitrary convention — as for instance, when the red light at the street corner signifies that drivers are ordered to halt. In contrast to this purely external connection, a symbol 'participates in that to which it points'. To use Tillich's example, a flag participates in the power and dignity of the nation that it represents. Because of this inner connection with the reality symbolized, symbols are not arbitrarily instituted, like conventional signs, but 'grow out of individual or collective unconscious' and consequently have their own span of life and (in some cases) their decay and death. A symbol 'opens up levels of reality which otherwise are closed to us' and at the same time 'unlocks dimensions and elements of our soul' corresponding to the new aspects of the world that it reveals. The clearest instances of this two-fold function are provided by the arts, which 'create symbols for a level of reality which cannot be reached in any other way', at the same

* 2nd edn, © 1973. Reprinted by permission of Prentice-Hall, Inc., Englewood Cliffs, N. J.

time opening up new sensitivities and powers of appreciation in ourselves.

Tillich holds that religious faith, which is the state of being 'ultimately concerned' about the ultimate, can only express itself in symbolic language. 'Whatever we say about that which concerns us ultimately, whether or not we call it God, has a symbolic meaning. It points beyond itself while participating in that to which it points. In no other way can faith express itself adequately. The language of faith is the language of symbols.'

There is, according to Tillich, one and only one literal, nonsymbolic statement that can be made about the ultimate reality which religion calls God – that God is Being-itself. Beyond this, all theological statements – such as, that God is eternal, living, good, personal, that he is the Creator and that he loves his creatures – are symbolic.

There can be no doubt that any concrete assertion about God must be symbolic, for a concrete assertion is one which uses a segment of finite experience in order to say something about him. It transcends the content of this segment, although it also includes it. The segment of finite reality which becomes the vehicle of a concrete assertion about God is affirmed and negated at the same time. It becomes a symbol, for a symbolic expression is one whose proper meaning is negated by that to which it points. And yet it also is affirmed by it, and this affirmation gives the symbolic expression an adequate basis for pointing beyond itself.

Tillich's conception of the symbolic character of religious language can – like many of his central ideas – be developed in either of two opposite directions and is presented by Tillich in the body of his writings as a whole in such a way as to preserve its ambiguity and flexibility. I shall, at this point, consider Tillich's doctrine in its theistic development, indicating in a later section, in connection with the view of J. H. Randall, Jr, how it can also be developed naturalistically.

Used in the service of Judaic-Christian theism, the negative aspect of Tillich's doctrine of religious symbols corresponds to the negative aspect of the doctrine of analogy. Tillich is insisting that we do not use human language literally, or univocally, when we speak of the ultimate. Because our terms can only be derived from our own finite human experience, they cannot be adequate to apply to God, when used theologically, their meaning is always partially 'negated by that to which they point'. Religiously, this doctrine constitutes a warning against the idolatry of thinking of God as though he were merely a greatly magnified human being (anthropomorphism).

Tillich's constructive teaching, offering an alternative to the doctrine of analogy, is his theory of 'participation.' A symbol, he says, participates in the reality to which it points. But unfortunately Tillich does not define or clarify this central notion of participation. Consider, for example, the symbolic statement that God is good. Is the symbol in this case the proposition 'God is good' or the concept 'the goodness of God'? Does this symbol participate in Being-itself in the same sense as that in which a flag participates in the power and dignity of a nation? And what precisely is this sense? Tillich does not analyse the latter case – which he uses in several different places to indicate what he means by the participation of a symbol in that which it symbolizes. Consequently, it is not clear in what respect the case of a religious symbol is supposed to be similar. Again, according to Tillich, everything that exists participates in Being-itself; what then is the difference between the way in which symbols participate in Being-itself and the way in which everything else participates in it?

The application to theological statements of Tillich's other 'main characteristics of every symbol' summarized above, raises further questions. Is it really plausible to say that a complex theological statement such as 'God is not dependent for his existence upon any reality other than himself' has arisen from the unconscious, whether individual or collective? Does it not seem more likely that it was carefully formulated by a philosophical theologian? And in what sense does this same proposition open up both 'levels of reality which are otherwise closed to us' and 'hidden depths of our own being'? These two characteristics of symbols seem more readily applicable to the arts than to theological ideas and propositions. Indeed, it is Tillich's tendency to assimilate religious to aesthetic awareness that suggests the naturalistic development of his position, which will be described later.

These are some of the many questions that Tillich's position raises. In default of answers to such questions, Tillich's teaching, although valuable and suggestive, scarcely constitutes at this point a fully articulated philosophical position.

Peter Donovan, 'Ian Ramsey on Religious Language' from *Religious Language*, pp. 31ff

Readers of *Punch* will remember the regular feature which comes on the last pages of that magazine, where readers are invited to supply a caption to a cartoon taken from earlier issues. The winning effort is later published, along with the caption which appeared when the cartoon was first published (often many years before). The humour of the exercise lies in seeing how quite different captions, sometimes reflecting a complete change of mood or point of view, can make a striking difference to the way we see the picture and appreciate its point.

The way an effective caption leads us to appreciate the message of a cartoon or drawing gives us a parallel with the way religious words enable people to find meanings in the phenomena of life, with the help of imagery and concepts drawn from religious traditions. The words seem to produce a new apprehension of what is observed, bringing out otherwise unnoticed meaning and giving the observed facts an overall point.

In his book *Religious Language*, and in numerous other places, Ian Ramsey has attempted to show that religious discourse functions in an empirically based way, yet enables meanings of a profound and transcendent kind to be expressed. The oblique and often problematic words and phrases of religious statements, according to Ramsey, are admittedly 'logically odd'. But that is not a failing, for it enables them to function like the captions mentioned above. As models or stories, qualified in various ways, they are set alongside facts in such a manner as to bring about a discernment or disclosure of significance; this, where religious words are involved, leads to a peculiarly religious kind of response, a commitment of a total kind.

While religious assertions may look much like ordinary statements in form, to take them as such is to miss their distinctive characteristics, and the peculiar connection with the situations of discernment and commitment which they evoke. Ramsey produces many examples to illustrate situations where there is a discernment of *depth*, going far beyond the mere observation of matters of fact by the senses. He uses a wide range of common examples to make this point, occasions which 'come alive', in which 'the light dawns', 'the ice breaks', 'the penny drops' and so on, as the result of the use of certain words or the telling of a suitable story.

Religious language will only be understood, on this view, when it is seen in relation to the discernment and commitment situations from which it arises, and to which it continues to apply. For instance, traditional statements about God's attributes, especially the negative ones like immutability, impassibility, etc., are understood,

If we see them as primarily evocative of what we have called the odd discernment, that characteristically religious situation which, if evoked, provokes a total commitment. (Ramsey, *Religious Language* (SCM Press 1957, p. 50.)

Similarly with the puzzling metaphysical descriptions of God as First Cause, Almighty or Infinitely Wise, and with references to God's Eternal Purpose and to Creation *ex nihilo*. For Ramsey, theological formulae like these are to be regarded as models, qualified in certain ways so as to produce a disclosure of cosmic significance – at least that is what happens on the occasions when such terms are genuinely understood in the properly religious way, and not mistaken for straightforward assertions about a supernatural subject-matter.

At some points Ramsey sounds rather like Braithwaite who was discussed above, for instance, in the freedom he allows in the choice of religious expressions and stories from which discernments may come:

> . . . we must recognise that while some people are impervious to some models and qualifiers, to some routes and to some stories, they may not be to others. The characteristic situation may be evoked for some by telling causal stories, for others by telling wisdom stories, for others by telling stories of good lives, for others by telling creation stories, for others by telling purpose stories. In fact there is no word which, in principle, cannot lead to a story which might evoke the characteristic situation in which God is known. (Ibid., p. 80.)

But he rejects Braithwaite's limiting of the function of Christian language to the expression of commitment to an *agapeistic* way of life (Braithwaite's abbreviation for the New Testament ideal of self-giving love – from the Greek agape). Discussing Braithwaite's view of religious belief Ramsey objects:

> when the Christian asserts 'God is love' he declares *primarily* not his commitment to *agape* or to an agapeistic way of life, but his commitment to certain 'facts' somehow or other described in the Gospels. (Ramsey, ed., *Christian Ethics and Contemporary Philosophy* (SCM Press 1966, p. 86.)

He argues against Braithwaite, that a thoroughgoing empiricism will take account not only of this-worldly experience but also of the kinds of experience to which he tries to draw attention, discernment of cosmic depth, of 'the universe and more' evoked by the religious words and stories.

Religious Language

Does Ramsey succeed in avoiding the naturalism implicit in Braithwaite's and Miles's accounts of religious language? It is clearly his desire to do so, and he constantly speaks as though he intends the 'disclosure of depth' to be taken as having objective content, of supernatural origin. But there are some major difficulties, which critics of Ramsey's views have not been slow to point out. The difficulties arise from the attempt to treat so-called disclosure situations as providing 'empirical anchorage' for religious claims and statements. Experiences described by metaphors like 'the light breaking in' or 'the penny dropping' may be of considerable psychological interest. Ramsey assembles a good many examples to remind us how familiar such experiences are. But it is obvious that the mere occurrence of some disclosure-like experience is in itself no clear guide to the actual discernment of anything. A genuine discovery of information or achievement of insight may or may not be accompanied by any sudden sense of illumination or disclosure. It is easy for us to think the light has dawned, and yet to go on and show that we have got the thing completely wrong. (Anyone trying to follow a road map in a strange city will have had *that* experience.)

If the meaningfulness of oblique and figurative religious statements rests entirely on their power to lead to disclosures of profound significance, evoking total commitments, who is to be sure that heretical or blasphemous combinations of religious words, or even total nonsense, might not in some situations produce the same effect? And are the claims of religions to lose all their meaning, if it comes about that no one responds in the appropriate way to them? If that were so, they could scarcely be called truth-claims. Here our distinction . . . between evocative power and informative content becomes relevant. Ramsey's theory makes meaningfulness turn entirely on the evocative power of certain combinations of words. He fails to show how they can also be informative.

That is not to say that disclosures of some kind, from a transcendent source, are out of the question. Ramsey's cosmic disclosures are not unlike the kinds of mystical consciousness of higher levels of reality, supposed to be produced by paradox and negation and other meditational devices. Ramsey may be correct in holding that *some* religious word use is of that kind. His difficulty, like that of the mystics, is that if this is to be the only meaningful function of religious language, how are we to find any meaning in the language left over, so to speak, by which the supposed *content* of the mystical discernment is spelt out –

attributing it, for instance, to one holy God, to whom worship is the appropriate response? A theory of the meaningfulness of religious claims, which does no more than give them the function of evoking disclosures, fails to account for the informativeness they must have for anything to be known about the object (if any) so disclosed.

Ramsey has sought to describe an empirically-anchored function for religious statements. But the sort of anchoring his theory suggests turns out, like Braithwaite's, to be largely a psychological or causal function, rather than the kind of anchoring in observable, testable matters of fact needed if the claims of religions are to count as factually informative. Admittedly Ramsey thinks religious language has far greater causal power than Braithwaite does, taking man's discernment beyond the here and now and discerning things of divine origin. But without a further account of how facts beyond the perceived world can be known and spoken about, Ramsey's account fails to answer the empiricist challenge.

Many of Ramsey's suggestions about models and qualifiers, and other non-descriptive functions of religious and theological discourse, are subtle and perceptive, and may yet be developed into a more philosophically-convincing theory. In the meantime, it is necessary to tackle the empiricist challenge head-on and see if religious claims, taken as in some sense descriptive and cognitive, can be shown testable and open to confirming or disconfirming observations within human life and experience.

John M. Hull, *Sense and Nonsense about God*, pp. 14ff

PART FIVE *Some more replies*

5.1 Many Christians are dissatisfied with the replies to the challenge of the philosophers of language given so far. They point out that if this sort of reply is all that can be made, then Christians must stop talking of religion as truth. Christians may speak of religious experiences and religious attitudes, but if they admit that their claims do not refer to any reality beyond themselves, there can be no question of an objective religious truth. Many Christians maintain that statements such as 'God created the world' and 'Jesus Christ is Lord of all' are in some sense stating facts. Unusual facts no doubt, but there is some element of fact in them. . . .

5.2 Attention has also been given by philosophers to certain weaknesses in the principle of verification. The main criticisms are as follows:

First criticism: How can we tell if the principle of verification is itself meaningful? You will remember that the famous principle states that the meaning of any statement is the methods by which it could be verified. Now we must ask whether this statement will itself fit into any of the classes of meaningful, i.e. verifiable, statements. Is it analytic or is it synthetic? If it is analytic, then it is merely a definition of terms, e.g. that meaning equals method of verification. It would not tell us anything about actual sentences, for, as you recall, analytic propositions define words and do not impart actual information about states of affairs. There would, therefore, seem to be no particular reason why anyone should accept this definition of these particular words. The linguistic philosopher may reply that the verification principle is just a handy and convenient rule of thumb for the use of language. And the religious believer may quite logically reply that it is not handy and convenient to *him* and he will not use it but will adopt some other definition of meaning.

5.3 On the other hand, the principle of verification may be synthetic. In this case, it would be an observation drawn from sense experience, and we would have to ask what kind of sense experience we would use to verify it. But here we notice that the verification principle rests upon a logical distinction, a distinction between analytical and synthetic statements. This is a logical observation about the nature of things, not a generalization drawn from examining a lot of different actual sentences. Because it is a logical distinction, no sense experience could possibly upset it. You could not 'come upon' a sentence which to everyone's amazement did not fit into either category and which made philosophers create a third category into which the new discovery could be fitted! No, nothing like this is possible. Logical distinctions are not established by sense experience and cannot be overthrown by sense experience. If the principle of verification is synthetic it must on its own terms be a bit of nonsense, since it is impossible to verify it by reference to experience. . . .

5.4 Second criticism: The School of philosophers who have made most use of the principle of verification has been in the great tradition of English empirical philosophy, a tradition which includes such famous names as Locke, Berkeley and Hume. This tradition of philosophy believes that all true knowledge comes to us through our physical

Religious Language

senses. This teaching can be developed into an attack on religious beliefs (as for example in the work of Hume), since, however knowledge of God may be attained it is not through the physical senses. The empirical background of the modern linguistic philosophy may be seen in the insistence that synthetic statements should be verified by reference to sense experience.

5.5 From this it follows that one way of attacking the linguistic philosophers is therefore to question its theory about how we obtain knowledge and to ask whether in fact it is true that all our knowledge comes to us through the senses.

5.6 (i) *The law of contradiction*, i.e. the belief that it is absurd to contradict oneself. Where do we get this basic conviction from? What makes us feel that it is absurd to contradict ourselves? Although our experience of being found to look stupid when we do contradict ourselves no doubt impresses the truth deeply on us, 'the validation of it does not depend directly on experience. But this principle is basic to all our thinking, and there seems thus to be something non-empirical at the centre of all thought and experience.'

5.7 (ii) *Truths of mathematics*. Although it is often said that these are mere definitions and do not therefore give us any new knowledge about anything, H. D. Lewis suggests that this is true only of the elementary forms of maths. 'We know what 245 and 367 mean without having *any notion what they will yield when multiplied. That* would take time to discover, and the solutions to some problems require exceptional gifts and in some cases genius. Surely we learn something new in the process.'

5.8 (iii) *Value judgements in morals and art*. Many thinkers, of course, regard ethical judgements as derived from our experience, the pressures of society, and so on. Others regard them as merely expressing emotional attitudes of approval or disapproval. But there remain important ethical philosophers who believe that the most basic ethical judgements (e.g. that it is wrong to cause pain and right to promote happiness) are insights which come to us from a source other than our own sense experience. The same is said to be true of theories of beauty.

5.9 All these points are hotly debated. But it is worth mentioning them if only to point out that the empirical philosophers have not got the thing sewn up completely. There are important areas of human experience within which there is at least room for manoeuvre on the part of the religious believer. If he can show that some knowledge is not derived from the senses he can go on to claim that his knowledge of God is, in a similar way, not from the senses.

5.10 Third criticism: The philosophical school we are considering is not only rooted in empiricism. See para 5.4. Its other source of inspiration is the study of language. This is why these thinkers are often called 'linguistic philosophers'. Just as a moment ago we questioned whether their attitude to human knowledge and experience was sound, we may also ask whether their treatment of language is sound. Here are some examples of ways in which their view of the role of language may be criticized:

5.11 (i) These philosophers believe that language has but two functions — language either aids clarity of expression and thought by defining words (analytic propositions) or it informs us of new facts about the world (synthetic propositions). It is because language can be used only in these two ways that all meaningful propositions are reduced to the types which were outlined in part three, paras 3:1–3:5.

5.12 But it may be claimed that this is a serious over-simplification of how in fact we do use language. We do indeed say things such as 'Tom is tall' (synthetic) and 'People of six feet or more are tall' (analytic). But don't we also say things like 'Is he tall?' or 'I wish I were tall!' Suppose I said 'Tom is leaving the room.' That would be a meaningful statement because it could be verified empirically, e.g. by sticking a length of cotton over the doorway and seeing it were broken after Tom had seemed to pass through and so on. But suppose I said 'Tom! Leave the room immediately!' How could that sentence be verified? After all, nothing might happen and Tom might refuse to move. Does that mean that the command is without meaning? Surely not. Let us take another example. Sometimes language does not impart information so much as actually doing something in its own right. Examples are 'Arise, Sir Francis' and 'I name this ship Venus.' Here language is actually doing something but it would seem difficult to show how one would prove or disprove by appeal to the senses that it is really doing anything when the words are spoken.

5.13 These uses of language may be termed the imperative use, the interrogatory use, the performatory use and so on. They are all perfectly normal and in the ordinary common sense understanding of the expression, meaningful. Yet none of them will easily respond to the demand for verification. This suggests that there may be something wrong with the principle itself as a test of meaning.

5.14 (ii) Another example of the rigid attitude of the older type of linguistic philosophy may be seen in its attitude to paradox. When describing a woman with a Mona Lisa type of beauty, I might at first say 'Well she's beautiful, and yet again she's not beautiful.' In strict logical terms this sentence contains a flat contradiction and must therefore be meaningless. But we would all understand that such a sentence was seeking to draw attention to an enigmatic quality of the lady's expression. Such a sentence is saying that the word 'beautiful' is not quite sharply defined enough to convey this elusive quality, and the paradoxical way of putting it is an invitation to sharpen up the adjectives, or to suggest others of greater precision. So we see that paradox can be a way of pointing to a deeper insight. Paradox can also be a way of trying to hide the fact that one is talking nonsense. The point is that the principles of the logical positivists did not seem to have any resource by which the legitimate and the illegitimate uses of paradox could be distinguished.

. . . . . .

PART SIX *The Uses of Language*

6.1 In the last section it was pointed out that the attitude of the older type of linguistic philosophy towards language was rather narrow. It must not be thought that the objections raised are merely an attempt by Christians to avoid the force of the arguments of the linguistic philosophers, for in fact it is the leaders of that philosophical school who, after further reflection on the nature of language, have again led the way in pointing out many additional uses.

6.2 Here the philosopher Wittgenstein who was himself one of the pioneers of logical positivism lists some of the uses to which language is put:

Giving orders and obeying them –
Describing the appearance of an object, or giving its measurements –
Constructing an object from a description (drawing) –
Reporting an event –
Forming and testing a hypothesis –

Presenting the results of an experiment in tables and diagrams –
Making up a story and reading it –
Play acting – singing catches –
Making a joke – telling it –
Solving a problem in practical arithmetic –
Translating from one language into another –
Asking, thanking, cursing, greeting, praying –

He goes on 'It is interesting to compare the multiplicity of the tools in language and of the ways they are used, the multiplicity of kinds of word and sentence, with what logicians have said about the structure of language.' (*Philosophical Investigations* (Blackwell 1953), pp. 11e–12e.)

6.3 It became clear that the strict division into only two types of statement and the demand that to be meaningful a statement should submit to the demand for empirical verification was a good deal more tidy than the actual structure and use of language itself warranted. The earlier linguistic philosophers, although their valuable work had, in its time, marked an important advance, now seem to have been guilty of forcing language into their own preconceived notions of what it should be like.

6.4 'The image one gets of verificational analysis is too much that of a sausage grinder, receiving a great variety of cuts of meat, but turning out a neat row of uniform *wurst*.' (Ferré, *Language, Logic and God* (Eyre and Spottiswoode 1962), p. 55.)

How then are we to tell when a sentence is meaningful? For the problems about nonsense and meaning outlined in sections 1 and 2 are still just as pressing. We have seen enough to show that just because a sentence cannot be subject to empirical testing, it does not mean it is without any sense and meaning. As Professor Ferré puts it 'To say of a given sentence that it can be verified is not to say anything about the meaningfulness of the sentence, but to characterize it as being a sentence of a particular type, namely, an empirical sentence.' (Ibid., p. 63.)

6.5 We must state a new principle of meaningfulness as follows:

The meaning of language is found in its use.

This approach is often called *functional analysis* because it seeks to discover meaning in the role or function of a sentence.

R. B. Braithwaite, 'An Empiricist's View of the Nature of Religious Belief' from *The Philosophy of Religion*, ed. Basil Mitchell, pp. 77ff

Religious statements, however, are not the only statements which are unverifiable by standard methods; moral statements have the same peculiarity. A moral principle, like the utilitarian principle that a man ought to act so as to maximize happiness, does not seem to be either a logically necessary or a logically impossible proposition. But neither does it seem to be an empirical proposition, all the attempts of ethical empiricists to give naturalistic analyses having failed. Though a tough minded logical positivist might be prepared to say that all religious statements are sound and fury, signifying nothing, he can hardly say that of all moral statements. For moral statements have a use in guiding conduct; and if they have a use they surely have a meaning – in some sense of meaning. So the verificational principle of meaning in the hands of empiricist philosophers in the 1930s became modified either by a glossing of the term 'verification' or by a change of the verification principle into the use principle: the meaning of any statement is given by the way in which it is used. . . .

The meaning of any statement then, will be taken as being given by the way it is used. The kernel for an empiricist of the problem of the nature of religious belief is to explain, in empirical terms, how a religious statement is used by a man who asserts it in order to express his religious conviction. . . .

Unless a Christian's assertion that God is love (*agape*) – which I take to epitomize the assertions of the Christian religion – be taken to declare his intention to follow an agapeistic way of life, he could be asked what is the connection between the assertion and the intention, between Christian belief and Christian practice. And this question can always be asked if religious assertions are separated from conduct. Unless religious principles are moral principles, it makes nonsense to speak of putting them into practice.

The way to find out what are the intentions embodied in a set of religious assertions, and hence what is the meaning of the assertions, is by discovering what principles of conduct the asserter takes the assertions to involve. These may be ascertained both by asking him questions and by seeing how he behaves, each test being supplemental to the other. If what is wanted is not the meaning of the religious assertions made by a particular man, but what the set of assertions would mean were they to be made by anyone of the same religion (which I will call their *typical* meaning), all that can be done is to specify the form of behaviour which is in accordance with what one takes to be the fundamental moral principles of the religion in question. Since different people will take different views as to what these fundamental principles are, the typical meaning of religious assertions will be different for different people. I myself take the typical meaning of the body of Christian assertions as being given by their proclaiming intentions to follow an agapeistic way of life, and for a description of this way of life – a description in general and metaphorical terms, but an empirical description nevertheless – I should quote most of the 13th chapter of 1 Corinthians. Others may think that the Christian way of life should be described somewhat differently, and will therefore take the typical meaning of the assertions of Christianity to correspond to their different view of its fundamental moral teaching.

My contention, then, is that the primary use of religious assertions is to announce allegiance to a set of moral principles; without such allegiance there is no 'true religion'. This is borne out by all the accounts of what happens when an unbeliever becomes converted to a religion. The conversion is not only a change in the propositions believed – indeed there may be no specifically intellectual change at all; it is a change in the state of will. . . .

In assimilating religious assertions to moral assertions I do not wish to deny that there are any important differences. One is the fact already noticed that usually the behaviour policy intended is not specified by one religious assertion in isolation. Another difference is that the fundamental moral teaching of the religion is frequently given, not in abstract terms, but by means of concrete examples – of how to behave, for instance, if one meets a man set upon by thieves on the road to Jericho. A resolution to behave like the good Samaritan does not, in itself, specify the behaviour to be resolved upon in quite different circumstances. However, absence of explicitly recognized general principles does not prevent a man from acting in accordance with such principles; it only makes it more difficult for a questioner to discover upon what principles he is acting. . . .

The resolution proclaimed by a religious assertion may then be taken as referring to inner life as well as to outward conduct. And the superiority of religious conviction over the mere adoption of a moral code in securing conformity to the code arises from a religious conviction changing what the religious man wants. It may be hard enough to love your enemy but once you have succeeded in doing so it is easy to behave lovingly towards him. But if you continue to hate him it requires a heroic perseverance continually to behave as if you loved him. Resolutions to feel even if they are only partly fulfilled, are powerful reinforcements of resolutions to act.

But though these qualifications may be adequate for distinguishing religious assertions from purely moral ones, they are not sufficient to discriminate between assertions belonging to one religious system and those belonging to another system in the case in which the behaviour policies, both of inner life and of outward conduct, inculcated by the systems are identical. For instance, I have said that I take the fundamental moral teaching of Christianity to be the preaching of an agapeistic way of life. But a Jew or a Buddhist may, with considerable plausibility, maintain that the fundamental moral teaching of his religion is to recommend exactly the same way of life. How then can religious assertions be distinguished into those which are Christian, those which are Jewish, those which are Buddhist, by the policies of life which they respectively recommend if, on examination, these policies turn out to be the same? . . .

There must be some more important differences between an agapeistically policied Christian and an agapeistically policied Jew than that the former attends a church and the latter a synagogue.

The really important difference, I think, is to be found in the fact that the intentions to pursue the behaviour policies, which may be the same for different religions, are associated with thinking of different *stories* (or sets of stories). By a story I shall here mean a proposition or set of propositions capable of empirical test and which are thought of by the religious man in connection with his resolution to follow the way of life advocated by his religion. On the assumption that the ways of life advocated by Christianity and by Buddhism are essentially the same, it will be the fact that the intention to follow this way of life is associated in the mind of a Christian with thinking of one set of stories (the Christian stories) while it is associated in the mind of a Buddhist with thinking of another set of stories (the Buddhist stories) which enables a Christian assertion to be distinguished from a Buddhist one.

A religious assertion will, therefore, have a propositional element which is lacking in a purely moral assertion, in that it will refer to a story as well as to an intention. The reference to the story is not an assertion of the story taken as a matter of empirical fact: it is a telling of the story, or an alluding to the story, in the way in which one can tell, or allude to, the story of a novel with which one is acquainted. To assert the whole set of assertions of the Christian religion is both to tell the Christian doctrinal story and to confess allegiance to the Christian way of life.

It is not necessary, in my view, for the asserter of a religious assertion to believe in the truth of the story involved in the assertions: what is necessary is that the story should be entertained in thought, i.e. that the statement of the story should be understood as having a meaning. I have secured this by requiring that the story should consist of empirical propositions. Educated Christians of the present day who attach importance to the doctrine of the Atonement certainly do not believe an empirically testable story in Matthew Arnold's or any other form. But it is the fact that entertainment in thought of this and other Christian stories forms the context in which Christian resolutions are made which serves to distinguish Christian assertions from those made by adherents of another religion, or of no religion.

What I am calling a *story* Matthew Arnold called a *parable* and a *fairy-tale*. Other terms which might be used are *allegory*, *fable*, *tale*, *myth*. I have chosen the word 'story' as being the most neutral term, implying neither that the story is believed nor that it is disbelieved. The Christian stories include straightforward historical statements about the life and death of Jesus of Nazareth; a Christian (unless he accepts the unplausible Christ-myth theory) will naturally believe some or all of these. Stories about the beginning of the world and of the Last Judgement as facts of past or of future history are believed by many unsophisticated Christians. But my contention is that belief in the truth of the Christian stories is not the proper criterion for deciding whether or not an assertion is a Christian one. A man is not, I think, a professing Christian unless he both proposes to live according to Christian moral principles and associates his intention with thinking of Christian stories; but he need not believe that the empirical propositions presented by the stories correspond to empirical fact. . . .

Peter Donovan, *Religious Language*

The Bible as Authoritative Religious Language, p. 68

The view most commonly held by Christians throughout their history of their right to use religious language in the ways they do, has been quite simple. The Bible is the source of that authority. It contains not only the record of God's dealings with men and nations. It also gives the words in which God himself is to be talked about, his will for men known, and his way of salvation grasped. Though on the face of it, the Bible consists of the writings of many different people, over more than ten centuries, yet they are all inspired by God, so that their words become his words. Being God's words the Bible is infallible. It may be misunderstood or misinterpreted, but it cannot in itself be in error. . . . What reasons do such Christians give for taking a diverse collection of sixty six books, written by various Jewish and Christian authors, most of them unknown, as uniquely and exclusively the words of God? That view may have been the prevailing opinion of the Church until modern times. But can such a confident choice of a final verbal authority be given any rational basis today?

Defenders of the view argue that it is the Bible's own view of itself. Certain verses are taken to show explicitly the Bible 'witnessing to its own authority', as being of more than human origin, and the uniquely inspired and authoritative form in which divine revelation is given to man. . . .

But, of course, 'the Bible's own view of itself' (even if a meaning for that phrase can be agreed on) is still only binding on the Christian if he already believes the Bible to be authoritative in all its views. The argument in fact is circular – it assumes what it sets out to prove. . . .

The traditional view discussed above may be called a *deductive* approach; it holds that because the words of the Bible are divinely inspired, truths about God can be simply deduced or read off from those words. In contrast to this is an inductive view, according to which divine inspiration is not uniformly pre-supposed, but the varying circumstances and intentions of the writings themselves are first of all taken into account. In general terms, the Biblical writings represent many centuries of religious experience and document the emergence and development of a living religious tradition. This gives the writings the authority of the work of specialists and significant contributors to a body of faith. In addition to that general authority, Christians find in the Bible a uniquely particular authority, insofar as they take it to be not just a record of developing religious insight, but an account of progressive acts of God, leading to an incarnation in the person of Christ, to achieve man's salvation and establish the beginnings of his Kingdom on earth. . . . The Bible's authority, on the inductive view, still lies not in its words, so much as in what it records and communicates to man today, of the progressive dealings of God with mankind, centred on his decisive self-revelation in Jesus Christ.

. . . . . .

Religious Language

The authority of sacred books or scriptures is not self-evident, even if that authority is taught by certain religious figures, themselves taken as authorities. Like any other appeal to authority, it needs to be backed up with reasons. No one can object to another's decision to treat a certain book, or religious figure, as authoritative about God, even when he cannot spell out grounds which make it reasonable to decide in that way. All that is necessary (to avoid arbitrariness and irrationality) is that he believes there to be such grounds. But that is a belief which may or may not be well founded. . . .

The Christian who justifies his words about God by an appeal to the language of Jesus which he takes as authoritative is not being illogical in doing so. But neither is his position self-evidently secure. There have been many others, informed and sensitive theists amongst them, who do not respond in the Christian way to the records of the person of Jesus or experience any authoritative impact from the New Testament; any more than most Christians respond to the records of the prophet Muhammad, or experience the impressiveness which the Muslim finds in the Qur'an.

'Taking someone's word for it' in religious matters, would make a great deal of sense if we knew for sure that the words in question were from God, or from some reliable authority. But the establishing of that position itself seems to depend on appeals to claims about divine sonship, inspired scripture, revelation, God speaking to men, and the like – the very kinds of religious statement we have seen to be most problematic.

By whatever means their authority is defended, the sacred scriptures of religions and the words of authoritative figures recorded in them must be recognized as fundamental in understanding religious language-use. They are the primary source of the stories, imagery, concepts and propositions used to express beliefs about God and the human condition. They provide the greatest fund of ideas for interpreting the continuing religious experience of believers and their communities. But the observation that religious people for the most part take their language on trust from the founders of their religions and the sacred scriptures of their traditions does not relieve the philosopher of his task of assessing the validity of that language. While it may show him the right place to begin his investigations, it in no way bypasses the questions about informativeness and testability, which we have been considering in previous chapters.

Getting at the Truth in Religions, p. 105

I have spoken throughout this book of religious *claims, assertions* or *statements*, since that is how they appear to those who make them as believers. But it may be more accurate, philosophically, to describe religious claims as *proposals* or *suggestions* (or even as theories or hypotheses, though the use of those terms may for some suggest too close an analogy with scientific testing procedures).

I have accepted the view that if central religious claims or proposals are to carry information for mankind they must have some points of contact with human experience. If their truth (or falsity) makes no difference at all to what human beings can envisage, expect to meet with, or undergo in this or any other life, then they cannot be seriously regarded as the supremely important and profound claims to knowledge they have characteristically been taken to be. When attention is turned from the statements in religious language to the phenomena which those statements purport to interpret, the basis for that approach becomes clearer. The question of religion's truth and informativeness can be seen as more extensive than merely looking for observational tests sufficient to verify some theological statement or doctrinal claim. The question has to be directed rather to the phenomena from which those claims arise, and the responses to those phenomena which the claims attempt to articulate.

Thus instead of asking 'Is belief in divine providence true?' (in the sense of 'Is there such a thing as divine providence?') we should ask rather: 'Do the kinds of event and experience religious believers look to when they talk about divine providence carry anything like the sort of significance for human belief and response which those people think they find in them, and express by talking about them in such language?' For that is what it would *mean* for belief in divine providence to be true. In other words, the first thing to be investigated, to evaluate the truth of religions, is not the truth or falsity of statements and claims made in religious language, but the interpretation of phenomena, mostly non-verbal, on which those claims rest. What is there about such things that has led people, on the strength of them, to speak in those ways? How, if at all, might those things support such interpretations and sustain such responses?

All that has been said above about the ways of testing religious claims has an important bearing on these questions. But the search for tests and relevant observations can now be seen as not so tightly tied to the verifying of certain fact-claiming utterances, and more loosely related to the evaluating of ways of regarding certain phenomena. It has generally been assumed that the validity of religious interpretations and responses depends on the truth of the doctrinal beliefs they reflect. But the order can just as well be reversed, so that the doctrines are taken to reflect the interpretations, rather than *vice versa*. What it means for the beliefs or the doctrines to be true, sound or well founded, is that the interpretations they rest on are somehow or other supported by the phenomena to which they are directed, and indeed, in crucial cases, better supported than any of the alternative ways of responding and making sense of those phenomena.

We have in past chapters looked briefly at the wide range of phenomena which receive religious interpretations. ... The main concern throughout has been to show how some degree of testability for religious claims is possible; to show that despite their oblique and elusive character, religious beliefs and utterances can have informative content. ... But deciding what informativeness religious claims have in fact, what truth they genuinely convey, is a far larger task, and one which philosophers of religion certainly ought not to consider tackling on their own. For a task like that the resources of all who investigate human religious interpretations, behaviour and phenomena must be called upon; and that includes those who know the interpretations thoroughly themselves, as sensitive participants in religious life, as well as those who are equally sensitive to alternative interpretations, both from other religious points of view, and from the points of view of those who do not live by any religion.

On not having the Last Word

I have throughout taken as the chief worry of the philosopher the possibility of *illusory* meaningfulness in religious claims; the fear that the believer is misled, and misleads himself by religious language which seems to carry great meaning, but which is in no way supported by fact. The central issue in our study of religious language, then, has been showing how there can be sufficient consistency with experience and openness to objective tests for at least the possibility of genuine informative content in religious claims. There is a further possibility, however, less often discussed in philosophy of religion, since little can be done about it apart from noting it as a possibility. There may be phenomena with meanings which would bear on religious questions and pursuits if they were recognized as such, yet which are thought irrelevant to religion simply because they are not appreciated; their significance slips through the net of existing religious conceptions. We have spoken of the danger of over-interpretation of things in religious words. What we are now considering is the possibility of their *under*-interpretation. . . .

If there is truth within religions, and real significance for human life amongst the things religions deal with, that significance may not be anything like adequately reflected in the things religions have so far said, the doctrines they have up till now constructed.

The obscurity of religious language is in fact an advantage, so far as the possibilities of development go. For oblique language is always open to amendment and clarification, which can often take place without seriously negating or denying what was understood before. Religious traditions themselves have illustrated that time and again. Existing religious interpretations may, then, be reliable guides up to a point, without necessarily saying all there is to be said, or even saying what they do say in anything like the best, most accurate way.

It is a mistake to think there can be no meaning where people at a certain time and place in human history happen to find none. Many people doubtful about a future for religion point to the narrowness and naivety of religious interpretations of the majority of mankind up to the present day. But optimists about religion hold that our very recognition of the shortcomings of the past may give grounds for hope; they feel there is no good reason to assume that in the late twentieth century man cannot expect to come across anything further in the way of spiritual or religious significance for his life. Whatever the future of religion may be, people will inevitably go on putting into words the things and experiences they believe to be deeply significant. And so long as they do, there will continue to be a point in attempts by the philosophically minded to appreciate religious language and to understand more about its uses.

Basil Mitchell, 'The Stranger' from *New Essays in Philosophical Theology*, ed. A. G. N. Flew and A. MacIntyre, pp. 103f

In time of war in an occupied country, a member of the resistance meets one night a stranger who deeply impresses him. They spend the night together in conversation. The Stranger tells the partisan that he himself is on the side of the resistance – indeed that he is in command of it, and urges the partisan to have faith in him no matter what happens. The partisan is utterly convinced at that meeting of the Stranger's sincerity and constancy and undertakes to trust him.

They never meet in conditions of intimacy again, but sometimes the Stranger is seen helping members of the resistance, and the partisan is grateful and says to his friends 'He is on our side.'

Sometimes he is seen in the uniform of the police handing over patriots to the occupying power. On these occasions his friends murmur against him: but the partisan still says 'He is on our side.' He still believes that, in spite of appearances, the Stranger did not deceive him. Sometimes he asks the Stranger for help and receives it. He is then thankful. Sometimes he asks and does not receive it. Then he says 'The Stranger knows best.' Sometimes his friends, in exasperation, say 'Well, what *would* he have to do for you to admit that you were wrong and that he is not on our side?' But the partisan refuses to answer. And sometimes his friends complain 'Well, if *that's* what you mean by his being on our side, the sooner he goes over to the other side the better.'

The partisan of the parable does not allow anything to count decisively against the proposition: 'The Stranger is on our side.' This is because he has committed himself to trust the Stranger. But he of course recognizes that the Stranger's ambiguous behaviour *does* count against what he believes about him. It is precisely this situation which constitutes the trial of his faith.

J. H. Hick, 'The Road' from *Philosophy of Religion*, pp. 91f

Two men are travelling together along a road. One of them believes that it leads to the Celestial City, the other that it leads nowhere; but since this is the only road there is, both must travel it. Neither has been this way before, therefore neither is able to say what they will find around each corner. During their journey they meet with moments of refreshment and delight, and with moments of hardship and danger. All the time one of them thinks of his journey as a pilgrimage to the Celestial City. He interprets the pleasant parts as encouragements and the obstacles as trials of his purpose and lessons in endurance, prepared by the king of that city and designed to make him a worthy citizen of the place when at last he arrives. The other, however, believes none of this, and sees their journey as an unavoidable and aimless ramble. Since he has no choice in the matter, he enjoys the good and endures the bad. For him there is no Celestial City to be reached, no all-encompassing purpose ordaining their journey; there is only the road itself and the luck of the road in good weather and in bad.

During the course of the journey, the issue between them is not an experimental one. They do not entertain different expectations about the coming details of the road but only about its ultimate destination. Yet, when they turn the last corner, it will be apparent that one of them has been right all the time and the other wrong. Thus, although the issue between them has not been experimental, it has, nevertheless, been a real issue. They have not merely felt differently about the road, for one was feeling appropriately and the other inappropriately in relation to the actual state of affairs. Their opposed interpretations of the situation have constituted genuinely rival assertions, whose assertion-status has the peculiar characteristic of being guaranteed retrospectively by a future crux.

This parable, like all parables, has narrow limitations. It is designed to make only one point: that Judaic-Christian theism postulates an ultimate unambiguous existence *in patria*, as well as our present ambiguous existence *in via*. There is a state of having arrived as well as a state of journeying, an eternal heavenly life as well as an earthly pilgrimage. The alleged future experience cannot, of course, be appealed to as evidence for theism as a present interpretation of our experience; but it does suffice to render the choice between theism and atheism a real and not merely an empty or verbal choice.

STUDY TOPICS

1. What are the strengths and weaknesses of the views of the logical positivists on the meaninglessness of religious language? Is it possible to show that RL is meaningful?
2. If God is a 'mystery' how can we believe in him? Is it possible to believe in something you don't understand or pin down accurately?
3. If RL is meaningful does this have any implications for the claims of the various religions of the world. Can they all be right?
4. Why do you think people take up positions of belief or disbelief and stick to them? Do we need some sort of philosophy to guide us through life? How do we come to construct such a philosophy and how can it be defended against attack?

5. Apart from RL what other means are available for communicating religious sentiments? What tests of verification would you apply to them (if any)?

BIBLIOGRAPHY

(Here and in Further Reading sections numbers in brackets indicate source books quoted; for details see Bibliography on pp. 229–30.

The amount of literature on this subject is so vast that it is only possible to scratch the surface of it here. All the books from which extracts are taken are worth reading. This is especially true of Peter Donovan's *Religious Language* (8) which is an excellent introduction to the subject, as is John M. Hull's brief leaflet *Sense and Nonsense about God* (16). Braithwaite's essay is printed in full in Basil Mitchell's *Philosophy of Religion* (25) as is the discussion on *Theology and Falsification* between Flew, Hare, and Mitchell (in 11). This last is essential reading for those who wish to pursue the wider implications of the verification theory. It also has the double advantage of being relatively short and of being broken up into brief articles. John Hick's *Philosophy of Religion* (15) has sections on RL and the problem of verification which are well worth reading in full (pp. 69–96). Ian Ramsey's *Religious Language* (SCM 1969) and James Richmond's *Faith and Philosophy* (Hodder and Stoughton 1966) are more difficult but contain some valuable material.

FURTHER READING

Ayer, A. J., *Language, Truth and Logic*. Gollancz 1946 rev., pp. 38–54. The book that popularized logical positivism in Britain. Not easy.

Charlesworth, M. J., *Philosophy of Religion: The Historic Approaches*. Macmillan 1972, pp. 145–174. Advanced. Gives some useful comments on Braithwaite.

Crombie, I. M., 'Theology and Falsification' in *New Essays in Philosophical Theology*, ed. A. Flew and A. MacIntyre (11), pp. 109–130.

Ferré, Frederick, *Language, Logic and God*. Eyre and Spottiswoode 1962.

Lewis, H. D., *Teach Yourself the Philosophy of Religion* (21). Chapters 7, 8, 13.
Macquarrie, John, *God-talk*. SCM Press 1967.
McPherson, Thomas, *Philosophy and Religious Belief* (24). Hutchinson 1974.
Mitchell, Basil, ed., *Faith and Logic*. Allen and Unwin 1975.
Robinson, J. A. T., *Honest to God*. SCM Press 1963.
Santoni, R. F., ed., *Religious Language and the Problem of Religious Knowledge*. Indiana University Press, Bloomington and London 1969.
Van Buren, Paul, *The Secular Meaning of the Gospel*. SCM Press 1963.
Wilson, K., *Making Sense of it*. Epworth Press 1973, p. 65.
Wilson, John, *Language and Christian Belief*. Macmillan 1959.
Wilson, John, *Language and the Pursuit of Truth*. Cambridge University Press 1956.
Wilson, John, *Philosophy and Religion*. Oxford University Press 1961.

2
Revelation

INTRODUCTION

Sometimes people speak of Christianity as a 'revealed' religion. The point of saying this is to distinguish it from a 'non-revealed' or 'natural' religion. The basis of 'natural' religion is the claim that by looking at nature we can see enough evidence of a God to be able to say things about him. Thus a 'natural theology' is concerned to show that this is possible. Although, as far as Christianity is concerned, most theologians nowadays seem to think this is not so, some (e.g. Macquarrie and Brown) still think that 'natural' theology of some sort is required.

However, Christianity suffers from 'the scandal of particularity'. A vital part of the Christian religion is that God has communicated certain information about himself and our relationship to him. The Christian claims to be able to make some quite specific statements about the nature of God and his wishes concerning us. This information was not derived from looking at the natural world of earth, sea, and sky, but was conveyed to mankind through particular people in particular historical situations. The fullest example of God's revelation was in his Son Jesus Christ, who, so Christians claim, was alive on earth in Palestine about 2,000 years ago.

The 'revelation' of the Christian God through the prophets of the Old Testament, historical events, Jesus of Nazareth, and the workings of the Holy Spirit, poses certain problems. For example, if God has revealed himself to mankind why did he do it so ambiguously? There is so much room for doubt and debate that many people question whether or not God even exists. Why did he not reveal himself in such a way as to put the matter beyond all doubt?

Another problem is that of the content of revelation. How do we know what is true revelation and what are the mere ravings of a lunatic? (There was a time, as shown in the Old Testament, when to be called 'one of the prophets' was not very complimentary.) Flew presses the point home that, even admitting that some men believe they have had a message from God, there is no way of checking that this is in fact the case. The two brief extracts from William James are striking examples (of which there are many more in the Bible) of a religious experience, but Flew's point about objectivity still remains valid.

The arrival of biblical criticism last century also raised questions about the nature of revelation and the Bible. Many people in the past (see Jurgens) believed that the Bible contains the revelation of God, true in every word and detail. The results of biblical criticism have made this an impossible position but its simplicity still appeals to many. Modern Protestant theologians like Barth want us to concentrate on Jesus as the Word of God. Revelation is the movement of God towards man, seen in perfection in Jesus. It is absolute, final, and totally derived from God. But here another question raises its head: What is the role of man when he receives revelation? Is he active or passive? Is there any way the recipient can tell if he has been misled? Religious experiences are ultimately ambiguous and essentially incommunicable. Each man must make his own decision, because revelation has always left room for faith over and above what has been revealed. Even those who saw Jesus perform miracles were able to interpret what they saw as acts of the devil.

Many modern theologians (e.g. Hick, Macquarrie) do not see revelation as a set of 'facts' or 'propositions' about God, but prefer a more existentialist approach, placing revelation in the context of human experience and talking in terms of 'insight' and 'interpretation'.

It is impossible to have an overall view of Christianity without first making up your mind about what revelation is. The questions of its reception, authenticity, content, and interpretation are central to any coherent understanding of Christianity, and from your answers to the foregoing questions many consequences follow.

W. A. Jurgens, *The Faith of the Early Fathers*

Origen – De Principiis, p. 194

Although no one, certainly, is able to speak worthily of God the Father, it is nevertheless possible for some knowledge of Him to be obtained by

Revelation

means of visible creatures and from those things which the human mind naturally senses; and it is possible, moreover, for such knowledge to be confirmed by the sacred Scriptures.

St Cyril of Jerusalem – Catechetical Lectures, p. 351

Keep always in mind this seal, which I have until now but briefly summarized for you in my discourse, but which, the Lord willing, shall after this be stated to the best of my ability with the proofs from the Scriptures. In regard to the divine and holy mysteries of the faith, not the least part may be handed on without the Holy Scriptures. Do not be led astray by winning words and clever arguments. Even to me, who tell you these things, do not give ready belief, unless you receive from the Holy Scriptures the proof of the things which I announce. The salvation in which we believe is proved not from clever reasoning, but from the Holy Scriptures.

Colin Brown, 'Natural theology' from *Philosophy and the Christian Faith*, pp. 271–6

Natural theology has something of the irrepressible quality of a yo-yo. However much it is repulsed, there has always been someone or other who has tried to bring it back. A few years ago it was called 'the sick man of Europe'. Certainly it has taken quite a battering from the philosophers on the one hand and the Barthians on the other. But more recently, in 'Soundings', Howard Root has entered a wistful plea for its revival. His essay combines something of the tone of don't-shoot-the-pianist-he's-doing-his-best and the claim that theology inevitably involves metaphysical theology. And by implication this means natural theology. Admittedly, the matter is not so naïvely straightforward as philosophers such as Descartes imagined it was. Nor does Professor Root say what form he envisages that it will take (apart from dropping a hint that future natural theology should look more to the arts and creative imagination).

What are we to say to all this? On the basis of our survey the following points may be suggested as guidelines for future thought: (1) The traditional rationalistic arguments for the existence of God will not hold water. Their logic is suspect and they fail to bring us to the God of Christian faith and experience. We saw this right at the outset when we discussed Anselm and Aquinas. The point was underlined when we looked at the classical debates of thinkers such as Descartes and Kant. In our own day the ventures of John Robinson and Paul Tillich into the realms of natural theology have proved equally fruitless. (2) But this, in the opinion of the present writer, is no great loss. It brings no honour to God to resort to dubious arguments in his defence! Nor does it help the faith of the believer to be propped up by such proofs, which are drawn from outside the Christian revelation. Moreover, as we saw in looking at the influence of medieval philosophy, natural theology opened the door to all kinds of speculation which had the effect of obscuring the Christian gospel. Instead of opening up man's mind to the challenge of the Christian revelation, it has proved a perennial temptation to fashion God in the image of man.

(3) On the other hand, writers like the early Barth fall into the opposite error when they insist that man has no knowledge at all of God apart from the gospel. It would seem to be both the common experience of men and also the testimony of several important strands of Scripture, that men have an awareness of God regardless of whether they have heard the gospel and regardless of whether they respond or not. This awareness may be dim. It is certainly not that intimate, personal knowledge of God in Christ through the Holy Spirit to which the apostle Paul testified and claimed to be unique to Christian experience. Christians all down the ages have endorsed Paul's claim at this point. On the other hand, it is precisely this awareness of God as one to whom we are ultimately responsible which provides a point of contact for the Christian message and which clinches man's guilt in his persistent turning away from God.

This general awareness of God gains added point when we reflect on the question whether we really believe that the universe that we live in with all its apparent evidence of design is purely the product of accidental chance or whether it points to some sort of connection with a rational mind. To my mind the former alternative is incredible, however incomplete and puzzling the universe may be. I think that Professor Root has something when he directs attention to men's awareness of God in art, literature and experience. But this does not seem to add up to anything capable of being called a theology except in the most rudimentary sense. Natural theology (in the sense of a coherent knowledge of God and his relationship with the world without recourse to the Christian revelation) is a blind alley. On the other hand, it seems legitimate on the basis of both common experience and the witness of the biblical writers to speak of a revelation in nature and a natural awareness of God. And these deserve due attention in preaching, apologetics and the philosophy of religion.

(4) It would be interesting to investigate in more detail Howard Root's plea for a new type of natural theology in the light of Van Til's and Schaeffer's views on the importance of presuppositions. In discussing the latter it was suggested that the Christian faith could be seen as a hypothesis. It suggests explanations for phenomena which are otherwise inexplicable. It makes sense of what at first seemed senseless. It gives a wholeness to life which is missing in other views. This is so whether we look at the universe in general or at personal experience of life. On atheistic, humanistic premises the whole universe is the product of blind chance. All human values are accidental and arbitrary. If this is so, life is what Macbeth said it was, 'a tale told by an idiot, full of sound and fury, signifying nothing'. On these premises, it would be right simply to live for oneself. Pleasure, profit, drugs – whatever gave the individual the maximum of pleasure and the minimum of discomfort – would be the obvious options. But there is something in man which cries out against this. Is it merely wishful thinking? Does it make best sense of this highly complicated universe to say that it just happened, that it is a purely fortuitous collection of atoms?

Van Til and Schaeffer say that the universe in general and human life in particular make real sense only on Christian premises. What they are saying is not natural theology in the accepted sense of the term. The key to meaning is not derived simply from reflecting on phenomena. The latter is more like a jig-saw puzzle with vital pieces missing, or perhaps one so complex that the pieces just do not make sense without the aid of a picture from outside. By beginning with himself and his rationalism man just cannot make sense of it as a whole.

To say this is not to claim that the Bible explains everything. Clearly it does not. It does not pretend to do the job of the scientist for him. It does not say everything there is to know about God himself. But it does provide a key which gives coherence and meaning to life as a whole. To argue in this way is not to relapse into the discredited God-of-the-gaps arguments of old-fashioned apologetics. It is not a case of saying that we have a gap here in scientific explanation, therefore, God must have done it, only to find later on that there was a natural explanation. The argument here is on a different plane. It concerns the presuppositions of naturalistic explanation. By itself scientific explanation gives an account of particular phenomena. The question then arises whether we are to say that these rational accounts are, in the last analysis, about the irrational and absurd.

To adopt this line of thought is not to say that Christian theology is merely a presupposition or hypothesis. (In any case, presuppositions are not just arbitrary ideas picked out of the air. Their validity is tested by whatever is built upon them. If they are incapable of bearing the weight, they must be scrapped, and others sought.) The Christian belief that God created all things outside of himself is a presupposition of Christian thought about life generally. But the Christian interpretation of life does not remain in the realm of the theoretical. What the Bible says about forgiveness, faith, being born again, about love and the whole range of human activity, is validated by the Christian as he tries it out in life. It gives meaning to experience. It is precisely at the conjunction of experience and interpretation through the gospel that there takes place that encounter with God which in Christian theology is termed revelation.

(5) All too often in the past it has been assumed that the philosophy of the Christian religion was synonymous with natural theology. No doubt this was partly due to the fact that those Christians who were interested in philosophy tended to be devotees of some established brand of secular philosophy or advocates of the methods of natural theology. But in fact this is not the only option. There remains the possibility that the philosophy of the Christian religion should be worked out on the basis of the Christian revelation and the practising Christian's experience of God.

This is not an attempt to turn the Christian message into an esoteric philosophy. Men encounter God in their total personalities through the gospel presented by the church, and not through abstruse arguments. Philosophy is not everybody's cup of tea. A man can be a perfectly good Christian without any great grasp of the subject. Nevertheless, because the Christian faith lays claims to a type of knowledge and asserts that certain events in the past are decisive for humanity, Christianity inevitably raises philosophical questions. In so far as the phenomenon of the gospel raises philosophical issues, it is this which should provide the subject-matter for the philosophy of the Christian religion. This is, in fact, what has happened to some extent in recent years in those philosophical circles which have been interested in examining the nature and function of religious language. To that extent the analytic movement in philosophy is something to be welcomed by the Christian, as is the renewed interest of the past couple of decades in the philosophy of history.

The point can be put another way round. The Christian gospel must henceforth stand or fall – from the philosophical point of view – by itself. Christianity must be capable of vindicating itself by itself. Our proof of the existence of God must derive from our experience of God *'through the whole gospel'* and not be made dependent upon hypothetical abstract arguments borrowed from outside. All too often in the past the Christian apologist has put himself in the position of the schoolboy who knows how the theorem should come out, but, through not following the proper proof, has found himself obliged to 'cook' it. Just as the shrewd eye of the maths. master soon spots the cooking, so the modern secular philosopher refuses to be taken in by the lame arguments of natural theology. In future Christian philosophers must be prepared to vindicate Christianity by a more thorough investigation of the Christian revelation, or quit the field altogether.

D. M. Baillie, *The Idea of Revelation in Recent Thought*

The Good News, pp. 49–50

We have said that it is not enough to think of God as giving us information by communication, but that we must rather think of Him as giving Himself to us in communion. Two things are implied in this. With the first we were concerned in the foregoing chapter, and we said then that it is one of the points on which there appears a remarkable breadth of agreement in recent discussions about revelation. It is that what is fundamentally revealed is God Himself, not propositions about God. Equally remarkable, however, is the recent agreement on the second, which is this: that God reveals Himself 'in action' – in the gracious activity by which He invades the field of human experience and human history which is otherwise but a vain show, empty and drained of meaning. In the sequel we shall have to examine very closely the nature of this relation between revelation and history, but meanwhile we shall stay within the area of fairly general agreement.

The Bible is essentially the story of the acts of God. As has often been pointed out, its most striking difference from the sacred books of all other religions lies in its historical character. Other sacred books are composed mainly of oracles which communicate what profess to be timeless truths about universal being or timeless prescriptions for the conduct of life and worship. But the Bible is mainly a record of what God has done. Those parts of it which are not in a strict sense historiographic are nevertheless placed within a definite historical frame and setting which they presuppose at every point. The Mosaic law differs from other law books in that all its prescriptions presuppose the sealing of a covenant between Yahweh and Israel – a covenant which is conceived as being no part of a universal and timeless relation between God and man, but one which was sealed on Horeb-Sinai on a particular historical occasion.

The Mighty Acts of God – Event and Interpretation, pp. 62–5

No affirmation runs more broadly throughout recent writing on our subject than that which in the last chapter we were concerned to make, namely, that all revelation is given, not in the form of directly communicated knowledge, but through events occurring in the historical experience of mankind, events which are apprehended by faith as the 'mighty acts' of God, and which therefore engender in the mind of man such reflective knowledge of God as it is given him to possess. It is clear that this represents a very radical departure from the traditional ecclesiastical formulation which identified revelation with the written word of Scripture and gave to the action of God in history the revelational status only of being among the things concerning which Scripture informed us. Thus, for instance, Aquinas, having defined the revealed (as distinct from the natural) knowledge of God as resting 'upon the authority of Scripture confirmed from heaven by miracles', (*Summa Contra Gentiles I*, ch. ix) goes on to subdivide this knowledge into (a) suprarational information concerning God's nature, (b) information concerning His suprarational works – the Incarnation and its sequel, and (c) information concerning suprarational events to be expected at the end of earthly history. Dr Barth may be suspected of remaining still more biblicist in the traditional sense than most of the other contemporary writers from which we have been quoting, yet it is clear that the same fundamental change has accomplished itself in his thinking. The following may here be added to the quotations already made from his treatment of the subject:

> What has generated Scripture and what Scripture in its turn asserts is something that really and definitively, once and once for all, happened. What happened was . . . that God was with us. . . . He was with us as One like unto ourselves. His word became flesh of our flesh, blood of our blood. His glory was seen here in the depth of our predicament, and only when it was there and then illuminated by the glory of the Lord was the deepest depth of that predicament made manifest. . . . That did happen, and that is what the Old Testament as the word of prophecy and the New Testament as the word of

fulfilment are concerned to announce, but in both cases as having 'happened' – happened conclusively, completely, sufficiently. (*Church Dogmatics*, vol. 1 (T. & T. Clark 1936), p. 118.)

It is well known that the general concept under which Dr Barth works out his theology is that of the Word of God. This Word of God, he teaches, always reaches us in a three-fold form – as preached, as written, and as revealed. In order of knowledge the preaching comes first, but all Christian preaching is dependent upon the witness of prophet and apostle as handed down to us in Scripture.

Revelation is therefore originally and directly what the Bible and the Church's proclamation are derivatively and mediately – the Word of God. (Ibid.)

We must, however, think very carefully what we mean when we say that revelation is given in the form of events or historical happenings. For it is not as if all who experience these events and happenings find in them a revelation of God. The question thus arises as to whether even such events as are in themselves 'mighty acts of God' can properly be spoken of as revelation if, in fact, there should be nobody to whom they reveal anything. To take the human analogy, do all my efforts to make myself plain amount to a real self-disclosure, if none succeeds in grasping what is in my mind? Surely not. We must therefore say that the receiving is as necessary to a completed act of revelation as the giving. It is only so far as the action of God in history is understood as God means it to be understood that revelation has taken place at all. The illumination of the receiving mind is a necessary condition of the divine self-disclosure. Here again we find general agreement among contemporary theologians. It is to be noted, for instance, that it is only the prophetic and apostolic 'witness' to the revelation, and not the illumination of the prophetic and apostolic minds themselves, that Dr Barth makes posterior to the event of revelation. The witness does indeed come afterwards, but the illumination is an integral part of that to which witness is borne. Similarly Dr Brunner has it that 'The fact of the illumination necessarily belongs to the process of revelation itself; without it an event is no more revelation than light is light without a seeing and illuminated eye. . . . Jesus Christ is not revelation if He is recognized by nobody as the Christ, any more than He is redeemer if there is nobody whom He redeems.' (*Offenbarung und Vernunft*, p. 34. Translated as *Revelation and Reason* by O. Wyon. Copyright 1946 by W. L. Jenkins. Published by The Westminster Press.)

Karl Barth, 'The Christian Understanding of Revelation' from *Against the Stream*, pp. 205–12, 214

I

Revelation means the publication of something private, something hidden. The Greek concept 'Phanerosis' signifies the appearance of something hidden, and the parallel concept 'Apokalypsis' the unveiling of something veiled. A closed door is opened; a covering removed. A light shines in the darkness, a question finds its answer, a puzzle its solution. In general terms, this is the process we call 'revelation'. In this general sense the concept covers many things that are not contained in the Christian connotation of revelation. Let us first make a brief survey of this general connotation of the term in ten points.

1. In the general sense of the term there are revelations which man may find good and useful, enriching and deepening his life, but which are not necessary, vital or indispensable. There are many things we do not need to know even if we could know them. Is there also such a thing as a necessary, and indispensable revelation?

2. There are revelations which man may find interesting, stimulating and exciting and possibly useful in some way or other, but which are nevertheless dangerous and therefore of doubtful value. As everyone knows, it has been questioned whether the revelation on the basis of which Prometheus discovered fire was not rather a curse for man, and the question is all the more pertinent in regard to the invention of gunpowder and certain discoveries which are making our own age so remarkable. Is there a revelation of which it can be said that it is clearly a good and wholesome revelation for man?

3. There are revelations which occur today and which may be superseded by others tomorrow. There are therefore relative revelations. Is there, on the other hand, an absolute revelation, independent of the changes and chances of time?

4. There are revelations which are vouchsafed to possibly only a few, even very few people. There are therefore esoteric and exoteric relations to such revelations. Is there, in contrast to such special revelations, a general revelation which concerns all mankind?

5. There are revelations which are disclosures of matters of fact which

were only temporarily unknown – that is, contingent revelations. Is there, in contrast to these, something like a necessary revelation?

6. There are revelations which consist in the translation into reality, life and activity of hidden but existing possibilities which are available to and can be realized by man. Is there, on the other hand, a revelation which cannot be effected by man at all, which does not consist in the realization of an existing possibility, but can only be interpreted as a gift?

7. There are revelations which, when they take place or have taken place, pass into human possession, so that man can muster them and do as he likes with them. Such revelations may be said to be open to exploitation. Is there, on the other hand, a free revelation, free in the sense that man cannot use it for his own purposes at all?

8. There are revelations which occur in the form of partial and approximate revelations in the course of intellectual inquiries, whether conducted by individuals or groups. Is there, in contrast to such merely approximate revelations, an original and definitive revelation?

9. There are revelations of which man can establish the existence, constitution and quality, and which he can contemplate with more or less pleasure and insight: we may call such revelations 'speculative' revelations. Is there, on the other hand, such a thing as a 'practical' revelation?

10. Everything that has been said so far may be summed up as the self-revelation of something that already exists, a self-revelation of man in the cosmos or a revelation of the cosmos in relation to man: in other words, immanent, this-worldly revelation, which occurs in the human and cosmic realm. Is there, in contrast to this, such a thing as a transcendent, other-worldly revelation?

II

Revelation in the Christian sense is the wholly other revelation which only appears on the brink of all the above-mentioned possibilities.

Revelation in the Christian sense is:

1. A revelation which man needs not relatively, but absolutely for his very life and being as man, a revelation without which he would not in fact be man at all, a revelation which decides being and non-being: in

other words, one which man cannot please himself whether he accepts or not.

2. Revelation in the Christian sense is a revelation which accepts man absolutely, which takes place for his salvation, for his perfect salvation. Revelation in the Christian sense is an affirmation of man, however much it may be bound up with threats and judgement.

3. Revelation in the Christian sense is a revelation which was completely new to man yesterday and the day before yesterday, which is completely new to him today and will be new again tomorrow. It is absolute, not relative.

4. Revelation in the Christian sense is a revelation which comes to all men with equal strangeness from outside, but which concerns all men with equal intimacy. It is not a revelation intended for a few men only, but for all men.

5. Revelation in the Christian sense means the unveiling of certain facts that are fundamentally hidden from man, things no eye has seen, no ear has heard, no human heart conceived. Revelation in the Christian sense is not contingent.

6. Revelation in the Christian sense is the revelation of a reality outside man. It is the realization of a possibility which lies wholly in the place where the revelation takes place, not in the human realm. It is therefore a revelation which man is powerless to bring about by his own will.

7. Revelation in the Christian sense is a revelation which remains free in its relation to man. It cannot be capitalized.

8. Revelation in the Christian sense is a revelation which is complete and final, which fulfils past, present and future, which fulfils time itself. It is anything but merely approximate.

9. Revelation in the Christian sense is not an object which man can observe from outside; it is rather one which takes possession of man, seizes hold of him and calls him to action. It is anything but merely speculative.

10. We may sum up what has been said so far by saying that revelation in the Christian sense is the self-revelation of the Creator of all that is, the self-revelation of the Lord of all Being. It is not an immanent, this-

Revelation

worldly revelation, but comes from outside man and the cosmos. It is a transcendent revelation.

This is what is meant by revelation in the Christian sense of the term. It is useful to realize what revelation in this sense connotes, whatever the personal attitude may be that one adopts towards it. In any case it is the question we are to consider in this lecture.

We have seen that there are many kinds of revelation. In the ten points which we started with we tried to indicate the nature of the relevations that occur in all the spheres of human life, art, science, history, nature, and in man's personal life and experience. We contrasted this with the Christian understanding of revelation. You must decide for yourselves whether the two kinds are merely aspects of the same reality. But is it really feasible to lump together what we call revelation in all the fields of human experience and what the Christian means by the same term? Is it feasible, as happens so often, to derive, explain and justify the Christian interpretation on the basis of what we are in the habit of calling 'revelation' in everyday life? Is it even possible to compare the two realities? Is not revelation in the Christian sense rather a specific reality of its own, a revelation which begins at the very point where all the others end? We shall come back later to the significance, from the Christian point of view, of the existence of other revelations and meanings of revelation. What is certain is that Christian and non-Christian revelations are two quite distinct realities which must not be confused. We are concerned here with the sphere of Christian revelation which cannot be seen or penetrated from the sphere of any other revelation, but which has a special content and constitutes a special order of its own.

Revelation in the Christian sense is the revelation of God. For the Christian there is no need of a special enquiry and a special proof to know and to declare who and what God is. For the Christian the revelation is itself the proof, the proof furnished by God himself. The Christian answer to the question as to who and what God is, is a simple one: he is the subject who acts in his revelation. This act of revelation is a token of his Being and the expression of his nature.

III

Keeping to the sequence of our original ten points, we may define the Christian understanding of God as follows:

Who is God?

1. God is he who is absolutely necessary to man, God decides man's being or non-being.

2. God is he who accepts man with the utmost seriousness and in the deepest love. He is his saviour.

3. God is he who was, who is and always will be new to man. He is absolute.

4. God is he who is above all and for all: 'Before thee none can boast but all must fear.'

5. God is he who meets man as the inherently necessary and fundamentally hidden reality.

6. God is he who is able to come quite close to man, though he is farthest away from him. Though unknown, he is able to become most intimately known to man.

7. God is he who in revealing himself to man, is and remains free.

8. God is he who was, is and shall be, the Lord of time, the eternal God, the God of the aeons.

9. God is also the Lord and Master of man, who makes demands on man.

10. God is the Creator and as such acts upon man, without whom no other being, including man, could exist.

God is he who acts in his revelation and thereby describes himself. The revelation of God, that is, the action of the Subject who reveals himself in this revelation, is what is meant when Christians speak of revelation. They mean the revelation of this God, the one, the only God. There seem to be many gods, just as there are many revelations. In accordance with this multiplicity of revelations there are many religions, theologies, philosophies, ideologies and, therefore, many and multiform images of God. Sometimes God is said to be that which is most necessary or even most dangerous to man, sometimes he is merely a general ideal or an individual dream, sometimes the embodiment of an historical ideal or a temporary exigency, sometimes the essence of the universal cosmic possibilities of man in their known and unknown depths. Sometimes God may be the longed-for opium of a personal or general development, sometimes the exponent of some human caprice; ultimately and really all these gods are simply some form of man himself

Revelation

in his relationship to the cosmos. I must leave you to decide for yourselves whether God, in the Christian understanding of revelation, is simply one of these gods, or whether the *Deus non est in genere* (Tertullian) is not true, whether the antithesis between the true God and the false gods, the 'nonentities', as the old Testament calls them, is not valid and true. God is not an abstract category by which even the Christian understanding of the word has to be measured, but he who is called God here is the One God, the Single God, the Sole God.

IV

What is this revelation, what is the subject of the revelation of which we have been speaking? What is the frame of mind which is open to receive what we call revelation? What is the theory of cognition for which revelation in the Christian sense is a valid object of knowledge?

And on the other hand: is there a conception of the world, a basic view of existence which can include what we have called God? If the general conception of the world and the general pattern of human thought are the criteria, can such a thing as revelation in the Christian sense exist at all? Does this God exist, of whom we have spoken as the subject of this revelation? What are we in fact talking about? Are we possibly talking nonsense talking about *non-ens*? There are theories of knowledge which can account for what we have called the self-revelation of that which exists, and there are ontologies which can embrace the gods corresponding to these revelations. But as far as one can see there is no theory of knowledge and no pattern of thought which can embrace revelation in the Christian sense of the term. We can work through the whole history of philosophy from Thales to Martin Heidegger, and we shall be forced to the same conclusion. There is no room for revelation in the Christian sense in any human inquiry or any human faculty of reason. And the same applies to what we have called God in the Christian sense. There may be conceptions of the world which provide for gods, but the God of Christianity cannot appear in any imaginable human conception of the world. Try to map out a conception of the world in which God, as understood in Christian thought, would have room. And so we must say that if a purely human conception of the world is the measure of all things, then neither revelation nor God in the Christian sense exist at all. We would in fact have been speaking about 'nothing' when we were speaking about revelation and God.

We have not, however, been speaking about 'nothing', but about a reality, something incomparably more real than anything that can be called real in the sphere of human thought and knowledge. When the Christian language speaks of revelation and God it means a reality which is very insignificant-looking and outwardly most unpromising; it speaks quite simply of a single concrete fact in the midst of the numberless host of facts and the vast stream of historical events; it speaks of a single human person living in the age of the Roman Empire: it speaks of Jesus Christ. When the Christian language speaks of God it does so not on the basis of some speculation or other, but looking at this fact, this story, this person. It cannot place this fact in relationship to any system of principles and ideas which would illuminate its importance and significance; it cannot explain and establish it from any other source; it makes no presuppositions when it points to this event. Its sole concern is with the event itself; all it can do is to refer to the existence, or rather, more precisely, the presence of this fact and the reception of the news of its presence as recorded in a tiny sheaf of news about the existence of this Person.

With its eyes concentrated on this news, Christianity speaks of revelation and of God as the subject of this revelation. Looking at this fact, it speaks with absolute assurance. Here – but only here – it sees revelation (in the sense of the criteria we have stated) and it sees God (again, in the sense of the criteria we have stated). Revelation in the Christian sense takes place and God in the Christian sense is, in accordance with the news of Jesus Christ, his words and deeds, his death and resurrection. . . .

Inasmuch as this creative Word, which is superior to all being, is spoken and heard in him, revelation takes place: transcendent, not immanent revelation. Revelation from the origin of all being. And it is God who speaks this Word.

The concept of revelation and the concept of God in the Christian sense coincide, therefore, in the contemplation of Jesus Christ, in which they are both related to reality. And in contemplation of him it is decided that God is and what God is; that God is a person and not a neutral thing. And that revelation is his acting and speaking and not a blind occurrence or an un-articulated sound.

William James, 'Mysticism' from *The Varieties of Religious Experience*, pp. 376ff

This has the genuine religious mystic ring! I just now quoted J. S. Symonds. He also records a mystical experience with chloroform, as follows:

> After the choking and stifling had passed away, I seemed at first in a state of utter blankness; then came flashes of intense light, alternating with blackness, and with a keen vision of what was going on in the room around me, but no sensation of touch. I thought that I was near death; when, suddenly, my soul became aware of God, who was manifestly dealing with me, handling me, so to speak, in an intense personal present reality. I felt him streaming in like light upon me . . . I cannot describe the ecstasy I felt. Then, as I gradually awoke from the influence of the anaesthetics, the old sense of my relation to God began to fade. I suddenly leapt to my feet on the chair where I was sitting, and shrieked out, 'It is too horrible, it is too horrible, it is too horrible', meaning that I could not bear this disillusionment. Then I flung myself on the ground, and at last awoke covered with blood, calling to the two surgeons (who were frightened), 'Why did you not kill me? Why would you not let me die?' Only think of it. To have felt for that long dateless ecstasy of vision the very God, in all purity and tenderness and truth and absolute love, and then to find that I had after all had no revelation, but that I had been tricked by the abnormal excitement of my brain.
>
> Yet, this question remains, Is it possible that the inner sense of reality which succeeded, when my flesh was dead to impressions from without, to the ordinary sense of physical relations, was not a delusion but an actual experience? Is it possible that I, in that moment, felt what some of the saints have said they always felt, the undemonstrable but irrefragable certainty of God? (Benjamin Paul Blood, The *Anaesthetic Revelation and the Gifts of Philosophy* (Amsterdam, N. Y. 1874), pp. 78–80 abridged.)

. . . . . .

It was Dr Bucke's own experience of a typical onset of cosmic consciousness in his own person which led him to investigate it in others. He has printed his conclusions in a highly interesting volume, from which I take the following account of what occurred to him:

I had spent the evening in a great city, with two friends, reading and discussing poety and philosophy. We parted at midnight. I had a long drive in a hansom to my lodging. My mind, deeply under the influence of the ideas, images, and emotions called up by the reading and talk, was calm and peaceful. I was in a state of quiet, almost passive enjoyment, not actually thinking, but letting ideas, images, and emotions flow of themselves, as it were, through my mind. All at once, without warning of any kind, I found myself wrapped in a flame-coloured cloud. For an instant I thought of fire, an immense conflagration somewhere close by in that great city; the next, I knew that the fire was within myself. Directly afterwards there came upon me a sense of exultation, of immense joyousness accompanied or immediately followed by an intellectual illumination impossible to describe. Among other things, I did not merely come to believe, but I saw that the universe is not composed of dead matter, but is, on the contrary, a living Presence; I became conscious in myself of eternal life. It was not a conviction that I would have eternal life, but a consciousness that I possessed eternal life then; I saw that all men are immortal; that the cosmic order is such that without any peradventure all things work together for the good of each and all; that the foundation principle of the world, of all the worlds, is what we call love, and that the happiness of each and all is in the long run absolutely certain. The vision lasted a few seconds and was gone but the memory of it and the sense of the reality of what it taught have remained during the quarter of a century which has since elapsed. I knew that what the vision showed was true. I had attained to a point of view from which I saw that it must be true. That view, that conviction, I may say that consciousness, has never, even during periods of the deepest depression, been lost. (*Cosmic Consciousness: a study in the evolution of the human mind* (Philadelphia 1901), p. 2.)

A. Flew, 'Religious Experience' from *God and Philosophy*, pp. 124ff

6.1 It is common ground among all schools of theologians and anti-theologians that the maximum which any natural theology could hope to offer must be much less than the minimum which we should be prepared to accept as constituting Christianity, Islam, or Judaism. So even if it were to have been conceded that arguments such as we have been examining ... do establish the existence of God, in the sense

Revelation

indicated and criticized, there would still be two urgent issues outstanding. These are: first, which, if any, of the various candidate systems of revelation is in fact authentic; and, second, how this is supposed to be determined. When, on the contrary, the pretensions of natural theology are not conceded, then everything hinges on these questions of revelation. Revelation now for us becomes the only possible source of knowledge of God. What it undertakes to provide can no longer be seen as any sort of supplement, however important: for it has to include the primary presupposition, that there is a God to reveal.

6.4 The expression *religious experience* is enormously comprehensive. *Experience* can embrace almost everything which is, in a wide sense, psychological: visions of all kinds, dreaming and waking; all the analogues of visions connected with the other senses; emotions, affections, sensations, dispositions; even convictions and beliefs. It also has a fundamental and crucial ambiguity. This ambiguity, which the generic term *experience* shares with many of its species labels, is that between, first, the sense in which it refers only to what the subject is undergoing and, second, a sense in which it implies that there must be an actual object as well. It is, therefore, as easy as it is both common and wrong to pass without warrant from what is supposed to be simply a description of subjective experience to the conclusion that this must have, and have been occasioned by, some appropriate object in the world outside. . . .

6.5 The crucial point is put, in his usual succinct and devastating way, by Hobbes; 'For if any man pretend to me that God hath spoken to him . . . immediately, and I make doubt of it, I cannot easily perceive what argument he can produce to oblige me to believe it. . . . To say he hath spoken to him in a dream, is no more than to say that he dreamed that God spoke to him. . . . So that though God almighty can speak to a man by dreams, visions, voice, and inspiration; yet he obliges no man to believe he hath done so to him that pretends it; who (being a man) may err, and (which is more) may lie.' (Thomas Hobbes, *Leviathan* (1651) in *Works*, ed. W. Molesworth (Bohn 1839–40), ch. 32.)

6.7 We are, therefore, not entitled, because a man truly has certain subjective experiences, immediately to infer that these are experiences of what is truly and objectively the case: nor must we assume, because such experiences are in some sense truly religious, that they must as

Revelation

such or consequently represent religious truths. The mere fact of the occurrence of subjective religious experience does not by itself warrant the conclusion that there are any objective religious truths to be represented. A vision may be a vision of the Blessed Virgin, in the senses either that it resembles conventional representations or that it is so described by the subject, without this constituting any sort of guarantee of its being a vision of the Blessed Virgin, in the very different sense that it actually is produced by the presence in some form of Mary the wife of Joseph and mother of Jesus. . . .

6.9 In the same way, in the present slightly trickier case, to analyse the notion of God wholly in terms of human beliefs is to make your God a sort of Tinker-Bell: a figure whose existence is entirely dependent on, and is indeed a function of, these beliefs. Any analysis of this sort must be dismissed as an irrelevant mockery – notwithstanding that it may be presented in respectful innocence as a psychologist's or a sociologist's view of religion. This dimissal also has its price. And the price is that we may not draw inferences about the existence and character of the Christian God directly from the occurrence of the phenomena of Christian belief. If talk about God is to be more than a mere literary flourish there has to be a fundamental distinction between, on the one hand, the facts that people believe in God and that their having this belief has expressions and consequences, and, on the other hand, the facts, if they be facts, that this God exists and brings about effects both in human lives and elsewhere.

6.10 The difference is so great and, once it has been pointed out, so obvious that any failure to appreciate the importance of the distinction may well appear impossibly stupid. But the confusions become more credible, and rather more excusable, when they are found in the context of a doctrine of Incarnation. We may, indeed we must, acknowledge the driving dynamic of the religious convictions of Jesus bar Joseph; and in particular of his belief that he was constantly in contact with and directed by the will of the living God. Yet neither the strength of convictions nor the fact of their vast influence in generating similar convictions in others, by itself provides sufficient – or even any – reason for concluding that these beliefs were or are actually true. Consider and compare the similar but secular case of Lenin. It is certainly no exaggeration to say, in the words of a slogan to be seen in Moscow in 1964: 'Lenin's words and Lenin's ideas live; he is an inspiration to millions.' In this second case there is no temptation to think that Lenin is still alive today, producing immediate effects. But in the first case, supposing you once in some way identify Jesus bar Joseph with God, then you may become inclined to mistake what in the second you would unhesitatingly recognize as some of the long-term consequences of a man's life, for the immediate effects of his living presence. Jesus as man is no more and no less dead than Lenin. But Jesus as God would presumably be eternal and, as such, perhaps a possible object of present experience.

6.12 Once we are seized of the pivotal importance of such distinctions we might expect to find that those who propose to rest a lot of weight upon the evidence of religious experience would take it as their first and inescapable task to answer the basic question: How and when would we be justified in making inferences from the facts of the occurrence of religious experience, considered as a purely psychological phenomenon, to conclusions about the supposed objective religious truths? Such optimism would almost always be disappointed; so regularly indeed that this very fact tends to confirm suspicion that the crucial question cannot be adequately answered. It seems that those who have really taken the measure of the essential distinction have abandoned all hope of developing a valid independent argument from religious experience. Certainly it is significant that the Roman Catholic Church is always chary of any appeal to personal experience not disciplined and supported by (its own) authority. For this insistence on the need for external checks and props surely springs from a wise acknowledgement that religious experience is not suited to serve as the evidential foundation which is needed if anyone is to be entitled to claim religious knowledge. (D. J. B. Hawkins, *The Essentials of Theism* (Sheed & Ward 1949), pp. 5ff.)

6.13 The difference between using religious experience as the premise of an independent argument, and using it to illustrate what is supposed to be known already, can be brought out here by referring to the way in which apologists sometimes first point to (some of) the effects or expressions of strong beliefs in and about God, and then, without any further argument, require that these be construed as instances of God's working in and through his particular servants. This construction, unless some further argument is being taken as read, must involve precisely the illegitimate move, from the mere fact that certain things are believed to the conclusion that these beliefs are true, which we have been labouring to expose. . . .

Revelation

6.14 ... However, as we said before, it is most remarkable how those who consider religious experience to be evidence so often fail to appreciate the fundamental distinctions, and hence fail to address themselves to the basic question. This weakness is not confined to the most popular levels of discussion. For instance: in a recent volume of the proceedings of a conference of professional philosophers and theologians it is only at the fifty-seventh of sixty pages on 'Religious Experience and its Problems' that anyone presses our sixty-four-dollar question: 'Suppose it does seem to us that we are "encountering God", how can we tell whether or not we really are?'; and the outline answer given offers as a criterion: 'the difference of quality between the inner experience of acting and that of being acted upon'. (N. Clarke, 'Some Criteria Offered' in *Faith and the Philosophers*, ed. J. Hick (Macmillan 1964), p. 59.)

6.15 This suggestion is breathtakingly parochial and uncomprehending. It is parochial in that it takes no account whatsoever of the inordinate variety of religious experience: if we were to try to employ this criterion we should establish the existence of the entire pantheon of comparative religion. It is uncomprehending in that it has not seen that the question arises precisely because it is impossible to make direct and self-authenticating inferences from the character of the subjective experience to conclusions about the supposedly corresponding objective facts. The impossibility here is logical. ...

6.17 ... Another influential Protestant theologian claims that Christian experience of God '... in the nature of the case must be self-authenticating and able to shine by its own light independently of the abstract reflections of philosophy, for if it were not, it could hardly be living experience of God as personal'. (H. H. Farmer, *The World and God* (Nisbet 1935), p. 158.)

6.18 ... If Farmer were right in thinking that Christian experience of God must be self-authenticating then the proper conclusion would be that there could not be such experience: for, in so far as it is experience of God in the sense which involves the actual existence of the object, it cannot be self-authenticating; whereas, if it really is to be self-authenticating, it cannot demand a reference to an actual God. There is, however, no necessity in the nature of the case which demands that anything has to satisfy these two incompatible requirements simultaneously. The apparent necessity of this impossibility is the paradoxical product of an understandably human but inherently insatiable desire both to eat cake and have it. What Farmer, and Lewis and others, want is that they and their co-religionists should be able to make a sort of assertion which would at one and the same time fulfil two logically inconsistent specifications: first, that of involving only their own experience, without any falsifiable reference to anything beyond; and, second, that of entailing the truth of the essentials of their religion. But one thing that really is in the nature of the case, and rock-bottom fundamental, is that all assertion must involve a theoretical possibility of error precisely proportionate to its content. You cannot make the enormous advances involved in the second clause while exposing only the narrow and virtually impregnable front opened by the first. Yet the charm of this impossible combination is plain, even without Farmer's own broad hint. It would put basic religious presuppositions comfortably beyond the range of philosophical criticism.

6.19 The immunity so humanly desired is not obtainable. Instead the position is that anyone equipped with the intellectual tools already provided has the means to demolish all similar pretensions to a knowledge of God grounded incorrigibly in immediate acquaintance. . . .

6.20 The vital but often neglected distinction is that between, on the one hand, biographical questions about how as a matter of fact a person may come to believe and, on the other hand epistemological questions about the adequacy or otherwise of the grounds which can be deployed in support of a claim that a belief constitutes knowledge. The fact that Baillie thinks that he, and others, have been confronted by the personal presence of the Father, Son, and Holy Spirit is, of course, of biological and sociological interest. But what it certainly is not is a sufficient reason for thinking that they actually have. Nor, even supposing that they in fact had, would it be superfluous to ask whether and on what grounds their admittedly strong convictions could be said to constitute knowledge. For it is not the case that all beliefs, or even all true beliefs, do. The decisive issues of justification are not to be dismissed so conveniently.

6.21 A more subtle version of the same fundamental confusion centres on the notion of inference. Later in an article from which Baillie quotes with approval we read: 'If we think of the existence of our friends . . . merely inferential knowledge seems a poor affair. . . . We don't want merely inferred friends. Could we possibly be satisfied with an inferred God?' (J. Cook Wilson, *Statement and Inference*, vol. II (OUP 1926), p. 853.)

6.23 Once the epistemological question is squarely put, and as squarely faced, it must become extremely hard to deny either of two things: first, that, however great the positive analogy between everyday encounters with other flesh and blood people and these putative confrontations with 'His personal Presence as Father, Son, and Holy Spirit', still the dissimilarities also are very great indeed; and, second, that any serious attempt to answer the question is bound to lead us away from the bold, direct claim that we have ourselves been honoured – and that's final – with a series of face to 'Face' interviews. . . .

6.24 The first point is one which it is embarrassing to press. Yet it has to be pressed if we are to show, what does apparently need to be shown, that it is arbitrary and question-begging for anyone to rest his case finally upon blank unsupported assertions that he – and some of his religious associates too – just do have experience 'of the God within whose purpose he is conscious that he lives and moves and has his being'. So we have simply to resign ourselves to any consequent embarrassment; reflecting perhaps that in philosophy it is often valuable actually to state what, when once stated, no one would be willing directly to deny. Surely, then, it is not in dispute that, where Farmer and Baillie and others believe that they are enjoying personal relations with the Christian God, to the outside observer it must seem that they are just imagining things? For there is nothing there which he can discern for them to be having their personal relations with. Such an enquirer may, and indeed should, be perfectly prepared to acknowledge: both that their 'encounter' experience seems very real to them, that they are almost irresistibly inclined to think that they are being acted upon, and so on; and that in his own failure to discern the putative object it may conceivably be his powers of discernment which are shown to be at fault. What, and all, the surely undisputed fact shows is that there has got to be an adequate answer to the basic epistemological question if claims to know (a particular) God through personal encounter are to be anything better than gratuitous and parochial dogmatism.

6.25 We have already, directly or by implication, suggested some of the reasons why people frequently ignore, or even deny, this by now painfully evident conclusion. First, there is the failure to distinguish two

Revelation

senses of *experience, being conscious of,* and so on; and in so doing to take the full measure of the fundamental difference thus marked. Next, there is the parochial but always tempting refusal to recognize that the different religious experience of other people may seem as veridical to them as yours does to you. Then there is the general Cartesian delusion that knowledge can and must be self-certifying. Again the equation assumed between the Christian God and the man Jesus bar Joseph also eases the way for the otherwise utterly implausible claim to be immediately aware, without even implicit reference to any supporting reasons, of the presence of that triune God; and not – say – of the unequivocally monotheist Gods of Israel or Islam, or of some undifferentiated Transcendent. . . . Consider Baillie's 'revelation of His personal Presence as Father, Son, and Holy Spirit'. This is, as Hepburn points out in his excellent treatment of these problems, a deal of theological theory to be allegedly derived from immediate observation. (R. W. Hepburn, *Christianity and Paradox* (C. A. Watts 1958), chs. 3–4.)

. . . . . .

6.28 The second point forced by pressing the epistemological question is that any sustained attempt to meet the challenge must lead away from the brazen finality of the thesis that (some) believers are personally acquainted with their God, and that's that. Even if we were dealing only with a claim about an ordinary flesh and blood person, an utterly convinced assertion would not necessarily be the last word. We must not be misled by Hick and his 'husband' or by Cook Wilson and his 'friends'. Certainly in such cases epistemological questions may be in fact superfluous. This is because the answers are in these cases obvious, not because the questions themselves would be logically inept. Where – as may sometimes be – the answers happen not to be obvious and the facts are in dispute, the questions are very much to the point. But, whereas questions about the existence of people can be answered by straightforward observational and other tests, not even those who claim to have enjoyed personal encounters with God would admit such tests to be appropriate here: if indeed they were appropriate then the question would by common consent be accounted settled, and in the negative. Yet if, as we have shown, the epistemological question is inescapable, and if, as everyone agrees, it cannot be met by reference to immediate observation or other commonplace tests; then the whole argument from religious experience must collapse into an argument from whatever other credentials may be offered to authenticate the revelation supposedly mediated by such experience.

C. Brown, 'Revelation and History' from *Philosophy and the Christian Faith*, pp. 276–84

We shall not attempt to work out here a comprehensive account of revelation and history. But these themes have cropped up repeatedly in our survey, and some comment here is justified.

We have suggested that revelation is the significant self-disclosure of God. Although we have spoken of a revelation in nature, the chief locus is personal experience of God in Christ interpreted by the Word of God in Scripture. This is a complex phenomenon which, though basic to Christian faith, requires even more careful investigation than has hitherto been given it. It is no less complex than the involved questions of Christology in the early church, where some parties said that Jesus was a mere man, others that he was not human at all, and others that he was some kind of hybrid. It is tempting to pursue the point that modern radicalism, with its stress on some things at the expense of others, is falling into all the old pitfalls all over again, but we must content ourselves by saying that in revelation there is both a human element and a divine element. If we are to understand it, we must be careful not to play off one against the other.

Modern thinkers are in danger of falling into opposite extremes. The existentialist radical says that the Bible is a collection of largely unhistorical stories about human self-understanding. They are of value today because they still help us to understand human existence better. In reply the Evangelical is apt to say that there is no truth in this at all, and that the Bible is the means of communicating a number of divinely-revealed truths which could not otherwise be known.

As a matter of fact, there is some truth in both positions. It is almost, though not quite, a case of men being right in what they affirm and wrong in what they deny. The Evangelical is apt to overlook in theory (though not altogether in practice in his preaching and devotions) that there is a very large existential element in Scripture. A great deal of it is devoted not to the communication of new facts but to getting us to see the old facts in a new light. . . . The main purpose of a parable, such as that of the Good Samaritan, is not so much to pass on facts, as to confront the hearer with himself and his motives, so that he will 'go and do likewise'.

Revelation

The Existentialist goes wrong when he says that there is no more to it than this. On his premises it is difficult to see why we should make such a fuss about Christianity and have all the bother of going to church and keeping an organization going which most people do not seem to want. In fact, this is precisely what the outsider thinks, and naturally he does not bother, especially when the radical tells us that we can know very little of what Jesus really said and did. He can enlarge his understanding of human existence simply by sitting at home, reading a novel or watching television (even if the latter is showing only a Donald Duck cartoon).

The radical, existentialist account of Scripture falls short on three counts. First, it fails to do justice to the claim of the biblical writers, that they are not just recounting any parabolic story, but that they are speaking in their own human words the Word of God. What they utter is, in the first instance, directed to a particular human situation. Nevertheless, they claim that what they say is God-given and is of decisive importance. We cannot disentangle the existential element without distorting the rest. Secondly, in Scripture the existential element is inextricably bound up with the communication of information. This ranges from statements about the character of God, the requirements he makes of man, and what he does for man, to the interpretation of particular events such as the Exodus and the life, death and resurrection of Christ. Again we cannot have the one without the other. Thirdly, the biblical understanding of life is bound up with historical events – acts of God in history. If the latter did not happen, then the Christian faith is groundless. Such events, plus the interpretation given them in Scripture, are all part and parcel of the Christian revelation. As such, they are relevant not only to the presentation of the Christian message to the modern world, but to any philosophy of the Christian religion.

The Christian faith claims to bear witness to what God has done and will do in time and space. The record of such past events is in principle open to the same verification and falsification as any other historical record. Otherwise, they would forfeit the claim to be historical events. Today the objection is sometimes raised that the supernatural cannot be entertained by the modern, critical historian. Everything must be interpreted in terms of a closed system of finite causes. Otherwise, the door is open to every superstition and fable. The supernatural and the miraculous are discounted from the start. Clearly, the historian needs criteria which will help him to sift fact from fiction. But to adopt this over-strict line seems to the present writer to misconceive the task of the historian. It decides beforehand to a large extent what may or may not have happened without even looking at the evidence.

The phenomenon of history is the sum total of events in the past. But the academic discipline that we call history is no such catalogue of events. It is not even, to use Ranke's celebrated phrase, the record of an event 'as it actually happened'. For one thing, the historian cannot get back into the past and see things for himself (unless he happened to be an eyewitness). For another thing, he does not write down everything that he unearths. He selects. He has to, in order to get it into a book. He discriminates. He tries to trace causes and assess influence. In doing this he is not reconstructing the past, for the past cannot literally be reconstructed. What he is doing is more like building a model. A model is a representation of something else which enables us to see what that something else is or was like. . . .

To describe history in this way might suggest that it is a highly arbitrary affair, depending a great deal upon the fads and fancies of individual historians. My answer to such a query would be that it sometimes is, but need not be so. The quality of a historian depends both upon his use of material and upon his interpretations. But the latter need not be something foisted upon the former. Although the historian will draw upon his own experience to help him envisage a personality or an event, his own background should not prejudice the issue. In fact, it is the very data which suggest the interpretation. . . .

The American philosopher of history J. W. Montgomery has suggested that facts and interpretations are like feet and shoes. The interpretation that the historian brings to his data should be neither too tight nor too loose. The point could be pressed even further. The critical historian is like a shoe salesman. He has at his disposal numerous pairs of shoes. His job is to look at the data before him and try on various interpretations until he finds one which is neither too big nor too small and which suits. This is especially important in trying to trace connections and assess significance. When he is confronted by the question of whether a particular event happened or not, he has to judge the most probable explanation in the light of the data before him, paying attention to the credibility of the data and its consistency with his model as a whole.

It may happen that the data before him may require the historian to revise his whole general scheme. He may, for example, start out from the premise that miracles do not happen today. This is the basic position of many radical New Testament scholars. They are then confronted by the alleged miracles of the Bible, not least the resurrection of Jesus. Some of them reject this as myth without more ado. But the present writer would submit that the proper course of action is to examine the data in detail, together with all possible alternative explanations, such as that Jesus did not really die, or that the disciples stole the body, or simply invented the story, or suffered from hallucinations. None of these theories actually tallies with the data. They all mean that the whole thing was a gigantic fraud. They all equally fail to explain the change that came over the disciples and their motivation and characters, if what they claimed had not in fact happened. It may sound naïve to some thinkers today, but if God is God, and the giver of life in the first place, there is nothing inherently incredible in the belief that he can restore life. To the present writer the most satisfactory explanation is that Jesus was actually raised from the dead. . . .

It has become fashionable today to talk about the 'live options' open to us in theology. The phrase is notoriously question-begging. It relieves its user of the solid slog of thinking out his approach from first principles, and helps to salve his conscience when he ignores the unwelcome opinions of others. We live in an age of mini-commentaries and popular paperbacks of pre-digested theology, when what is needed is scrupulous examination of primary sources. All too often, even in larger books, critical scholars begin by taking for granted certain theories of date and literary dependence, when what is needed is to start with the original text with a truly open mind, ready to examine all possible interpretations. It is not a case of ignoring critical theories, but of looking really critically at everything. It is the belief of the present writer that when this is done, scepticism is unwarranted; but when it is not done, scepticism is very much a 'live option'.

The American liberal theologian John Knox has claimed that historical scholarship could not impair faith. There is, I think, a fallacy here. A faith which goes on believing regardless of the evidence is not a faith worth having. The biblical idea of faith is trust in God because of what God has done and said. If it could be shown that there were no good reasons for believing that God has said or done these things, the faith would be empty and vain. In saying this, we are not tying faith to the latest book of the scholar who happens to be most fashionable at the time. But we are saying that scholarship has a real place. Its job is to strengthen faith by its demonstration of truth (or, if it cannot do this, it should say so plainly and throw faith overboard). In saying this we are only carrying on what the biblical writers themselves were doing. The

Bible is not a promise-box full of blessed thoughts. So much of it is devoted to arguments, demonstrations and appeals to history. To get the point, we need think no further than the Epistles of the New Testament or of the opening words of Luke's Gospel which stress the historicity of the story of Jesus as the basis of faith. It is on the truth of such arguments that Christian devotion depends. The ordinary believer is not required to work out all the arguments. But someone has got to do it somewhere for the sake of the faith.

J. H. Hick, *Philosophy of Religion**

The propositional View of Revelation and Faith, pp. 51–4

Christian thought contains two very different understandings of the nature of revelation and, as a result, two different conceptions of faith (as man's reception of revelation), of the Bible (as a medium of revelation), and of theology (as discourse based upon revelation).

The view that dominates the medieval period and that is officially represented today by Roman Catholicism (and also, in a curious meeting of opposites, by conservative Protestantism) can be called the 'propositional' conception of revelation. According to this view, the content of revelation is a body of truths expressed in statements or propositions. Revelation is the imparting to man of divinely authenticated truths. In the words of the 'Catholic Encyclopedia', 'Revelation may be defined as the communication of some truth by God to a rational creature through means which are beyond the ordinary course of nature.'

Corresponding to this conception of revelation is a view of faith as man's obedient acceptance of these divinely revealed truths. Thus faith is defined by the Vatican Council of 1870 as 'a supernatural virtue whereby, inspired and assisted by the grace of God, we believe that the things which he has revealed are true', . . .

These two interdependent conceptions of revelation as the divine promulgation of religious truths, and of faith as man's obedient reception of these truths, are related to a view of the Bible as the place where those truths are authoritatively written down. They were first revealed through the prophets, then more fully and perfectly through Christ and the apostles, and are now recorded in the Scriptures. It is

---

* 2nd edn, © 1973. Reprinted by permission of Prentice-Hall, Inc., Englewood Cliffs, N. J.

thus an essential element of this view that the Bible is not a merely human, and therefore fallible, record of divine truths. . . .

This same propositional conception of revelation as God's imparting to men of certain truths that have been inscribed in the sacred Scriptures and are believed by faith, leads also to a particular view of the nature and function of theology. The propositional theory of revelation has always been accompanied by the distinction between natural and revealed theology. This distinction has been almost universally accepted by Christian theologians of all traditions until the present century. Natural theology was held to consist of all those theological truths that can be worked out by the unaided human intellect. It was believed, for example, that the existence and attributes of God and the immortality of the soul can be proved by strict logical argument involving no appeal to revelation. Revealed theology, on the other hand, was held to consist of those further truths that are not accessible to human reason and that can be known to us only if they are specially revealed by God. For example, it was held that although the human mind, by right reasoning, can attain the truth that God exists, it cannot arrive in the same way at the further truth that he is three Persons in one; thus the doctrine of the Trinity was considered to be an item of revealed theology, to be accepted by faith. (The truths of natural theology were believed to have been revealed also, for the benefit of those who lack the time or the mental equipment to arrive at them for themselves.)

Many modern philosophical treatments of religion, whether attacking or defending it, presuppose the propositional view of revelation and faith. . . . Indeed, probably the majority of recent philosophical critics of religion have in mind a definition of faith as the believing of propositions upon insufficient evidence.

Many philosophical defenders of religion share the same assumption, and propose various expedients to compensate for the lack of evidence available to support their basic convictions. The most popular way of bridging the evidential gap is by an effort of the will. Thus, one contemporary religious philosopher says that '. . . faith is distinguished from the entertainment of a probable proposition by the fact that the latter can be a completely theoretic affair. Faith is a "yes" of self-commitment, it does not turn probabilities into certainties; only a sufficient increase in the weight of evidence could do that. But it is a volitional response which takes us out of the theoretic attitude.' (Dorothy Emmet, *The Nature of Metaphysical Thinking* (Macmillan 1945), p. 140.)

A 'Non-Propositional' View of Revelation and Faith, pp. 59–63

A different view of revelation, which can be called in contrast the nonpropositional view (or, if a technical term is desired, the 'heilsgeschichtliche' view), has become widespread within Protestant Christianity during the decades of the present century. This view claims to have its roots in the thought of the Reformers of the sixteenth century (Luther and Calvin and their associates) and further back still in the New Testament and the early Church.

According to this nonpropositional view, the content of revelation is not a body of truths about God, but God himself coming within the orbit of man's experience by acting in human history. From this point of view, theological propositions, as such, are not revealed, but represent human attempts to understand the significance of revelatory events. This nonpropositional conception of revelation is connected with the recent renewed emphasis upon the 'personal' character of God, and the thought that the divine-human personal relationship consists in something more than the promulgation and reception of theological truths. Certain questions at once present themselves.

If it is God's intention to confront men with his presence, as personal will and purpose, why has he not done this in an unambiguous manner, by some overwhelming manifestation of divine glory?

The answer that is generally given runs parallel to one of the considerations that occurred in connection with the problem of evil. If man is to have the freedom necessary for a relationship of love and trust, this freedom must extend to the basic and all-important matter of his consciousness of God. . . . God does not present himself to us as a reality of the same order as ourselves. If he were to do so, the finite being would be swallowed by the infinite Being. Instead, God has created space-time as a sphere in which we may exist in relative independence, as spatiotemporal creatures. Within this sphere God reveals himself in ways that allow man the fateful freedom to recognize or fail to recognize his presence. His actions always leave room for that uncompelled response that theology calls faith. It is this element in the awareness of God that preserves man's cognitive freedom in relation to an infinitely greater and superior reality. . . .

Faith, conceived in this way as a voluntary recognition of God's activity in human history, consists in seeing, apperceiving, or interpreting events in a special way.

In ordinary nonreligious experience, there is something epistemologically similar to this in the phenomenon of 'seeing as', which was brought to the attention of philosophers by Ludwig Wittgenstein (1889–1951) when he pointed out the epistemological interest of puzzle pictures. Consider, for example, the page covered with apparently random dots and lines, which, as one gazes at it, suddenly takes the form of a picture of (say) a man standing in a grove of trees. The entire field of dots and lines is now seen as having this particular kind of significance and no longer as merely a haphazard array of marks.

We may well develop this idea, and add that in addition to such purely visual interpreting, there is also the more complex phenomenon of 'experiencing as', in which a whole situation is experienced as having some specific significance.... Any individual would react in characteristically different ways in the midst of a battle and on a quiet Sunday afternoon stroll; he would do so in recognition of the differing characters of these two types of situation. Such awareness is a matter of 'experiencing as'....

Sometimes two different orders or levels of significance are experienced within the same situation; this is what happens when the religious mind experiences events both as occurring within human history and also as mediating the presence and activity of God. A religious significance is found superimposed upon the natural significance of the situation in the believer's experience.

Thus, for example, the Old Testament prophets saw the events of their contemporary history both as interactions between Israel and the surrounding nations and, at the same time, as God's dealings with his own covenant people – leading, guiding, disciplining, and punishing them in order that they might be instruments of his purpose. In the prophetic interpretation of history embodied in the Old Testament records, events which would be described by a secular historian as the outcome of political, economic, sociological, and geographical factors are seen as incidents in a dialogue that continues through the centuries between God and his people. It is important to realize that the prophets were not formulating a philosophy of history in the sense of an hypothesis applied retrospectively to the facts; instead, they were reporting their actual experience of the events as they happened. They were conscious of living in the midst of 'Heilsgeschichte', salvation-history. They saw God actively at work in the world around them....

The same epistemological pattern – the interpreting in a distinctive way of events that are in themselves capable of being construed either naturalistically or religiously – runs through the New Testament. Here again, in the story of a man, Jesus of Nazareth, and a movement which arose in connection with him, there are ambiguous data. It is possible to see him simply as a self-appointed prophet who got mixed up in politics, clashed with the Jerusalem priesthood, and had to be eliminated. It is also possible, with the New Testament writers, to see him as the Messiah of God, the one in whom the world was to witness the divine Son living a human life and giving himself for the renewing of mankind. To see him in this way is to share the faith or the distinctive way of 'experiencing as' which gave rise to the New Testament documents.

A Corresponding View of the Bible and Theological Thinking, pp. 63–7

The conception of revelation as occurring in the events of history – both world history and men's personal histories – and of faith as the experiencing of these events as God's dealings with his human creatures also suggests a different conception of the Bible from that which accompanies the propositional theory. Within the propositional circle of ideas the Bible is customarily referred to as 'the Word of God'. This phrase is understood in practice as meaning 'the words of God'. But within the contrasting set of ideas associated with the nonpropositional view of revelation, there is a tendency to return to the New Testament usage in which Christ, and only Christ, is called the divine Word (*Logos*). According to this view the Bible is not itself the Word of God but is rather the primary and indispensable witness to the Word. The New Testament (upon which the discussions have mainly centred) is seen as the human record of the Incarnation, that is, of the 'fact of faith' which is expressed in such statements as 'the Word became flesh and dwelt among us, full of grace and truth; we have beheld his glory, glory as of the only Son from the Father'.

On the one hand, the Bible is a book written by men as the record of God's actions in history. It is, indeed, not so much 'one' book as a library of books, produced during a period of about a thousand years and reflecting the various cultural situations within which its different sections were produced. In this sense it is a thoroughly human set of documents. On the other hand, the Bible is written from beginning to end from a stand-point of faith. . . . In the Bible, the chief agent upon the stage of history is not any human ruler, however powerful; it is the Lord who is invisible, yet ever present, never seen, yet never to be escaped, in one sense more remote than the farthest star but in another sense closer to a man than his own most secret thoughts. The faith of the biblical writers, which is their consciousness of God at work within human experience, constitutes the inspiration by virtue of which their writings still have the power to reveal the transcendent God to human consciousness. . . .

The non-propositional view of revelation also tends to be accompanied by a different conception of the function of theology from that operating in the propositional system of ideas. The strong emphasis upon God's self-revelation in and through the stream of saving history (Heilsgeschichte) recorded in the Bible, and upon the necessity for man's free response of faith, often leads to a rejection both of the distinction between natural and revealed theology and of the traditional conception of each member of this distinction. The notion of revealed theology is rejected as a series of attempts to establish without faith what can only be given to faith.

This modern theological rejection of natural theology is not necessarily motivated by an irrationalist distrust of reason. It may represent an empiricism which recognizes that human thought can only deal with material that has been given in experience. Just as our knowledge of the physical world is ultimately based upon sense perception, so any religious knowledge must ultimately be based upon aspects of human experience that are received as revelatory. Thus, reason can never replace experience as the source of the basic religious data. Nevertheless, in its proper place and when allowed to fulfil its proper role, reason plays an important part in the religious life. Negatively, it can criticize naturalistic theories that are proposed as ruling out a rational belief in the reality of God; and in this way it may have the effect of removing blocks in the way of belief. Positively, it must seek to understand the implications of what is known by faith: in a famous phrase of Anselm's, this is 'faith seeking understanding'. And, of course, reason is at work also in the systematic formulation of what is believed on the basis of faith. . . .

It is important to distinguish between the assertion of 'facts of faith' and the subsequent development of theological theories to explain them, for these fulfil distinct functions and have a different epistemological status. The 'facts of faith' upon which a given religion is based define that religion, and are (in intention at least) enshrined in its creeds. Theological theories, on the other hand, cannot claim the sanctity, within a particular religion, that is possessed by an affirmation of its basic 'facts of faith'. Much mental confusion, as well as ecclesiastical division, has been caused by attempts to treat the theological theories of some particular school as though they were themselves the basic articles of faith which they seek to explain. This kind of confusion is not unknown even today, as when the penal-substitutionary theory of the atonement is equated with the religious fact of man's reconciliation with God; or when the doctrine of the virgin birth of Jesus is equated with the Incarnation.

John Macquarrie, *Principles of Christian Theology*, pp. 75–92

A General Description of Revelation

We have now to consider more carefully what can be meant by the claim of the religious man that his faith is made possible by the initiative of that toward which his faith is directed; or, to put the same point differently, that his 'quest' for the sense of existence is met by the 'gift' of a sense of existence. He experiences this initiative from beyond himself in various ways. In so far as it supports and strengthens his existence and helps to overcome its fragmentariness and impotence, he calls the gift that comes to him 'grace'. In so far as it lays claim on him and exposes the distortions of his existence, it may be called 'judgement'. In so far as it brings him a new understanding both of himself and of the wider being within which he has his being (for the understanding of these is correlative), then it may be called 'revelation'. The word 'revelation' points therefore especially to the cognitive element in the experience.

Critics of religion and of theology have frequently attacked the notion of revelation. As Abraham Heschel has pointed out, resistance to the notion of revelation has had more than one motivation, and he mentions especially two conceptions that have militated against it: 'One maintained that man was too great to be in need of divine guidance, and the other maintained that man was too small to be worthy of divine guidance. The first conception came from social science, and the second from natural science.' Confidence in man, born of the success of the scientific method, and the naturalistic view of man, resulting from the application of the same method, seem to constitute a paradox, but they certainly combine to make anything like revelation improbable.

It looks as if the religious man, having no rationally defensible grounds for his faith, appeals to some private source of knowledge; but since such private knowledge cannot be tested by established logical procedures, it must be dismissed as illusory. Critics of the idea of revelation can point to the stubborn way in which theologians have defended alleged truths of revelation, as, for instance, the assertion that the earth does not move, and they argue that this belief in revelation has been a hindrance to the advance of genuine knowledge, which is not given but has to be won by strenuous efforts of thought. . . .

There is some substance in all of these criticisms of revelation. . . . However, while these points may be conceded, this does not mean that revelation is to be thrown out or its significance minimized. If its role has sometimes been exaggerated and distorted, it nevertheless retains an important place. . . .

Already we have explored the human side of the revelatory situation. We have taken note of the polarities and tensions of human existence, in which possibility and responsibility are conjoined with finitude and death. Out of this polarity is generated an anxiety (Angst) or fundamental malaise, a concern about existence itself with its potentialities and its precariousness. The quest for sense, coherence, a meaningful pattern, thus takes its rise from the very constitution of existence. The anxiety is heightened when, to the basic polarities of existence, there is added an awareness of its actual disorder and guilt. The quest for sense becomes also a quest for grace.

The anxiety is not a mere subjective emotion but a mode of awareness. But if we ask, Awareness of what? the answer must be a paradoxical one, Awareness of nothing! But here 'awareness of nothing' does not mean just that there is no awareness at all. Perhaps one should say 'awareness of nothingness' or 'awareness of nullity'. What is intended is the awareness of precariousness of existence which at any time may lapse into nothing or is already lapsing into nothing. It may 'cease' to be in death, and it 'fails' to be in guilt. We become aware of a nullity that enters into the very way in which we are constituted. The mood of anxiety may bring more than this. The world too sinks to nothing, it gets stripped of the values and meanings that we normally assign to the things and events that belong within it, and it becomes indeterminate, characterized by the same kind of emptiness and nullity that we know in ourselves. . . .

What is it then that confronts us and reveals itself when we have become aware of the nothingness of ourselves and our world? The answer is, Being. It is against the foil of nothing that for the first time our eyes are opened to the wonder of being, and this happens with the force of revelation. Being is all the time around us, but for the most part it does not get explicitly noticed. What we see are particular beings, the things and persons that are: only when these sink to nothing are we seized with the awareness of the being in virtue of which they are. This is not another being or a property of beings like their colour or size or shape. It is different from any particular being or any property, yet we are aware of it as more beingful, so to speak, than anything else, for it is the condition that there may be anything whatsoever. It falls under none of our everyday categories, so that we do not grasp it conceptually. . . .

More will need to be said in due course about the meaning of this word 'being' and how it is related to the key word of religious discourse, 'God'. Meanwhile, however, let it be said that the revelatory encounter with being, as it has been described here, is not, as has sometimes been claimed, 'self-authenticating'. It is indeed not too easy to know what this word means. In any case, it ought to be admitted that what we take to be this revelatory encounter or confrontation could be an illusion. . . . All that can be done is to offer a description of the experience, indeed, to trace it all the way from its sources in the way our human existence is constituted. We can only ask people to look at this situation as described, to compare it with what they know in themselves or their friends, to make some attempt at least to enter sympathetically into it, and then to decide. Actually, the scrutiny and analysis of this experience can be carried further, for instance, by comparing it with related types of experience, and this will be done in the later parts of the chapter. We need to test such an experience in every possible way, especially as its claims are so great. But in the long run, we shall still fall short of certitude. We cannot abolish faith to replace it by certitude, for our destiny as finite beings, seeing things from below up, so to speak, is that we have to commit ourselves in one way or another without conclusive proof. If there is an unclouded vision of being, it does not belong in our earthly existence.

Let me end this section by making three comments on the foregoing description of revelation.

1. It was called a 'general' description, and its general and formal character should be borne in mind. Any actual experience of revelation would be concrete, belonging to a particular person, at a particular place, in a particular situation, employing particular symbols. Karl Barth frequently insists on the particularity of God's self-revelation, telling us that the Bible does not permit us to set up the general thought of a being furnished with divine attributes but 'concentrates our attention and thought upon one single point and what is to be known at that point'. This insistence on concreteness and particularity is acceptable, provided it is not arbitrarily restricted to the biblical revelation. . . . Let us remember then that one can hardly speak of a

'general' revelation, though there is a universal possibility of revelation. . . .

2. In the account of revelation given here, it is assumed that the person who receives the revelation sees and hears no more than any other person in the situation might see and hear. What is revealed is *not* another being, over and above those that can be perceived by anyone. Rather, one should say that the person who receives the revelation sees the same things *in a different way*. We might say that he sees them in depth, though this expression is in danger of becoming trivialized. . . .

3. In the description of revelation given above, I have talked in terms of a directly given revelation. This, however, is probably a relatively rare occurrence, and we must remember from an earlier discussion the distinction that was drawn between 'classic' or 'primordial' revelations on which communities of faith get founded, and the subsequent experience of the community in which the primordial revelation keeps coming alive, so to speak, in the ongoing life of the community so that the original disclosure of the holy is being continually renewed. . . . For the moment, however, let us simply note that the general description of revelation given in this section is not meant to imply that every religious person has a direct revelation of being. For the great majority, it will be a case of reliving some classic revelation, but even such 'repeating', if it is not just a conventional attachment to a religious community, will mean something like a first-hand participation in the pattern of awareness that we have tried to trace, from the sense of finitude to the sense of the presence of the holy.

Revelation and the Modes of Thinking and Knowing

Continuing our analysis of revelation, we must now turn to the task of trying to locate the revelatory experience in the area of man's general cognitive experience. It has been said that the revelatory experience is not self-authenticating and might be illusory. . . . The philosophical theologian has a duty to try to show where this knowledge belongs within the entire field of knowledge. What is required is something like an epistemology of revelation, though the term 'epistemology' is somewhat presumptuous for the limited treatment which the question receives here.

I propose then to set out briefly a scheme or frame of reference in which we can locate the principal modes of thinking and knowing, and then ask whether we can find a place for revelation in this scheme.

Readers will notice that the outlines of the scheme reflect the philosophy of Martin Heidegger, though there are considerable differences in detail and the scheme as here presented is much more explicit than one finds in Heidegger....

The first level of thinking is the kind which Heidegger calls 'calculative' thinking — sometimes, indeed, in his polemics against its dominance, he will hardly allow it to be called 'thinking' at all. Nevertheless, this is probably the commonest mode of thinking and the one in which we are for the most part engaged in our everyday activities. Such thinking is in the subject-object pattern, for what we think about is an 'object' to us, that is to say, it stands over against us and outside of us. Our thinking is directed toward handling, using, manipulating this object, and incorporating it within our instrumental 'world'. The most sophisticated development of such thinking is, of course, technology....

The knowledge corresponding to this kind of thinking is objective knowledge. In all such knowing, we transcend what is known. We *subject* it, in the sense of rising above it and, to some extent, mastering it....

A second level of thinking we may designate, in the most general way, as 'existential' thinking. This kind of thinking is proper to existential or personal being. It does not aim, as calculative thinking does, at use or exploitation, though it may aim at well-being, either one's own or another's. This kind of thinking is also common in everyday existence. It does not take as its object what we think about, but rather recognizes what is thought about as another subject, having the same kind of being as the person who does the thinking. Most typically, then, this kind of thinking involves participation, a thinking into the existence of the other subject that is thought about, and this 'thinking into' is possible because of the common kind of being on both sides....

A special case of existential thinking, and a very important one, is what is called 'repetitive' thinking. The expression 'repetition' is to be understood as meaning much more than a mere mechanical going over again. It implies rather going into some experience that has been handed down in such a way that it is, so to speak, brought into the present and its insights and possibilities made alive again. This can happen with an historical happening, or again with a document, say a poem or a saying, that has been handed down from the past. If we are to understand it, we must think *into* it, and so think *again* and *with* the agent or the author....

Revelation

However, our consideration of the two modes of thinking and knowing, what we may call the 'subject-object' mode and the 'subject-subject' mode, raises the question whether we must not consider the possibility of a third mode, one in which I would be subjected to that which is known, one in which I am transcended, mastered and, indeed, known myself. Here Heidegger's philosophy does point us to still another mode of thinking which may be what we are looking for. He calls this 'primordial' or 'essential' thinking. It has a meditative character which contrasts with the probing activity of calculative thinking. This primordial thinking rather waits and listens. Heidegger can even talk of it as an 'occurrence of being' or as a thinking that 'answers to the demands of being'. This primordial thinking is a philosophical thinking, but it is described as a thinking which responds to the address of being and is explicitly compared both to the insights of religion and to those of poetry. This kind of philosophical thinking, then, provides a kind of paradigm for the understanding of what is meant by 'revelation', and shows where revelation is to be located in the range of man's cognitive experience.

What would seem to happen both in the primordial thinking of the philosopher and in the revelatory experience of the religious man (if indeed these two can be definitely distinguished) is that the initiative passes to that which is known, so that we are seized by it and it impresses itself upon us. But what is known is not another being, but rather being itself, the being which communicates itself through all the particular beings by which it is present, by which it manifests itself, and not least through the depth of our own being, for we too are participants in being and indeed the only participants to which being opens itself, so that we not only are but we exist.

The knowledge that corresponds to primordial thinking has a gift-like character, and this is precisely what the religious man points to when he talks of 'revealed' knowledge. We have seen, of course, that there must be a gift-like character even at the level of person-to-person knowing, but on the level of revelation, the gift-like character is enhanced and we have become almost passive recipients. Presumably, however, we are not 'entirely' passive. All knowing involves an element of appropriation. For this reason, it was insisted earlier that there is a capacity for revelation. . . .

In this section, we have been trying to locate the revelatory experience within the range of man's ways of knowing and thinking, and our argument could be strengthened by a brief consideration of some of the parallels between revelatory experience and esthetic experience. The latter seems to be another type of experience that touches upon the whole existence, strongly involving the feelings, yet certainly not without its cognitive aspect. . . . The artist sometimes testifies to his 'inspiration' in terms not unlike the testimony of the recipient of a revelation. It is not surprising then that Heidegger sees in the perceptive thinking of the poet something very similar to that primordial thinking which is, in turn, close to what we call 'revelation'.

Here let it be said again that presumably a genuinely primordial thinking or a primordial experience of the revelation of being is rare. For most of us there can be only the repetitive thinking that follows in the course of some classic experience of the holy, as that experience has come down to us in a concrete symbolism, and as it has subsequently been lit up further by generations of thought and experience in the community of faith which it founded. Yet such repetitive thinking does bring us sufficiently close to the primordial experience to know what the approach of holy being is, so that our present existence too can move in the grace and openness of being and thereby, we may hope, find some healing for its disorder and a new possibility of bringing its potentialities to actualization. . . .

Revelation and Moods

Anxiety has played a key role in the foregoing discussions, and perhaps some justification should be offered for its prominence. It would seem that anxiety, as it has been described above, has a peculiar significance insofar as it tends to light up not just some particular situation but man's total situation in the world – man as the being in whom are conjoined possibility and facticity, responsibility and finitude. But even if this is conceded, perhaps the question will be asked whether the stress upon anxiety does not introduce an unhealthy, neurotic tendency into the description. . . . Perhaps much of our religion is indeed a neurotic clutching after security, yet anxiety is at the centre of life because of the essential fragmentariness of our existence, and to recognize anxiety and attend to its disclosure is surely a mark of maturity. The man who thinks he has outgrown anxiety or that it is only a peripheral phenomenon may well be the immature person who has never been able to accept himself and who comforts himself with the illusion that all is in order. Let us remind ourselves again of the tensions between the polarities of existence, and of how easily we fall into imbalance, and move out to one extreme or the other. Aristotle's doctrine of the mean has some relevance here, for he applied it to feelings as well as to actions. The fact that anxiety can sometimes reach an extreme pitch where it becomes a pathological and disturbing factor should not disguise from us that there is a healthy anxiety or lead us to the opposite extreme of trying to suppress all anxiety or sweep it under the carpet. Anxiety belongs essentially to man's being and discloses him in the very centre of that being. . . .

Let us remember too that (as Heidegger also asserts) anxiety is near to awe. That is to say, it does not remain in the awareness of the nullity of existence, but opens our eyes to the wonder of being; and the religious experience of awe, as has already been pointed out, is an awareness of the grace of being as much as it is an awareness of the overwhelmingness of being. When these points are remembered, the objections to giving anxiety such an important role are lessened.

But perhaps a new objection will be raised here. It may be said that modern man does not feel awe. With the rise of science, the mystery has been taken out of things, so that they no longer excite awe but present a challenge to investigation. Whether this generalization can be accepted and whether our apprehension of phenomena would not be greatly impoverished if it becomes dominated by calculative thinking are questions we need not answer. More fundamentally, the objection rests on a failure to understand what the religious man means by 'awe'. This has nothing to do with gaps in scientific knowledge, or with a superstitious dread in the face of ignorance as to *how* this or that phenomenon occurs. It is the far more basic wonder *that* there are phenomena at all, and this wonder would remain untouched, perhaps enhanced, even if science had answered all its questions. As Ludwig Wittgenstein rightly saw, 'Not *how* the world is, is the mystical, but *that* it is.'

A Further Scrutiny of Revelation

The whole preceding part of this chapter has been a scrutiny of revelation, a description of the revelatory experience, and an examination of the conditions that would seem to be required for such an experience to be valid. But the matter is so important that we must scrutinize the claim of revelation in every way possible, and in this last section we shall consider what more, if anything, can be done to test revelation's credentials.

This brings us back to the question of revelation and reason. In discussing natural theology, we noted that a faith-conviction has always come prior to any attempt to prove the existence of God, and in the present chapter we have tried to push back the investigation beyond the rational arguments to the foundations of the prior faith-conviction. We have found these foundations in the revelatory experiences where man becomes aware of the presence and manifestation of holy being. It is now more than ever clear to us that the work of reason comes after the conviction that arises out of the revelatory experience, but reason's work is none the less important for being critical rather than speculative, subsequent to the religious conviction rather than foundational for it. . . .

These remarks bring us back to the traditional theistic proofs. Though they might never convince us starting from cold, as it were, they may have a confirmatory function. Especially in their modern formulations, they seek to bring together faith and reason by facing the question of whether the facts of the world, as known to us in science and everyday experience, are compatible with belief in the grace of being, as this is supposed to have been made known in revelation. We have already seen that the picture presented by our world is an ambiguous one, but it must at least be shown that the faith-conviction is compatible with what we learn about the world through our everyday experience.

Perhaps the religious man should be prepared to say what state of affairs he would acknowledge to be *incompatible* with his faith, and therefore one that falsifies it. Such a state of affairs, for instance, might be the presence in the world of massive, senseless, irremediable evil. But even to say this shows how difficult or impossible it would be to reach a conclusive demonstration. How could we definitely recognize such a state of affairs? However, the traditional preoccupation of theologians with the so-called 'problem of evil' shows their sensitivity to such questions.

Certainly, it would not seem to be the case that at the beginning one could bring forward any clinching arguments on behalf of the validity of a religious faith, and indeed all one could ever hope to do would be to show its *reasonableness*, for it remains faith, and not demonstrable knowledge – just as the opposite point of view is not demonstrable either. But the reasonableness of a faith or of its corresponding revelation has to be weighed throughout the whole theological exposition of the revelation's content. In Christianity, for instance, the question of its reasonableness has to be judged in the light of all its teachings about creation, sin, providence, atonement, eschatology and so on. In the end, the revelation must be judged as a whole, when all its implications have been unfolded. Does it make sense, and is it compatible with what we know of the world in everyday experience?

STUDY TOPICS

1. Can we know anything about God without revelation?
2. What consequences follow from the conclusion that the Gospel stories about Jesus are not totally historically accurate?
3. What is the importance of religious experience in establishing religious truth?
4. Is revelation merely 'seeing things' in a particular light?
5. What is man's part in revelation?

BIBLIOGRAPHY

The relevant section of A. Richardson's *Theological Wordbook of the Bible* (SCM Press 1964) contains an excellent distillation of the biblical understanding of revelation. For those who enjoyed A. Flew's attacking style, Chapter 9 of his book *God and Philosophy* (10) on faith and authority contains more thought-provoking comments. Although rather dated, John Baillie's book *The Idea of Revelation in Recent Thought* (1) is quite readable and has a useful first chapter on the history of the idea.

On natural theology, pp. 43ff of John Macquarrie's *Principles of Christian Theology* (23) contains a useful analysis of the situation and a plea for some sort of natural theology as essential. Similarly H. E. Root's essay 'Beginning all over again' in *Soundings*, ed. A. R. Vidler (32) suggests that natural theology is not quite as useless as people think. *Revelation Theology – A History*, A. Dulles SJ (Burnes & Oates 1970) is a brief survey of the history of thought by a Roman Catholic.

FURTHER READING

Barth, Karl, *Against the Stream. Shorter Post-War Writings 1946–52* (4). SCM Press 1954. p. 205.
James, William, *The Varieties of Religious Experience* (17).

Lewis, H. D., *Teach Yourself the Philosophy of Religion* (21). Chapters 20, 21.
Moran, G. FSC, *Theology of Revelation*. Burns and Oates 1967. Advanced.
Pannenberg, W., Rendtorf, R. and T., and Wilckens, U., ed., *Revelation as History*. Sheed and Ward 1969. Advanced.
Smart, Ninian, *Philosophers and Religious Truth* (30). Chapter 2.
Thornton, L. S., *Revelation and the Modern World*. Dacre Press 1950.

3

The Problem of Evil

INTRODUCTION

The problem of evil is perhaps the most persistent stumbling block to faith the would-be Christian has to negotiate. Augustine put it simply: 'either God cannot abolish evil or he will not. If he cannot he is not all powerful: if he will not he is not all good.' The Christian, believing as he does in a good, loving, omnipotent deity, who created all things and 'saw that they were very good', somehow has to reconcile the sufferings, pain, and disasters of this world and the human condition with the idea that his good, loving God is aware of all created things. Indeed, not only is he aware of them, the Christian believes he actively 'loves' them and cares for them; 'even the hairs of your head are all numbered'.

The idea of 'evil' is usually divided into two distinct but interrelated categories:

(1) 'Natural or physical evil', a phrase covering natural calamities of the world – earthquake, famine, flood, disaster, etc. If God created the world why did he not make a better job of it so that it functions smoothly?

(2) 'Moral evil', denoting evil and suffering arising from the actions of men, free agents who are held to be responsible for their actions and consequent results, e.g. murder, war, maiming, sadism, oppression, fear, hatred, envy, etc.

It is noteworthy that evil only becomes a problem for the believer when his concept of God is one of an all-powerful, active, good God. Buddhism, for example, has no such problems of evil, it is simply a fact of existence, 'to live is to suffer' say the Buddhists. For Christians, however, the problem of evil is a real one, both in rational-intellectual terms and in practical terms of constructing a working philosophy of life. We all have to come to terms with pain and suffering and death in our lives. Many people (see extracts from B. Russell and David Hume) find it an insuperable obstacle in the way of belief. It is questionable whether there is one simple answer to the problem of evil; it remains a 'mystery' which means different things to different people according to one's disposition and experience. Various suggestions have been made to ease the problem. John Hick, taking his lead from an early Christian writer, Irenaeus, has suggested that this world is a 'vale of soul-making', a place where men struggle against evil and so improve themselves in a way which would be impossible in the 'ideal world' of our dreams. Even so, problems remain. Some scholars (see A. Flew's extract) reject Hick's suggestion and demand a better explanation. The final extract provides a more general picture of how the religions of the world have dealt with the problem of evil.

TERMINOLOGY

Theodicy:
A justification of the righteousness of God in the face of apparent evidence to the contrary.

Monism:
A belief that the power behind the universe is one God/power/person.

Dualism:
A belief that behind the universe there are two powers (usually categorized as good *v.* evil, dark *v.* light, order *v.* chaos).

David Hume, 'Dialogues Concerning Natural Religion' from R. Wollheim, *Hume on Religion*, p. 186

Look round this universe. What an immense profusion of beings, animated and organised, sensible and active! You admire this prodigious variety and fecundity. But inspect a little more narrowly these living existences, the only beings worth regarding. How hostile and destructive to each other! How insufficient all of them for their own happiness! How contemptible or odious to the spectator! The whole presents nothing but the idea of a blind Nature, impregnated by a great vivifying principle, and pouring forth from her lap, without discernment or parental care, her maimed and abortive children!

Bertrand Russell, 'Has Religion made Useful Contributions to Civilisation?' from *Why I am not a Christian*, p. 31

Leaving these comparatively detailed objections aside, it is clear that the fundamental doctrines of Christianity demand a great deal of ethical perversion before they can be accepted. The world, we are told, was created by God who is both good and omnipotent. Before he created the world he foresaw all the pain and misery that it would contain; he is therefore responsible for all of it. It is useless to argue that the pain in the world is due to sin. In the first place, this is not true, it is not sin that causes rivers to overflow their banks or volcanoes to erupt. But even if it were true, it would make no difference. If I were going to beget a child knowing that the child was going to be a homicidal maniac, I should be responsible for his crimes. If God knew in advance the sins of which man would be guilty, he was clearly responsible for all the consequences of those sins when he decided to create man. The usual Christian argument is that the suffering of the world is a purification for sin, and is, therefore, a good thing. This argument is, of course, only a rationalization of sadism, but in any case it is a very poor argument. I would invite any Christian to accompany me to the children's ward of any hospital to watch the suffering that is there being endured, and then to persist in the assertion that those children are so morally abandoned as to deserve what they are suffering. In order to bring himself to say this, a man must destroy in himself all feelings of mercy and compassion. He must, in short, make himself as cruel as the God in whom he believes. No man who believes that all is for the best in this suffering world can keep his ethical values unimpaired, since he is always having to find excuses for pain and misery.

H. D. Lewis, *Teach yourself the Philosophy of Religion*, pp. 307–8

Evil is only a problem, in the proper intellectual sense, for a religious view or for some form of metaphysics which finds supreme goodness at the heart of things. It is, of course, a problem for everyone, agnostic and believer alike, in the practical sense that we have to cope with evil or overcome it. But as a problem in the strict sense it arises when we have to reconcile evil with the goodness of God – or whatever takes his place. In its simplest terms it is this. God is alleged to be all good and all powerful, how then does there come to be any evil in the world – or, as it is more popularly put – why does God allow it? This is not just a problem for speculative thought or detached reflection. It is for many a major obstacle to faith, and it is a constant source of strain and tension in the life of the believer; indeed there are few more testing experiences for saintly and sensitive persons than to be the witness of sustained and heart-breaking evil in one of its many forms. . . .

One way of dealing with the problem of evil is to think of God as a finite or limited Being. The notion of a 'finite God' has been mentioned already. It is found as a rule in philosophical and sophistical contexts more than at the live centre of religion. The suggestion is that while God is good in all he intends there are some things he cannot encompass; he is in the van of the struggle against evil, and he calls us to co-operate with him, but his triumph is not complete. This doctrine has the merit of making us very genuinely co-workers with God. It encourages and stimulates the good man, he feels that he is on the side of God but that something substantial is left to him. The weakness of the doctrine, and in my eyes it is a fatal one, is that the way we are forced to think of there being God rules out the possibility of his being anything but transcendent and thus utterly supreme.

J. H. Hick, 'Grounds for Disbelief in God' from *Philosophy of Religion*,* pp. 86ff

Certain solutions which at once suggest themselves, have to be ruled out as far as the Judaic-Christian faith is concerned.

To say, for example (with contemporary Christian Science), that evil is an illusion of the human mind, is impossible within a religion based upon the stark realism of the Bible. Its pages faithfully reflect the characteristic mixture of good and evil in human experience. They record every kind of suffering and sorrow, every mode of man's inhumanity to man and of his painfully insecure existence in the world. There is no attempt to regard evil as anything but dark, menacingly ugly, heart-rending and crushing. In the Christian Scriptures, the climax of this history of evil is the crucifixion of Jesus which is presented not only as a case of utterly unjust suffering, but as the violent and murderous rejection of God's Messiah. There can be no doubt, then, that for biblical faith evil is unambiguously evil and stands in direct opposition to God's will.

* 2nd edn, © 1973. Reprinted by permission of Prentice Hall, Inc., Englewood Cliffs, N.J.

The Problem of Evil

Again, to solve the problem of evil by means of the theory (sponsored, for example, by the Boston 'personalist' School) of a finite deity who does the best he can with a material, intractable and co-eternal with himself, is to have abandoned the basic premise of Hebrew-Christian monotheism; for the theory amounts to rejecting belief in the infinity and sovereignty of God.

Indeed any theory that would avoid the problem of the origin of evil by depicting it as an ultimate constituent of the universe, co-ordinate with good, has been repudiated in advance by the classic Christian teaching, first developed by Augustine, that evil represents the going wrong of something that in itself is good. That is to say, it is the creation of a good God for a good purpose. He completely rejects the ancient prejudice that matter is evil. There are, according to Augustine, higher and lower, greater and lesser goods in immense abundance and variety; but everything that has being is good in its own way and degree, except in so far as it may have become spoiled or corrupted. Evil – whether it be an evil will, an instance of pain, or some decay or disorder in nature – has not been set there by God, but represents the distortion of something that is inherently valuable. Whatever exists is, as such, and in its proper place, good; evil is essentially parasitic upon good, being disorder and perversion in a fundamentally good creation. This understanding of evil as something negative means that it is not willed and created by God; but does not mean (as some have supposed) that evil is unreal and can be disregarded. On the contrary, the first effect of this doctrine is to accentuate even more the question of the origin of evil. . . .

We may now turn more directly to the problem of suffering. Even though the major bulk of actual human pain is traceable to man's misused freedom as a sole or part cause, there remain other sources of pain that are entirely independent of the human will, for example, earthquake, hurricane, storm, flood, drought and blight. In practice, it is often impossible to trace a boundary between the suffering that results from human wickedness and folly and that which falls upon mankind from without; both kinds of suffering are inextricably mingled together in human experience.

For our present purpose, however, it is important to note that the latter category does exist and that it seems to be built into the very structure of our world. In response to it, theodicy, if it is wisely constructed, follows a negative path. It is not possible to show positively that each item of human pain serves a divine purpose of good; but, on the other hand, it does seem possible to show that the divine purpose as it is understood in Judaism and Christianity could not be forwarded in a world that was designed as a permanent hedonistic paradise.

An essential premise of this argument concerns the nature of the divine purpose in creating the world. The sceptic's assumption is that man is to be viewed as a completed creation and that God's purpose in making the world was to provide a suitable dwelling place for this fully formed creature. Since God is good and loving, the environment that he has created for human life to inhabit will naturally be as pleasant and comfortable as possible. Since our world, in fact, contains sources of hardship, inconvenience and danger of innumerable kinds, the conclusion follows that this world cannot have been created by a perfectly benevolent and all powerful deity.

Christianity, however, has never supposed that God's purpose in the creation of the world was to construct a paradise whose inhabitants would experience a maximum of pleasure and a minimum of pain. The world is seen, instead, as a place of 'soul making' or person making in which free beings, grappling with the tasks and challenges of their existence in a common environment may become 'children of God' and 'heirs of eternal life'. A way of thinking theologically of God's continuing creative purpose for man was suggested by some of the early Hellenistic Fathers of the Christian Church, especially Irenaeus. Following Hints from St Paul, Irenaeus taught that man has been made as a person in the image of God but has not yet been brought as a free and responsible agent into the finite likeness of God, which is revealed in Christ. Our world, with all its rough edges, is the sphere in which this second and harder stage of the creative process is taking place.

This conception of the world (whether or not set in Iranaeus's theological framework) can be supported by the method of negative theodicy. Suppose, contrary to fact, that this world were a paradise from which all possibility of pain and suffering were excluded. The consequences would be very far reaching. For example, no one could ever injure anyone else; the murderer's knife would turn to paper or his bullets to thin air; the bank safe, robbed of a million dollars, would miraculously become filled with another million dollars (without this device, on however a large scale, proving inflationary); fraud, deceit, conspiracy, and treason would somehow always leave the fabric of society undamaged. Again, no-one would ever be injured by accident; the mountain climber, steeplejack or playing child falling from a height would float unharmed to the ground; the reckless driver would never meet disaster, for in such a world there could be no real needs or dangers.

To make possible this continual series of individual adjustments, nature would have to work by 'special providences' instead of running according to general laws that men must learn to respect on penalty of pain or death. The laws of nature would have to be extremely flexible; sometimes gravity would operate, sometimes not; sometimes an object would be hard and solid, sometimes soft. There could be no sciences, for there would be no enduring world structure to investigate. In eliminating the problems and hardships of an objective environment, with its own laws, life would become like a dream in which, delightfully but aimlessly, we would float and drift at ease.

One can at least begin to imagine such a world. It is evident that our present ethical concepts would have no meaning in it. If, for example, the notion of harming someone is an essential element in the concept of a wrong action, in our hedonistic paradise there could be no wrong actions – nor any right actions in distinction from wrong. Courage and fortitude would have no point in an environment in which there is, by definition, no danger or difficulty. Generosity, kindness, the agape aspect of love, prudence, unselfishness and all other ethical notions which presuppose life in an objective environment would be very ill adapted for the development of the moral qualities of human personality. In relation to this purpose it might be the worst of all possible worlds!

It would seem, then, that an environment intended to make possible the growth in free beings of the finest characteristics of personal life must have a good deal in common with our present world. It must operate according to general and dependable laws; and it must involve real dangers, difficulties, problems, obstacles, and possibilities of pain, failure, sorrow, frustration and defeat. If it did not contain the particular trials and perils that – subtracting man's own very considerable contribution – our world contains, it would have to contain many others instead.

A. Flew, 'Theology and Falsification' from the University Discussion, in *New Essays in Philosophical Theology,* ed. A. Flew and A. MacIntyre, pp. 98–9

Now it often seems to people who are not religious as if there was no conceivable event or series of events the occurrence of which would be admitted by sophisticated religious people to be a sufficient reason for conceding 'there wasn't a God after all' or 'God does not really love us then'. Someone tells us that God loves us as a father loves his children. We are reassured. But then we see a child dying of inoperable cancer of the throat. His earthly father is driven frantic in his efforts to help, but his Heavenly Father reveals no obvious sign of concern. Some qualification is made – God's love is 'not merely a human love' or it is 'an inscrutable love', perhaps – and we realize that such sufferings are quite compatible with the truth of the assertion that 'God loves us as a father (but, of course . . .)". We are reassured again. But then perhaps we ask: what is this assurance of God's (appropriately qualified) love worth, what is this apparent guarantee really a guarantee against? Just what would have to happen not merely (morally and wrongly) to tempt but also (logically and rightly) to entitle us to say 'God does not love us' or even 'God does not exist'? I therefore put to the succeeding symposiasts the simple central questions, 'what would have to occur or to have occurred to constitute for you a disproof of the love of, or the existence of, God?'

Harold K. Schilling, *The New Consciousness in Science and Religion*, pp. 202ff

I, for one, do not share the derogatory view that the basic biblical beliefs are insufficiently critical and discriminating in the sense that they cannot be validated by the process called falsification. The charge is that the belief that all happenings fit into a pattern for good is held in spite of much evidence to the contrary; and, similarly, that God is held to be love no matter how much unlove or actual hatred or diabolical evil there is in the world. How bad, it is asked, would the situation have to be before such beliefs would be relinquished? If they were retained under any and all conceivable circumstances, and if no conceivable conditions whatsoever would cause their denial, could they possibly be genuine truth-claims? Surely a claim that something is true, that does not thereby also declare its opposite to be untrue, has no genuine truth-value.

Now for me this charge of the unfalsifiability of theological assertions is not convincing. In the first place, it is simply not true that biblical beliefs are maintained despite all evidence to the contrary. In the second place, in their more mature stages of growth they rest not only on direct experience but also on careful analysis and critical reflection. Their central insight – namely, that the universe is fundamentally good and its Source therefore God, and that God is love – would not be espoused under all conceivable circumstances.

After all, the world is recognized to be contingent. It need not have been as it is. 'The way things are' *could* conceivably have been otherwise, exhibiting a radically different matrix of given entities and causal relationships – or with no causality at all. There might have been no love in it, or loving *might* normally have resulted in hatred or misunderstanding or confusion; in which case, according to the methodology of biblical thought, its 'Source, Guide, and Goal' would have had to be designated as *Diabolus* rather than *Deus*. The world *could* conceivably have been such that brotherhood and community, mutuality and sharing, sensitivity and redemptive suffering could not have emerged in it. Natural beauty *might* have been an impossibility; and the physical act of looking at the sunrise or waterfall, or of listening to the songs of birds or the sighing of the wind, *might* have been intolerably painful rather than pleasurable and beneficial. So could the act of touching anything, say, one's mate. Events *might* have been utterly predictable and unmanageable, the naturalness of 'nature' inconceivable, and rationality non-existent. There *might* have been no possibility of human creativity, and therefore of the arts, sciences, and religions, and of business and politics. Evil *might* have been not only present but completely irremediable and ineradicable. Life *might* have been unmitigated boredom or hell. Surely in such a world it would have made no sense to claim that God is love. And referring to the quote from Roger Shinn, life would indeed have been 'a bad joke' or 'dirty trick'. The fact is, then, that it is not at all difficult to state what some of the conditions might be – within a cosmic scheme different from ours – which would make faith as we know it impossible and our present basic beliefs or truth-claims unacceptable, or even unimaginable. It is not the case, therefore, that biblical beliefs are inevitably unfalsifiable.

To be sure, given the present cosmos with its general scheme of things *as it is*, the believer cannot point to any event that could possibly occur therein that would itself invalidate his fundamental belief that all happenings fit into a scheme for good. This does not mean, however, that he is gullible or willing blindly to believe anything whatsoever, regardless of the pros and cons. Rather, it means that he is simply being consistent in his conviction that the world is not self contradictory and that it would not, therefore, bring forth anything that would not 'fit' or would in this sense be an anachronism in violation of its fundamental, constitutive matrix. The scheme could conceivably have been different, but *as it is* it is consistently purposive for good. Had the scheme been radically different, self contradicting and 'for evil', so also would have been the character of the creative ground of its being – and it would not have generated faith and qualified as God.

Ninian Smart, 'F. R. Tennant and the Problem of Evil' from *Philosophers and Religious Truth,* pp. 148ff

6.22 But though all this, it may be objected, is a way of reinterpreting the traditional Christian picture in the light of the evolutionary picture, it still does not answer the problem of evil. First, it has to be shown that creating a theatre for moral and spiritual endeavour was worth all the cruelty and misery. Second, do we not feel uneasy about the many individual victims of this process? The two points can be distinguished in that we wish to take rather a qualitative view of the first problem, and not of the second. For it is easy to look upon the first problem as being solved as follows: by pointing out that the sum of human misery, though great, is more than outweighed by the sum of human happiness and achievement and so, on balance, the whole project has been worth while. But this surely is too superficial. For one thing, how do we reckon the sum? And, for another, there is the second problem. Is it just that the individual, who may have been tortured or raped or driven mad, should be sacrificed to the greater glory of the human race? Are we to say to him that what matters most is that the race should be capable of marvellous things? You cannot, of course, make omelettes without breaking eggs.

6.23 But it is not eggs, but human beings, of which we are speaking. Is there not a contradiction in saying that, in the interests of the growth of morality and creativity, it may be necessary for individuals to be destroyed? For surely the highest point in morality is to recognize the claims and worth of the individual. Is not the victim entitled to protest at his being made into a human sacrifice?

6.24 But still: What is the victim really trying to say? If the whole human enterprise is bought at too great a price, because of the victim's personal tragedy, then it would surely have been better if it had never been. Of course, it is too late now to effect this. But suppose the victim had a super-bomb which could painlessly destroy the human race, just

The Problem of Evil

by his pressing a button. Would he regard it as right to press that button, to prevent more tragedies?

6.25 Surely, if the victim accepts the whole human enterprise and failing to press the button would signalize such acceptance, then he is already substituting a new moral attitude for the sense of injustice at his own suffering. It is this: that his torturers really "know not what they do'; that, regarded as representatives of a race which strives, in its freedom, towards great and noble things, they are as it were part of that enterprise. Their evil actions themselves, besides paradoxically springing from the nobility of freedom, also teach each other the terrible truth of what freedom means. In adopting such an attitude, the victim sees himself as a sacrifice, and a willing one, rather than the petulant accuser of men or God. It is perhaps, therefore, of the deepest significance that God himself, if Christian teaching be true, having created beings who, he knew, would in their freedom multiply acts of good and evil, should accept the moral standpoint of the victim. In Christ's sacrifice there is, as well as the religious act, the moral act of one who sees the human enterprise as good and yet accepts the evil that comes with it.

6.26 So the substance of the present argument is that the human enterprise, evolutionary and creative as it is, rather than statistically 'perfect', may after all constitute the best kind of crown with which the cosmos could be endowed. In creating such a crown, God limits himself and stands a handbreadth off. Thus, though the general pattern of freedom is his handiwork, and though too in intervening in the cruel history of men he co-operates in an intimate way with human creativity, God is not, so to say, the individual author of human events. He did not kill six million Jews; it was we ourselves. If God did it, human freedom becomes meaningless.

6.27 But why should we place so much stress upon the universe as a theatre for morality, as though morality were an end in itself? Surely the point of virtue is that it promotes human welfare and reduces human suffering. Those who stress the intrinsic importance of morality seem to be taking the peculiar view that the happiness and suffering of men are really rather irrelevant and secondary, that what counts is the state of mind of the torturer rather than the agonised cries of the victim. Thus (so the objection runs) we should distinguish between first level goods, such as happiness, absence of suffering, etc., and second level ones, such as courage, temperance and the like. And the point of the second level goods is that they promote the first level ones. Thus to see the cosmos as a theatre for the promotion of second level goods is to get the order wrong. What counts is whether there is welfare, not ultimately as to whether there is virtue.

6.29 In the course of the argument so far we have not in any way *established* that this is the best of all possible worlds, or that God is free from blame for the moral evils implicit in human existence. But we have at least made out some sort of general case for saying that perhaps after all the human enterprise is worthwhile, and that maybe an evolutionary and creative world is superior to static perfection. Moreover, though God cannot be held to account for the particular evils of human history, he has through his self-sacrifice upon the cross, identified himself with the painful human enterprise, which has already achieved some glories and may in the end rise to sublime heights. But all this, though it suggests an answer to the problem of human evil, does not touch the question of physical evil.

J. L. Mackie, 'Evil and Omnipotence' (from *Mind*, April 1955)

If there is no logical impossibility in a man's freely choosing the good on one, or several occasions, there cannot be a logical impossibility in his freely choosing the good on every occasion. God was not, then, faced with a choice between making innocent automata and making beings who, in acting freely, would sometimes go wrong; there was open to him the obviously better possibility of making beings who would act freely but always go right. Clearly, his failure to avail himself of this possibility is inconsistent with his being both omnipotent and wholly good.

J. H. Hick, *Evil and the God of Love*

Augustine, p. 51

Here then is the central theme of Augustine's thought: the whole creation is good; the sun moon and stars are good, angelic and human beings are good ... all are good, expressing as they do the creative fecundity of perfect goodness and beauty. So Augustine rejects the ancient Platonic, Neo Platonic, Gnostic and Manichaean prejudice against matter and lays the foundation for a Christian naturalism that rejoices in this world, and instead of fleeing from it as a snare to the soul, seeks to use it and share it in gratitude to God for his bountiful goodness.

Where then, in a creation that is all good, consisting of a multitudinous host of greater and lesser, higher and lower goods, is the place of evil; and whence does it arise? Having rejected, in the name of the absolute sovereignty of God, the idea that there can be any independent force of evil or of resistance to good in the universe, coeternal with the Almighty, what account was Augustine to give of the undoubted power and presence of evil? His answer – adapted rather than adopted from Plotinus – is that evil is not any kind of positive substance or force, but consists rather in the going wrong of God's creation in some of its parts. Evil is essentially the malfunctioning of something that in itself is good. For 'omnis natura bonum est' and yet everything, other than God himself, is made out of nothing and is accordingly mutable and capable of being corrupted; and evil is precisely this corruption of a mutable good.

Irenaeus, p. 220

There is thus to be found in Irenaeus the outline of an approach to the problem of evil which stands in important respects in contrast to the Augustinian type of theodicy. Instead of the doctrine that man was created finitely perfect and then incomprehensibly destroyed his own perfection and plunged into sin and misery, Irenaeus suggests that man was created as an imperfect, immature creature who was to undergo moral development and growth and finally be brought to the perfection intended for him by his Maker. Instead of the fall of Adam being presented, as in the Augustinian tradition, as an utterly malignant and catastrophic event, completely disrupting God's plan, Irenaeus pictures it as something that occurred in the childhood of the race, an understandable lapse due to weakness and immaturity rather than an adult crime full of malice and pregnant with perpetual guilt. And instead of the Augustinian view of life's trials as a divine punishment for Adam's sins, Irenaeus sees our world of mingled good and evil as a divinely appointed environment towards the perfection that represents the fulfilment of God's good purpose for him.

The Traditional Free-Will Defence, p. 301

Why has an omnipotent, omniscient and infinitely good and loving creator permitted sin in his universe? To this question the Christian answer, both in the Augustinian and in the Irenaean types of theodicy, has always centred upon man's freedom and responsibility as a finite personal being. This answer has recently been critically discussed in the philosophical journals under the name of the free will defence, and it falls into three stages.

The first stage establishes a conception of divine omnipotence. It is argued that God's all power does not mean that he can do anything if 'anything' is held to include self-contradictions such as making a round square, or an object whose surface both is and is not red all over at the same time. The self contradictory, or logically absurd, does not fall within the scope of God's omnipotence; for a self contradiction, being a logically meaningless form of words, does not describe anything that might be either done or not done. Thus for example, God will never make a four sided triangle. . . .

The second phase of the argument claims that there is a necessary connection between personality and moral freedom such that the idea of the creation of personal beings who are not free to choose wrongly as well as to choose rightly is self contradictory and, therefore, does not fall within the scope of the divine omnipotence. If man is to be a being capable of entering into personal relationship with his Maker and not a mere puppet, he must be endowed with the uncontrollable gift of freedom. In order to be a person man must be free to choose right or wrong. He must be a morally responsible agent with a real power of moral choice. No doubt God could instead have created some other kind of being, with not freedom of choice and, therefore, no possibility of making wrong choices.

It is upon the third phase that discussion centres. Granted that God is going to make finite persons and not mere puppets or automata; and granted that persons must be genuinely free; could not God nevertheless have so made them that they would always freely do what is right? For human persons, though all endowed with some degree of freedom and responsibility, nevertheless vary markedly in their liability to sin.

John MacQuarrie, *Principles of Christian Theology*, p. 233

Natural Evil

In denying to evil any kind of positive being of its own we likewise turn away from ultimate dualism. There is a dualism of sorts between Being and nothing, but not an ultimate dualism, since we do not have two

The Problem of Evil

positive principles opposed to each other. Since the Christian faith rejects an ultimate dualism, as we have seen in sketching the typology of religions, then it would seem that a Christian view of evil must represent it as negation, as *privati boni*. This is the view to which St Augustine came after having passed through a Manichaean phase in which he had accepted that evil expresses a distinct will in the universe, contrary to that of God; but the negative character of evil had already been succinctly expressed by Christian writers, notably St Athanasius, who wrote: "What is evil is not, but what is good is.' To understand this statement, however, we have to set it in the context of St Athanasius' view of creation. Evil is not simply to be identified with nothing or what is not, for presumably this nothing is neutral and without any characteristics at all, either good or evil. As St Athanasius understands the matter evil is rather 'lapsing into nothing' or 'ceasing to be' which is a standing threat to all created beings. These beings have been created out of nothing, and it is possible for them to slip back into nothing or to advance into the potentialities for being which belong to them. Evil is this slipping back into nothing, a reversal and defeat of the creative process.

I have earlier maintained that creation involves risk, and the time has come to look more closely at this. In creation, God gives being, and he gives it to the plurality of particular beings. But what constitutes a particular or finite being is just that it is determinate; and whatever is determinate is what it is in so far that it is *not* anything else. To have any determinate character is to be without some other characters. Hence creation may be considered as the going out of being into nothing and the acceptance by Being of the limitations of determinate characteristics. All this makes possible the expression of Being in a richly diversified community of beings that would utterly transcend in value and interest what we can only visualise as a hypothetical limiting case, namely, a purely undifferentiated primal being. But this creative process inevitably involves risk. There is a genuine self-giving of Being. We have already seen that this imposes a self-limitation on God, when we discussed the problem of his omnipotence. But more than this, it means that God risks himself, so to speak, with the nothing; he opens himself and pours himself out into nothing. His very essence is to let be, to confer being. He lets be by giving himself, for he is Being; and in giving himself in this way, he places himself in jeopardy, for he takes the risk that Being may be dissolved into nothing. Did Bonhoeffer have something like this in mind when he talked about the 'weakness' of God, the God who manifests himself in the crucified Christ as placing himself at the mercy of the world? One would have to say, however, that this weakness of God is his strength. We have seen that a God who securely hoarded his being would be no God, and perhaps nothing at all. Only the God who does confer being and so goes out from himself into creation and into the risks of finite being that is bounded by nothing – only this God is *holy* Being and lays claim to our worship and allegiance. Only this God is a God of love, for love is precisely his self giving and letting be.

Brian Hebblethwaite, *Evil, Suffering, and Religion*, pp. 100ff

Coping with Evil and Explaining Evil

It can be seen, then, that the religions of the world have had a marked tendency to develop ideas of resurrection and a future life, in which men and women pass beyond the range of evil and enter upon a state of bliss that makes all their sufferings worthwhile. This tendency is particularly strong in the case of the monotheistic world religions, but it is to be seen also wherever the note of personal devotion comes to the fore in an otherwise mystical or non-theistic religion. We can see how such beliefs can help men both to cope with suffering and evil in this present life, and also to explain, if not the presence of suffering and evil in the world, then at least the worthwhileness of creation despite the world's ills.

In chapter two we distinguished five ways of coping with suffering and evil exemplified to different degrees and in different combinations by the religions of the world. Of those five ways, only the way of mystical knowledge is essentially independent of a future hope. Admittedly, in conjunction, say, with Christian faith, mystical experience has been thought of as a foretaste of heavenly bliss, but in most religions the mystical state in itself, whether interpreted as union with God or with the Absolute, or as the isolation of the pure self, is sufficient as a way out of human suffering. Not so the other ways. More often than not, the way of renunciation and way of works have been practised in the interests of a higher heavenly reward. Even when this somewhat mercenary attitude to discipline and goodness has been transcended, and human goodness thought of rather as the natural consequence of the faith-response to God, it has still been widely felt that God must have an eternal destiny in mind for his personal creatures. Thus we have seen the way of devotion, in the monotheistic faiths, developing strong doctrines of resurrection or immortality.

Similarly it has not been possible, in the context of devotional religion, to see the way of sacrifice as an ultimate end in itself. Whatever may be the case with the Bodhisattva who sacrificed himself to feed the hungry tigress, in the monotheistic faiths self-sacrifice is not the end. Jewish, Christian and Muslim martyrs have gone to their deaths in the confident hope of resurrection. There is no doubt, then, that this pervasive feature of religion has contributed greatly to the manner in which men and women have been enabled to cope with suffering and evil.

It has also helped them to make sense of the world as the creation of a good and all-powerful God. Taken in conjunction with the various ways of explaining the presence of evil in the world, which we examined in chapter three, the hope of resurrection, whether thought of crudely in terms of reward, or more spiritually in terms of insight into God's ultimate destiny for man, creates a new perspective in which to judge the worthwhileness of creation. Moreover the more convincingly one can show that the risks of present evil are a necessary condition of the fashioning of persons separate from God, the more plausible will be the claim that the ultimate consummation of God's creative process will be seen to justify the whole enterprise, despite the suffering and evil.

Heaven and Hell

The widespread belief in the eternal damnation of the wicked in hell, which in one form or another characterizes most theistic traditions, militates against such an optimistic conclusion. Admittedly, from time to time, particularly in the history of Christianity, we find the belief that *all* men will in the end be saved – the view known as universalism – but it is a minority view, and the larger part even of Christian teaching about 'the last things' includes the doctrine that men have the freedom and the power to reject God and cut themselves off from him through all eternity. Their fate is vividly pictured in the art and literature of Christendom, as of other religious traditions, concerning the day of judgement.

The possibility of hell is often held to demonstrate the dignity and seriousness of human moral choice. Thus T. S. Eliot wrote: 'It is true to say that the glory of man is his capacity for salvation; it is also true to say that his glory is his capacity for damnation.' But just as we have seen reason in earlier chapters for the reflective theist to treat the devil as a symbolic figure for all that opposed God in the human world, so now similar considerations will support the view that hell and eternal punishment are also figurative and symbolic notions, and do not literally describe permanent aspects of reality in the final consummation of the divine purpose. For a permanent or eternal sphere of malice and rebellion and suffering is not conceivable as part of the ultimate destiny of creation. It makes neither metaphysical, moral nor religious sense. Metaphysically speaking, the theist is bound to suppose that the final state of created being will be good without qualification, and the existence of hell would undoubtedly introduce a major permanent qualification. Morally speaking, the idea of eternal punishment has to be rejected by the sensitive moral conscience quite independently of religion. But also religiously speaking, at any rate the Christian moral conscience, if it is really responsive to the love of God claimed to be revealed in Jesus Christ, cannot in consistency tolerate the literal idea of hell.

If the literal idea of hell is rejected, the question remains, what does the language of hell and damnation in scripture and tradition symbolize? There seem to be two possibilities for the rational theist. Either he must affirm universalism, and hold that in God's eternity all men will be won over and saved. In this case the language of hell and damnation will certainly symbolize the horror of existence turned in upon the self and alienated from God, but it will not be regarded as portraying a permanent actuality. Among the Fathers of the Christian Church, Origen claimed that 'Christ remains on the Cross so long as the last sinner remains in hell', the implication being that the patience of God is such as to wait upon the repentance and renewal of all men in God's future. This is undoubtedly a morally and religiously attractive view.

However, it may be an over-optimistic view. It may be that the theist will have to admit that if freedom is to be real, it must be possible for a man to persist in the rejection of God, and so to embrace evil that he renders himself incapable of redemption. In such a case, one could only suppose that there is no point in God's keeping him in being. Such a man will be 'lost eternally' only in the sense that he has made himself incapable of taking part in God's future, and therefore suffers annihilation. The language of hell would in this case be taken to symbolize the awesome possibility of such an ultimate loss.

In either case – that of universalism or the annihilation of the irredeemable – there can be no permanent state of real being which remains in rebellion against God through all eternity. Consequently it is possible to hold that the absolute good of the transformed and perfected creation will in the end be seen to justify the total creative process despite its inevitable risks and temporary evils.

STUDY TOPICS

1. What can we learn from the story of Job in the Old Testament? Do you find this an adequate answer to the problem of evil?
2. Is it possible to be free and yet always choose to do the right? In such a situation what does 'right' mean? (See (11), p. 144ff.)
3. What is to be gained by studying an apparently 'insoluble' problem like this one? Do Christians have an answer other than that of saying 'it is all a mystery'? What are the advantages and disadvantages of Hick's suggestion of 'eschatalogical verification' (i.e. all evils will be remedied in the last things/next world)?
4. How do other religions deal with the problem of evil? (See (13.)) Which 'answer' appears to you to be most satisfactory?

BIBLIOGRAPHY

There are two very good books on this subject. One is J. H. Hick's *Evil and the God of Love* (14). It is rather long but not too difficult to read; Part IV gives the basis of Hick's position. (A much briefer outline of Hick's ideas is to be found in his *Philosophy of Religion* (15), pp. 37–43) and his *Christianity at the Centre* (SCM Centrebooks 1967, pp. 82–92). The other is Brian Hebblethwaite's recent book *Evil, Suffering, and Religion* (13) which examines what the religions of the world have to offer by way of an answer to the problem of evil.

Other shorter writings include Ninian Smart's treatment of F. R. Tennant's suggestions about the problem of evil, in *Philosophers and Religious Truth* (30), pp. 139–62. Also worth studying is A. Flew's essay in Chapter 8 of *New Essays in Philosophical Theology* (11), 'Divine Omnipotence and Human Freedom', of which the first ten pages are especially valuable.

FURTHER READING

Bowker, J., *Problems of Suffering in the Religions of the World*. Cambridge University Press 1970. For advanced students only.
Farrer, Austin, *Love Almighty and Ills Unlimited*. Collins Fontana 1962.

Lewis, H. D., *Teach Yourself the Philosophy of Religion* (21), pp. 307–14.
Macquarrie, John, *Principles of Christian Theology* (23). Mainly Chapter 11.
Pike, Nelson, ed., *God and Evil*. Prentice-Hall 1964. Advanced.
Plantinga, A., *God, Freedom and Evil*. Allen and Unwin 1975. Advanced.

4
Miracles

INTRODUCTION

The question of miracles has in the past provoked many writers to take up their pens and attack or defend Christianity as their inclination took them. The subject usually falls into three main areas: what is a miracle? what is the evidence for its occurrence? what is the position of the miraculous in Christianity today? Other related issues also raise their heads, such as the question of miracles in other religions, the presuppositions of the textual critic or the scientist, and the significance of miracles in general for religion.

Going back to the New Testament it is clear that there is a group of events called miracles (or signs) which were seen by the New Testament authors as a sort of 'proof' or mark of validation of the claims of Jesus. The working of miracles at that time was not restricted to Jesus (he refers to other miracle workers more than once), and it was a recognized way of attracting supporters (of which Jesus disapproved). The connection between belief and the performance of miracles is clear in Jesus's remark 'unless you see signs and wonders you will not believe'. It is noteworthy that nowadays miracles are often regarded as either irrelevant or as a stumbling-block to belief.

Hume's Essay on Miracles is the classic exposition of the argument against the miraculous. In his short but brilliant essay Hume tries to prove that miracles are against reason and that, quite apart from the prima facie case against them, there has never been any miracle story that can stand up to close scrutiny. His biting irony and the provocative subject matter of his work ensured great interest in his argument and the debate has gone on in various forms until today, when miracles are somewhat 'out of favour' at the moment.

Ninian Smart subjects Hume's argument to close analysis and uncovers some flaws in it. Smart goes on to maintain that the idea of a miracle, properly understood, does not necessarily involve the destruction of the 'laws of science'. He suggests that an unusual event can be seen in various ways. The scientist might see it as a random event whilst the religious believer could regard it as an act of God. The Bible gives us plenty of examples of great signs from God being ignored by the people, but the sceptic will reply, how do we know they were signs from God and not just mere happenings? The reply is that true miracles (like true prophecy) fit into a pattern of previous religious experience and provide their own persuasive force to the mind of the individual.

This brings us to a consideration of the problems of the general presupposition of men today. Some argue that we have closed our minds to miracles and therefore fail to see them even if they occur. The attitude of the Christian 'modern mind' is strongly attacked by C. S. Lewis and H. H. Farmer as having the wrong basic presuppositions. On the other hand McPherson and Macquarrie seem to be able to dispense with miracles; indeed, Macquarrie goes so far as to suggest that the traditional way of looking at miracles is 'outdated and outmoded'. This division amongst the theologians reflects the divide amongst Christians at large. For many people, miracles are an essential part of their faith, and Christians look for them today as in years past (see for example the recent instance of the Roman Catholic Church officially approving of the occurrence of a miracle in the case of a sick man recovering from inoperable cancer). Others (for example New Testament scholars like Bultmann) claim that the miracle stories about Jesus (and in other religions too) have taken their present form as the result of certain pressures on them as they were told and retold in the period after Jesus's death before they were finally written down, and that they do not give an accurate account of the historical events on which they are based. Attempts are sometimes made to retrieve this 'historical core' from the mass of additional material (see Macquarrie's treatment of the crossing of the Red Sea), but these 'reductionist' versions of the miracles often provoke adverse comment on many counts.

All this raises the question: 'just how important are miracles to Christianity?' In the time of Hume it was assumed that to disprove the miracles was to disprove the religion they supported, but this is no longer the case. Many scholars no longer feel that the truth of Jesus stands or falls on the miracles. H. D. Lewis and E. and M-L. Keller try to put the issue in perspective. The problem of the miracles is more than a storm in a theological teacup but it no longer shakes the foundations as it used to do. Many now regard belief in miracles as an 'optional extra' for Christians rather than as a basic requirement for faith.

Whatever conclusion you finally come to, your decision will have far-reaching effects in other areas of belief. For example a postive acceptance of miracles will mean that you are more likely to see the hand of God at work in the world today in unusual events than someone who denies that God ever 'works in that sort of way'. Similarly, total rejection of the miracles is difficult to square with an acceptance of the doctrine of biblical inerrancy. The heart of the matter is, 'what is a miracle?' Careful consideration of this question is a necessary prerequisite of any tentative conclusions about their occurrence or significance for Christianity today. The first extract from P. Nowell Smith's essay is a good example of how the conclusion to the question of miracles can be hidden in unspoken assumptions made at the start.

Patrick Nowell-Smith, 'Miracles' from *New Essays in Philosophical Theology*, ed. A. Flew and A. MacIntyre, p. 244

Before coming to my main point I shall first summarize Mr Lunn's argument and put out of the way two minor points. Mr Lunn's main argument is as follows:

(a) A miracle is defined as 'an event above or contrary to or exceeding nature which is explicable only as a direct act of God'.

(b) Miracles certainly occur. (There is plenty of evidence for them, if only people will bother to investigate it instead of rejecting miracles out of hand.)

(c) Miracles are 'evidence provided by God to demonstrate the existence of a divine order'.

(d) Therefore we must believe that reality is not 'coterminous with the natural order' and must answer in the negative the momentous question 'whether all phenomena recorded and witnessed by man are due to purely natural causes, such as the actions of the human will or physical causes'. Moreover, it is on the authority of the scientists themselves that we declare that a particular phenomenon is inexplicable as the effect of natural agents and must therefore be ascribed to supernatural agents.

Before coming to my main point, I have two objections to make to this thesis; the first will certainly be familiar to Mr Lunn and he has probably answered it elsewhere; the second is more important. In the first place, every religion has its own stock of miracles, some of which are as well attested as the Christian miracles. Would Mr Lunn deny that these miracles occurred? And, if he does, must it not be from an arbitrary standpoint such as he himself condemns? If he is willing to accept them, must there not be some flaw in the argument by which the devotees of the other religions prove the existence of their Gods from such evidence? And might not this flaw also appear in the Christian case? Or are we to accept the God of Muhammad and the whole Greek and Hindu pantheons?

My second, and more serious, point is that Mr Lunn *defines* 'miracle' in such a way that, whatever scientists may say, it can well be doubted whether miracles have in fact occurred. If any scientist has said that a certain phenomenon 'is inexplicable as the effect of natural agents and must *therefore* be ascribed to supernatural agents' he is not speaking as a scientist, but as a philosopher; and whatever authority he may have in his own scientific field he is by no means a safe guide here. We may trust him, as a trained observer, accurately to describe the phenomenon; we may believe him when he says that no scientific method or hypothesis known to him will explain it. But to say that it is inexplicable as a result of natural agents is already beyond his competence as a scientist, and to say that it must be ascribed to supernatural agents is to say something that no one could possibly have the right to affirm on the evidence alone. Mr Lunn defines a miracle not merely as an event exceeding nature but also as one which is *explicable only as a direct act of God*. But to say that a phenomenon is a direct act of God is to offer an explanation, not to report its occurrence. Let us accept all the evidence for miracles; what this shows is that extraordinary phenomena occur, and it is only in this sense that the evidence forces us to admit that miracles occur. If we define 'miracle' in the way that Mr Lunn does, we could only be forced to admit the occurrence of miracles by means of some *argument*, such as Mr Lunn himself offers. Mr Lunn has, in short, smuggled his explanation of these phenomena into the evidence for them, and this he has no right to do. Evidence must be kept distinct from explanatory theory; otherwise in accepting the evidence, we are already committed

Miracles

to accepting the theory. But, no matter how strange an event someone reports, the statement that it must have been due to a supernatural agent cannot be a part of that report". . . .

p. 251

What I reject is the theory of science which makes it possible to claim that any phenomenon is essentially inexplicable, the leap to 'supernatural agencies' and the view that such agencies in fact explain the phenomenon. If miracles are 'lawful' it should be possible to state the laws; if not, the alleged explanation amounts to a confession that they are inexplicable.

. . . . . .

Having said that miracles must be attributed to supernatural agencies, Mr Lunn goes on to claim that they are 'evidence provided by God to demonstrate the existence of the divine order'. But what, in detail, can they prove? If we can detect any order in God's interventions it should be possible to extrapolate in the usual way and to predict when and how a miracle will occur. To expect accurate and detailed predictions would be to expect too much. But we must be able to make some predictions, however vague. Otherwise the hypothesis is not open to confirmation or refutation. As far as I can see, we are limited to saying that God has in the past intervened in such and such a way. If Mr Lunn would say more than this, I would ask how his method differs from that of a scientist. . . .

Mr Lunn passes from unusual or abnormal events (for which there is evidence) to the miraculous, from the miraculous to the supernatural and from the supernatural to God. He cannot mean each successive phrase to be a mere synonym for the previous one; each step in the argument is intended to explain the last and to add something more. But, to make use of an old-fashioned way of putting this, we have no right to postulate in the cause any power greater than what is necessary to produce the effect. The difficulty with the argument from miracles as with other arguments for the existence of God, is that it is first claimed that certain evidence requires us to postulate an unknown X; we then call this X 'God' and then we claim to have proved the existence of a being endowed with characteristics by no means warranted by the original evidence. Now science too does this. The gravitational theory says much more than is necessary to describe the fall of an apple. But we can test the truth of this 'more' by predicting how other bodies will behave. It is the absence of such a test for supernatural explanations that makes them at once unscientific and also non-explanatory. . . .

The supernatural is either so different from the natural that we are unable to investigate it at all or it is not. If it is not, then it can hardly have the momentous significance that Mr Lunn claims for it; and if it is it cannot be invoked as an explanation of the unusual.

David Hume, 'An Enquiry Concerning Human Understanding' from R. Wollheim, *Hume on Religion*

Of Miracles, pp. 205–6

Nothing is so convenient as a decisive argument of this kind, which must at least *silence* the most arrogant bigotry and superstition, and free us from their impertinent solicitations. I flatter myself, that I have discovered an argument of a like nature, which, if just, will, with the wise and learned, be an everlasting check to all kinds of superstitions, delusion and consequently will be useful as long as the world endures. For so long, I presume, will the accounts of miracles and prodigies be found in all history, sacred and profane.

Though experience be our only guide in reasoning concerning matters of fact; it must be acknowledged that this guide is not altogether infallible, but in some cases is apt to lead us into errors. One who, in our climate, should expect better weather in any week of June than in one of December, would reason justly, and conformably to experience; but it is certain that he may happen, in the event, to find himself mistaken. . . .

A wise man, therefore, proportions his belief to the evidence. In such conclusions as are founded on an infallible experience, he expects the event with the last degree of assurance, and regards his past experience as a full *proof* of the future existence of that event.

In other cases he proceeds with more caution: he weighs the opposite experiments: he considers which side is supported by the greater number of experiments: to that side he inclines, with doubt and hesitation; and when at last he fixes his judgement, the evidence exceeds not what we properly call probability. . . . In all cases, we must balance the opposite experiments, where they are opposite, and deduct the smaller number from the greater, in order to know the exact force of the superior evidence. . . .

And as the evidence, derived from witnesses and human testimony, is founded on past experience, so it varies with the experience, and is regarded either as a proof ... or a *probability* according as the conjunction between any particular report of any kind of object has been found to be constant or variable. ... Where this experience is not entirely uniform on any side, it is attended with an unavoidable contrariety in our judgements, and with the same opposition and mutual destruction of argument as in every other kind of evidence. We frequently hesitate concerning the reports of others. We balance the opposite circumstances, which cause any doubt or uncertainty; and when we discover a superiority on any side, we incline to it; but still with a diminution of assurance, in proportion to the force of its antagonist. ...

We entertain a suspicion concerning any matter of fact, when the witnesses contradict each other; when they are but few or of doubtful character; when they have an interest in what they affirm; when they deliver their testimony with hesitation, or on the contrary, with too violent asseverations. There are many other particulars of the same kind, which may diminish or destroy the force of any argument, derived from human testimony.

Suppose, for example, that the fact which the testimony endeavours to establish, partakes of the extraordinary and the marvellous; in that case, the evidence, resulting from the testimony, admits of a diminution, greater or less, in proportion as the fact is more or less unusual.

p. 210

A miracle is a violation of the laws of nature; and as a firm and unalterable experience has established these laws, the proof against a miracle, from the very nature of the fact, is as entire as any argument from experience can possibly be imagined. ... Nothing is esteemed a miracle if it ever happens in the common course of nature. It is no miracle that a man, seemingly in good health, should die on a sudden; because such a kind of death, though more unusual than any other, has yet been frequently observed to happen. But it is a miracle that a dead man should come to life; because that has never been observed in any age or country. There must, therefore, be a uniform experience against every miraculous event, otherwise the event does not merit that appellation. And as a uniform experience amounts to a proof, there is here a direct and full *proof* from the nature of the fact, against the existence of any miracle; nor can such a proof be destroyed, or the miracle rendered credible, but by an opposite proof, which is superior.

The plain consequence is (and it is a general maxim worthy of our attention) 'That no testimony is sufficient to establish a miracle, unless the testimony be of such a kind, that its falsehood would be more miraculous, than the fact, which it endeavours to establish; and even in that case there is a mutual destruction of arguments, and the superior only gives us an assurance suitable to that degree of force, which remains, after deducting the inferior.' I weigh one miracle against the other; and according to the superiority, which I discover, I pronounce my decision, and always reject the greater miracle. . . .

p. 222

Upon the whole, then, it appears that no testimony for any kind of miracle has ever amounted to a probability, much less a proof, and that even supposing it amounted to a proof, it would be opposed by another proof; derived from the very nature of the fact, which it would endeavour to establish. It is experience only which gives authority to human testimony; and it is the same experience which assures us of the laws of nature. When, therefore, these two kinds of experience are contrary, we have nothing to do but subtract the one from the other and embrace an opinion, either on the one side or the other, with that assurance which arises from the remainder. But according to the principle here explained, this subtraction, with regard to all popular religions, amounts to an entire annihilation; and therefore we may establish it as a maxim, that no human testimony can have such force as to prove a miracle and make it a just foundation for any such system of religion. . . .

p. 225

I am the better pleased with the method of reasoning here delivered, as I think it may serve to confound those dangerous friends or disguised enemies to the *Christian Religion* who have undertaken to defend it by the principles of human reason. Our most holy religion is founded on faith not on reason and it is a sure method of exposing it to put it to such a trial as it is, by no means, fitted to endure. To make this more evident, let us examine those miracles, related in scripture, and not to lose ourselves in too wide a field, let us confine ourselves to such as we find in the *Pentateuch*, which we shall examine, according to the principles of these pretended Christians, not as the word of testimony of God himself, but as the production of a mere human writer and historian. Here then we are first to consider a book, presented to us by a barbarous and ignorant people, written in an age when they were still more barbarous and in all probability long after the facts to which it relates, corroborated by no concurring testimony, and resembling these fabulous accounts, which every nation gives of its origin. Upon reading this book, we find it full of prodigies and miracles. It gives an account of a state of the world and of human nature entirely different from the present; of our fall from that state, of the age of man extended to near a thousand years, of the destruction of the world by a deluge; of the arbitrary choice of one people, as the favourites of heaven; and that people the countryman of the author; of their deliverance from bondage by prodigies the most astonishing imaginable; I desire anyone to lay his hand upon his heart, and after a serious consideration declare, whether he thinks that the falsehood of such a book, supported by such a testimony, would be more extraordinary and miraculous than all the miracles it relates; which is, however, necessary to make it be received, according to the measures of probability above established.

... So that, upon the whole, we may conclude that the Christian religion not only was at first attended with miracles, but even at this day cannot be believed by any reasonable person without one. Mere reason is insufficient to convince us of its veracity; and whoever is moved by *Faith* to assent to it, is conscious of a continued miracle in his own person, which subverts all the principles of his understanding, and gives him a determination to believe what is most contrary to custom and experience.

Ninian Smart, *Philosophers and Religious Truth*, pp. 25ff

2.2 'It is true that Christians today feel much less inclined than were their predecessors in the 18th century to see in miracles a kind of guarantee of the authenticity of revelation. Christ (so it was fashionable to think) showed, in turning water into wine, in raising the dead, in healing the blind, that he brought God's message. This view of the miraculous suggested that these strange events were a kind of hall-mark placed upon his claims to show that they were authentic. Nowadays we feel somewhat uneasy about this rather simple view of miracles and of the way in which genuine revelation is validated. For one thing, there is an increasing awareness of the danger (remarked upon by Christ himself) of treating miracles as external signs, having nothing else to do with Christ's mission than to show its authenticity. To be a "proof" of Christ's divinity a miracle could take any form: and if the function of the miracles was to provide powerful evidence of his authenticity, why

Miracles

should he not have performed something much more spectacular? Moreover, if revelation is not just a matter of claims, teachings, propositions, but is properly speaking the self disclosure of God, then anything miraculous done by Christ must be an integral part of that self disclosure, and not an external guarantee of truth. For these reasons we can see that it is crude and naïve to think of miracles as guaranteeing the truth of scriptures.' . . .

2.9 Such is Hume's argument, and it appears powerful. But it has one or two paradoxical consequences. These we shall come to; but first let us glance at what Hume says elsewhere about the idea of a cause, for a miracle, by running contrary to a law of nature, may appear to be uncaused, or rather it is not physically caused, though supposedly caused by God, supernaturally. What he says elsewhere at first seems to contradict the notion that universal experience of a phenomenon amounts to proof that it will occur in the future. For Hume is at pains to argue that there is no *necessity* in causation. Though we have the idea that when an event causes another there is a necessary connection between the two, as though the occurrence of the one in some way makes it necessary that the other should occur, this idea cannot be given a basis in experience. From the empirical point of view, i.e. resting our argument solely on experience, all we are entitled to say is that whenever an event of type A occurs, we find that an event of type B occurs. There is a constant conjunction between the two; but we cannot observe anything over and above this which we can call a necessity. As we shall see, this view of Hume's had consequences about the nature of science which were important, and which roused Kant from what he called his 'dogmatic slumber' impelling him to think out afresh the basis of scientific explanation.

2.10 Hume's point about necessity may be seen in a different light by considering what it means about the future. If the connnection of causes and effects simply amounts to regular succession, then there is no necessity that this regular succession should continue in the future. The sun rises daily, with cheerful regularity. But how do we know that it will do so tomorrow? That there has been a regular sequence in the past does not imply necessarily that the sun will go on being regular. Indeed, there is no contradiction between saying

(1) The sun has always risen in the past; and
(2) The sun will not rise tomorrow.

This point of course applies not merely to the sun but to all regularities whatsoever, to all laws of nature, to all causal sequences. And this generates what philosophers have called 'the problem of induction'. Induction is when we arrive at conclusions on the basis of experience; as opposed to deduction, as in mathematics, where we work out conclusions without direct reference to experience. The problem is this:

2.11 Science discovers laws of nature, e.g. that water freezes at a certain temperature. But these laws refer both to past and future: what kind of a science is it if it says that water freezes at such and such a temperature, but not tomorrow! But the reference to the future is only valid upon the assumption that nature is uniform, that what has been will be. The uniformity of nature can only, however, be established upon the basis of observation. But observation is past observation and present observation, not future observation. I can't directly observe what will go on tomorrow. Consequently, we can only establish the uniformity of nature upon the assumption that what has been will be. But this is the very assumption of the uniformity of nature which we are trying to establish. The attempt to establish it is circular. Ergo, it cannot be established. The consequence is that science seems to rest upon an unprovable assumption. And this is seemingly a rather embarrassing situation.

2.12 It is one which was clarified by Hume. The point is immediately relevant to the discussion on miracles. For if it is not contradictory to suppose that water might not freeze in the same way tomorrow, it cannot be contradictory to suppose that an event occurs which 'violates a law of nature'. The miraculous is not self contradictory. At most it is incredible, and it is the latter which Hume is setting out to show. . . .

2.16 We should not say that because all conclusions about the observable world are in some measure, by comparison with mathematics, uncertain, therefore all are equally uncertain. We know what we mean by 'good evidence' when we are talking about murders, or the origin of an earthquake or who won the Test Match. So let us concede with a good grace that Hume is not talking nonsense when he says that we have 'proof' that the sun will rise tomorrow, in at least one quite respectable sense of 'proof'. If a man were to come up to me this evening and seriously contend that there was a good chance that the sun wouldn't rise tomorrow, I would, unless he had information about an

Miracles

impending cataclysm, say a star passing over close, be able to show him overwhelmingly good reasons why he was wrong.

2.17 But to admit this is not to admit that it is impossible that the sun should fail to come up tomorrow. Suppose we get up after the usual night's sleep and find no sun, and the world disordered and catastrophic about us — well, we have to face the fact, and we aren't involving ourselves in any self contradictions.

2.18 So we have arrived at two conclusions. First, it is not impossible that something quite contrary to our previous experience should occur. Second, we have proof, in certain cases, that nothing contrary to our previous experience will occur. In short, we can have the best possible evidence there is that X will not occur, and yet X might conceivably after all occur.

2.19 And this shows that there is a paradox in what Hume says. For according to his argument he must fail to believe in a miracle, the violation of a law of nature; and yet on his general philosophical principles, experience being the sole guide, he cannot rule out the theoretical possibility that such an event should occur.

2.20 Imagine Hume being present at someone's rising from the dead. What does he say to himself? 'Impossible, gentlemen, impossible. This is contrary to all my previous experience of mortality, and to the testimony of countless human beings. It would be a lesser miracle that my eyes deceive me than that this resurrection should have occurred.' Well, perhaps of course his eyes do deceive him. Let him test them. Let him investigate minutely the resurrected body. Can he still doubt?

2.21 Nor does it help for someone to defend Hume as follows by saying: 'There *may* be some perfectly natural explanation after all. Perhaps it's a kind of psychosomatic cure of death: you know how much the mind affects the body. Maybe one day we shall get round to understanding this sort of thing.' It is useless to say this, since, natural explanation or no, the event in question is quite contrary to previous experience. Nobody has seen this sort of thing happening, and lo! now it happens. On Hume's argument we have a proof that it cannot happen, and yet here it is happening. Better to disbelieve our eyes, however clear and eagle-like they may be.

2.22 Hume's general argument then fails. We cannot rule out *a priori*, i.e. without recourse to observing the way the world is, the possibility of

Miracles

miracles; and therefore we cannot frame a rule about believing them which would rule out the legitimacy of believing what we see, if we were to see a miracle. But this by no means shows that we have solved all the problems about belief in miracles. For one thing, Hume's particular reasons for holding that we never have, as a matter of fact, clinching testimony of their occurrence still remain. Again, there is a difficulty about saying that a miracle is a violation of a law of nature, as Hume's definition would have us describe it.

It follows from this that in order to disprove a law of nature all you have to do is to produce an exception, a negative instance. Then the supposed law of nature turns out not to be a law of nature. How then can a miracle violate a law of nature? If it is an exception to it, then the law of nature is already (so to speak) destroyed. There seems then to be a paradox in the definition of miracle. The miracle seems for ever frustrated in its attempt to violate; for as soon as it imagines that it has succeeded, it finds that there was nothing there after all to violate! It is like someone trying to live in a state of conjugal bliss with a bachelor: for as soon as there is conjugality there is (by definition) no bachelor.

2.24 These remarks, incidentally, bring out two important points about laws of nature. First, the use of the word 'laws' when we talk of them is not a satisfactory analogy. For laws in the primary sense, when we speak about the laws enacted by Parliament or about moral laws, are such that, even if they are often broken, they do not thereby cease to be valid. But this is not, as we have seen, possible with a scientific law. Indeed, one might say that the whole point of legal and moral laws is that they get broken: were it not for the fact that many human beings are inclined to commit adultery there would be no point in having a commandment about it.

2.25 The second lesson we can learn from the foregoing about scientific law is that, formally at least, it seems easier to disprove them than prove them. We are not in a position to search out every tiger that has existed, now exists or will exist, to check on whether it is a quadruped. It is just that all the ones we have come across have this property. That all atoms have a certain constitution is something we could not possibly verify conclusively. The best we can do is to sample a small slice of the universe. . . .

2.26 To return, however, to our paradox. What are we to say? We could perhaps alter the definition of 'miracle' and allow that a miracle is not a violation of a law of nature. But this lands us in certain difficulties. We could, for example, treat a miracle simply as a sign – that is, as an event which shows something about God to men on a particular occasion, but which occurs in a natural sequence of events. But it could not be a sign unless it were something rather extraordinary. The fact that it rained at 2 o'clock this afternoon could scarcely function as a particular sign of God's dealing with men. . . .

2.27 And to treat the miracle simply as a sign means that it has some special significance *for us* though it is capable of being explained naturally. But this seems too 'subjective'. A miracle would depend on the way it strikes us. Unless the way it strikes us is controlled by something 'objective' miracles would cease to be *evidence* of anything.

2.28 It might be more fruitful, if we can, to escape the paradox in another way. Could we somehow claim that a miracle has the peculiar property of violating but not destroying a law of nature, despite what we said about the deadly power of the negative instance? A digression upon the apparent villainy of the scientist might be useful here.

2.29 . . . It is not to be thought that the scientist does an experiment, finds a result contrary to all his previous experience and then good-naturedly shrugs his shoulders, sighing 'And there goes another scientific law.' Rather he concludes that he must have made a mistake in his experiment. And anything bizarre tends to be treated in the same way. . . .

But if he and his colleagues keep on finding the same thing, then there is nothing for it but to reject the law. Or at least to tinker with it in some way so that it is made to correspond with the new finding. Thus the law is scrapped or, as we might say, changed; but it must be remembered that even if it is only changed, then strictly speaking it is, in its original form, scrapped. But only, as I say, with reluctance. The moral of this digression is that science is not just observational: it is experimental. . . .

2.30 The fact that science is experimental is significant for our discussion. For experimentation involves controlled conditions and, thereby, repeatability. The great thing about an experiment is that it can be repeated. It is not, as we saw, the single experiment which produces the negative instance of deadly power. It is the repeated, the sifted, the scrutinised experiment which does this.

Miracles

2.32   The relevance of all this to miracles is readily apparent. Miracles are not experimental, repeatable. They are particular, peculiar events occurring in idiosyncratic human situations. They are not small scale laws. Consequently they do not destroy large scale laws. Formally, they may seem to destroy the 'Always' statements of the scientific laws; but they have not the genuine deadly power of the negative instance.

2.33   But we may well be unhappy at this solution to our paradox and say 'But in any given instance of a supposed miracle the strange anomaly must be caused by some condition which we have overlooked. Still, granting that it isn't, but that inexplicably contrary to all past and, no doubt, future experience, a man really rises from the dead, then this will be an uncaused event, a sudden bit of randomness in an otherwise orderly universe.' The trouble is that we seem to be in a cleft stick. Either all events are caused, in which case the violation of a law of nature seems to be ruled out; or we regard the miraculous as an uncaused – a random – event. But why should we attach any particular importance to random events?

. . . . . .

2.44   It is obvious from all this that the claim that an event is miraculous presupposes some kind of belief in God or the supernatural. As we have seen, the miraculous is more than the merely random, more than the merely (scientifically) inexplicable. But without the concept of God, and considered without relation to a miracle's religious context, it would seem to be merely a random or inexplicable event. There might then be two views of the same miraculous event, depending on the presuppositions and interests of the people investigating or contemplating it. From the strictly scientific point of view, the event would be merely inexplicable. From the religious standpoint it could be considered as directly caused by God.

2.45   We have been talking, though, as if it were a simple matter to say that an event was scientifically inexplicable. But how could we ever know that an event fell into this category? For we could never be absolutely sure that some new theory would not appear which would give us a means of explaining the event. All that we would be entitled to say, perhaps, would be 'Given the present state of knowledge, this event cannot be scientifically explained.' What once looked like miraculous healing might be accounted for by new advances in medicine (the phenomenon of psychosomatic disorders is much better appreciated nowadays). These remarks fit in with Hume's objection that miracles chiefly abound amid barbarous peoples, for clearly, the more ignorant people are, the more events there will be which are inexplicable to them in terms of natural processes.

2.47 ... First, miracles do not occur in the abstract, but in particular personal and historical situations. Perhaps a random event has just occurred at the top of Everest, a piece of snow rising inexplicably and hovering over the summit for ten minutes. But such an event has not the flavour of the genuine miracle. This is because in Western religious thought at least, the miracle has the characteristic of conveying to us something about God: it is a form of his self-disclosure. Thus it occurs in the context of a personal situation, and one which has a special religious significance. Thus one has to understand the religious context of the event, as well as having to presuppose the existence of a supernatural Being capable of causing the miraculous. It is the conjunction of the random and inexplicable event (looking at it merely from the scientific standpoint) with the religious context that constitutes the greatest wonder of all. If we really do find that a holy Teacher performs the inexplicable, it is a tremendous coincidence. . . .

... If the Christian claims that his faith is historical, he may mean one of two things. He may mean that it centres upon events which he believes occurred at a certain point in history; or he may mean that his faith can be validated by historical enquiry. For there are two senses of 'history'. First, the sequence of human events; second, the enquiry bearing upon them known in schools and universities as 'history'. In the first sense, you can record history, in the second sense you can *do* it. It may be useful to introduce some terminology to make this distinction clear. When we say that an event belongs to the sequence of events, we shall call it 'historical'. And let us use 'metahistorical' to refer to the type of enquiry pursued by the historian when he tries to find out what the sequence of events was. Now in the first sense Christianity is historical, or claims to be, for Christ's life belonged to the sequence of human events; but what of the second sense? Would the objective and 'scientific' historian, in reading the New Testament, be willing to concede that the miraculous might have occurred, that, metahistorically, it could be proved? It is one thing to agree, as the result of the kind of philosophical argument which we have been pursuing, that in theory a resurrection from the dead is possible. It is

Miracles

quite another thing to take this merely theoretical possibility into one's reckoning. . . .

Miracles can happen, but we would be rightly suspicious of a modern historian who set this event down as a fact.

2.57 Finally, let us look at the solution to the problem of miracles which has been proposed here, and consider what it implies about scientific laws and about causation. For a view about the nature of causes is rather central to any general philsophical theory, and indeed it was Hume's treatment of it that led to Kant's attempt to frame an alternative picture. Our solution, then, briefly is this. There is no reason in the nature of things why occasional random and inexplicable events should not occur. There is, and here we agree with Hume, no absolute necessity why things should always continue to operate in the way in which they have in the past. Thus we cannot rule out in advance the possibility that the miraculous, which is meant to be scientifically inexplicable, may occur. But supposing such an event does happen, it is not sufficient reason to abandon the natural law that the miracle has 'violated'. For what we mean by a genuine negative instance (the one which has the deadly power of destroying the law) is an experimentally repeatable exception. But the miracle does not fall into this category, otherwise it would itself be a new small scale law, not a 'violation' of regularity. But the miracle differs from the merely random in having a supposed unobservable cause (namely God) though from the purely scientific point of view, it would look random. Of course, one would have to have good reason for rejecting the hypothesis that after all the event may have an explanation (for does not science progress?); but in certain cases one might have practical assurance that it was inexplicable, e.g. if a person after the onset of physical decay genuinely rose to bodily life again. Such then is the general view that has been presented here. But it implies that we would not have to take scientific laws strictly as asserting, 'Whenever A then B', but rather saying that, 'There is an overwhelming tendency for an A to be followed by a B'. In other words, 'Every event must have a cause' (a principle which intuitively we feel we must hold, as a presupposition of scientific enquiry) is suspect. If it means 'Every event must of necessity fit into a pattern of regularities' it is false, even if we may use it in practice as a principle to guide our investigations. That we can so use it follows from the way in which we have interpreted the negative instance: for the random variety has no implications for the future, while the deadly exception (being a small-scale law) does. Thus all events which can be checked upon in a scientific manner can be found to fit into patterns of regularities. The merely random, because it does not repeat itself, can safely be neglected.

2.58 Further, though the miraculous does not fit into a pattern of observable regularities, it is believed to have a supernatural cause. So that from the religious point of view it is not a causeless event. But one could only appeal to this idea of a supernatural cause if it is legitimate to believe in such a transcendent Being. We shall have to come later to this all important question. But we can in the meantime note that it follows, from the view about miracles which has here been expressed, that miracles by themselves could not serve as conclusive evidence of a divine revelation. For, as we saw, one needs prior acceptance and understanding of the idea of God, and not just an abstract belief in him, but a knowledge in some degree of his character. A miracle, then, is not an external guarantee of the truth of revelation, but belongs with a pattern of revelation – a pattern of divine self-disclosure.

Thomas McPherson, *Philosophy and Religious Belief*, pp. 83ff

On a 'strong' definition of miracle – where miracle is defined in some way as 'an event in which the laws of nature are broken or suspended' – explanation of an event in terms of miracle and explanation of it in natural terms would be mutually exclusive. An event might be explained in terms of the operation of some natural law or in terms of divine suspension of the operation of natural law: obviously, however, it cannot be explained in both of these ways at the same time; for one of them excludes the other. On a weak definition of miracle, however, that is, where miracle is defined in some such way as 'unusual or unexpected event which is seen as having religious significance' – the two explanations are not mutually exclusive: there is no necessary impropriety in saying of a given event both that it can be explained in natural terms and that it is nevertheless at the same time both unusual and of religious significance. . . .

Some compromise between the strong and weak definitions would seem to be desirable, if it can be found. There would be an advantage in trying to retain something from the strong view. The notion of inexplicability seems to be part of what people generally intended by 'miracle' and the notion of inexplicability in natural terms is present in the strong view as it is not in the weak. A compromise might lie in the direction of regarding a miracle as an unusual or unexpected and (in a sense) inexplicable event which has religious significance. . . .

The view I wish to maintain is that a miracle is an event which both is and is not capable of being explained in natural terms. We may take it that every natural event is capable of a natural explanation. That is not to say that the natural explanation must be well known or even known at all. There may be a large element of uncertainty about it. But if the correct natural explanation has not yet been agreed upon or not yet even discovered, the proper assumption is not that there is no natural explanation but that its establishment lies in the future. We are not, generally, in the discussion of miracles, speculating about some imaginary event, which we can construct in any form we like, even incorporating elements of blatant physical or logical impossibility. We are usually discussing events which are alleged to have actually taken place. They have happened, or are believed to have happened, and what has happened could presumably happen again. . . .

The sense in which alleged miracles might be said to be inexplicable is clearly not such that it would rule out altogether all explanations in natural terms, for such explanations exist. It is rather that natural explanations alone seem inadequate. The force of the stories of Jesus' miracles is such that a purely natural explanation seems to miss the point – the point, that is, of calling them miracles.

The sense in which an alleged miracle may be said to be 'inexplicable' is that although it is not literally without the possibility of an explanation, in natural terms such an explanation is not adequate by itself. We may remind ourselves of the difference between two explanations that might be offered of a man's death. There may be no difficulty in establishing the cause of death as poison, self administered. But we may still want to say: 'It's inexplicable, he seemed so happy, successful, healthy.' What we are looking for is something that will give us his *reason* for taking his life. Without an acceptable explanation in these terms we may continue to regard the death as 'inexplicable'. If this parallel is apt, then miracles may be regarded as events which although capable of explanation in natural terms seem to call for explanation as well in terms of something like reasons: a man may suppose he glimpses a special divine purpose in them. Sometimes God seems to be operating like a natural cause, though in opposition to, or by 'suspension' of, what our knowledge of natural laws would lead us to expect. On such a view, the paradigm of a miracle would be something like the parting of the waters of the Red Sea, recorded in Exodus, taking this for present purposes to be purely an event in which natural laws are supposed to be violated. . . . But if explanation in terms of miracle is seen as parallel to explanation in terms of reason we are led to a different point of view. Here the escape of the Israelites against the odds is seen as miraculous, but the stress is not on extraordinary physical events but on a special divine purpose or plan. The parting of the waters of the Red Sea alone is not the miracle, this is the means (if we believe the story) to the miracle which lies in successful escape, because God had a *reason* for the escape of the Israelites, their escape was part of a divine plan, etc.

The concept of miracle is a religious concept. The non-religious man is much less likely than the religious man to want to use the term. 'Miracle' is part of the whole apparatus of religious terms: and part of what it means to be a religious man is that such a man is disposed to see the hand of providence at work in the world, and part of what this means is that he may be inclined to see some events as miracles. Not all religious believers will make much use of the notion of miracle: the tougher minded among them may use it hardly at all. But even if not all religious believers make much use of it, it is still a notion that belongs naturally in a religious context, and hardly belongs at all outside it. There is, of course, a use of 'miracle' in non-religious contexts (marvels, 'the miracles of modern science', etc.); but the use of 'miracle' that we are considering here is its use in the context of religious belief.

Hume pointed out to the Christian believers of his day that they do not give credence to stories of miracles told in pagan or superstitious societies, ancient or modern. Why not? A reason he did not give is that the miracle stories that Christians are inclined to accept are those that support their own religious beliefs. If they are inclined to reject a particular set of non-Christian beliefs, or beliefs that although Christian seem to them superstitious, they will not give credence to the miracle stories associated with those beliefs. Miracles are not to be considered except in relation to a particular religious (cultural, social) background. It has frequently been said that miracles ought not to be appealed to as proofs of Christian belief; the connection is rather the other way round; someone who is already a Christian believer will be disposed to take seriously Christian accounts of miracles. (The connection may in fact be a reciprocal one.) Hume's argument against miracles was not so much that there are no miracles as that:

'a miracle can never be proved so as to be the foundation of a system of religion'.

Even if belief in miracles were a straightforward matter of weighing up evidence – and we have expressed doubts on this – it is unlikely to be a matter of weighing up 'objective' evidence, equally available to all. What might seem evidence to one man will not appear as such to another. If a man is disposed to reject a particular set of beliefs as pagan superstition he will not accept as evidence for those beliefs any accounts of miracles: if the beliefs are untrue how can alleged miracles be evidence for their truth? Better to reject the stories of miracles as themselves untrue. The cultural or religious dependence of belief in specific miracles might be offered as an argument against their truth, but only on the assumption that no miracle could possibly be genuine unless it be capable of being seen and acknowledged to be genuine by everybody. But this assumption seems to be the same as the general assumption which we have in the previous chapter questioned, that nothing could be evidence for the existence of God that would not be acknowledged as evidence by a non-believer as well as a believer. But an important difference between believers and non-believers is that they see the world in different ways. If the non-believer saw as evidence for God – albeit in his opinion, insufficient evidence – the same things as the believer sees, then one fundamental difference between the believer and the non-believer would be on the way to disappearing.

In brief. The question of the truth or falsehood of a given story of an alleged miracle is not to be settled by an examination of 'objective evidence'. The question of what is to count as evidence is not to be divorced from a consideration of the contents and attitudes of a particular religion: and, furthermore, to the extent that we may regard this as a matter of evidence at all, the acceptability or otherwise of an alleged miracle is not to be discovered simply by a direct comparison between the evidence for a causal account (or account in natural or scientific terms) and the evidence, in the shape, say, of testimony, for an explanation in terms of miracle; for this is probably to regard explanation in terms of miracle as itself a kind of explanation in causal terms, that is, in terms of the super-physical effort of a super-physical being, which is an inadequate view of what explanation in terms of miracle is. It may well be that religious believers need not insist with any great force upon the truth of many, if any, alleged Christian miracles. But it has not been my concern to discuss this. I have not been arguing for the truth, or for that matter for the falsehood, of any particular miracle stories. I have tried rather to confine myself to the question of what sort of belief belief in miracles is.

H. D. Lewis, 'Some Outstanding Problems' from *Philosophy of Religion*, pp. 306, 302

p. 306

'Jesus, by his own example and teaching, also helps us to keep this subject in the right perspective. It is not a peripheral question, but neither is it a crucial one. The essential Christian claims, for example, are not jeopardised if the miracles are questioned. These are not the decisive indications of the divinity of Jesus. It is especially misleading to attempt, as alas many do, to establish the miracles in some secular way (by normal historical evidence for example) and then prove from this the doctrines of 'the Person of Christ'. That is to go to work crudely and in quite the wrong way. It puts entirely the wrong interpretation on the prominence of miracles in the Gospel narratives and much over-simplifies the issue. I think we shall find the position not radically different in the cases of other charismatic personalities or central figures of the great religions. Few topics have in fact been more misunderstood or mishandled than miracles; and this has often brought discredit on religion and made the way of its defenders hard. . . .

p. 302

If I were to stumble by chance on some substance containing penicillin and apply it to somebody's wound I might bring about a cure in unexpected and speedy ways. No one could perhaps account for it. But it is not hard for a scientist to give the explanation today. Accordingly, some would maintain, we have no reason for supposing that anything is in principle beyond explanation. We may never find the explanation, but that only shows how limited we are. If only we knew more or understood things a little better the explanation would be forthcoming. There are odd events but none that are inherently unaccountable. There must be some explanation for everything.

This is a natural line to take. It is also rather hasty. Those who adopt it are often influenced in one of two ways. They may take their start from an idealist position in philosophy or move in an intellectual atmosphere much affected by idealism, as was the case with much liberal theology earlier in this century. This would set up an initial presumption that there is an ultimate rational explanation of everything.

We have seen earlier how this should be. Others have been affected more by recent philosophy and led to the view that explanations depend on the map or grid through which we view the facts and that the suitable map would have some way of taking care of everything. Neither of these positions seems to me sound. . . .

The fact that explanations are in due course forthcoming for events which were wholly bewildering once remains disconcerting. Will there not always lurk in our thought the suspicion that, in fact, the most inexplicable happenings will eventually fit into place in 'The scheme of things'? Miracles may be possible but have there ever been any?

Many who are impressed by this difficulty or who are perhaps reluctant for reasons like those indicated earlier to admit any ultimate lack of continuity, will be apt to take refuge in some different notion of miracle. It will be held that an event could be miraculous although it is capable of a normal or scientific explanation. It will be a miracle because it has religious significance. This suggestion, as it stands, seems however to have much too wide a coverage. It could extend to all there is, and indeed some writers have boldly accepted that consequence. For the sun to rise each day is as much a miracle as it would be for it to stand, as alleged, 'upon Gibeon'. 'Every bush is a burning bush' as it was once eloquently put. But this will hardly do, for it seems pointless to speak of miracle if everything is a miracle; why not just say that the world is God's world and so on? The word 'miracle' becomes otiose here. But it seems also otiose on modifications of the present suggestion, such as the view very ably presented by thinkers like F. R. Tennant and H. H. Farmer, namely that a miracle is a very rare combination of events that have some distinctive significance for individuals or peoples – the crossing of the Red Sea in the Biblical account, for example, if ascribed to unusual combinations of winds and tide. My own impression after examining many variations on the theme that there can be miracles within an exhaustively rational scheme of things, is that it is much better to dispense with the term – or to deny that there are miracles – than to attempt to save the notion in a meaning so divorced from the one we normally give it as to be extremely misleading and confusing. Without the requisite 'break' there seems to be nothing which could not be properly treated in the terms we normally use in religion without recourse to the special notion of miracle. . . .

But here again the problem becomes acute of how could we ever know that miracles happen. Could we ever know that there is more than some rare or super-normal event? Does God, to put it in the sharpest and bluntest form, ever intervene? I think we could reply, if what has been maintained about religious experience is sound, that God does intervene in the normal course of things to shape such experiences — that is what divine disclosure involves. But again it will not do to treat this as miracle. For that would also give the word too wide and unusual a meaning. What we wish to know is whether God intervenes (or whatever approximation to this we may allow) beyond the disclosure in experience, and how is that established. . . .

But even with such difficulties out of the way, the question of fact remains. Granted that miracles are not on religious grounds out of place and that we may even reasonably expect them in some circumstances, can we ever know that they do happen? Could we recognise one? The root difficulty here has already been made plain. Strange things happen but for all we know they may admit of some natural explanation. 'But,' someone will say 'In the case I wish to instance, the end which came about had been prayed for — I was ill beyond all hope of recovery, but I prayed and behold I am well.' The difficulty with this is that many have prayed, devoutly and sincerely it would seem, and not been made well. The force of this objection can indeed be reduced — for some prayers are not worthy ones, it may not be God's will to grant all that we ask, our faith may be too weak. This would make it sensible to believe in petitionary prayer while allowing that many prayers are not granted. But it would not make it plausible to appeal to apparent instances of answer to prayer as a way of proving, in the first place, that God acts in this way. The reference to prayer does none the less give us our clue. For what we plainly need is some concomitance of events which seem to defy explanation in the ordinary way and of some religious factor. I have elsewhere suggested that this may be found in a heightening of religious awareness and its accompaniments in those instances where in other ways there appears to be an initially good case for a miracle. I think much might be learnt by investigating the subject afresh in this way. In the case of Jesus, as the Christian thinks of Him, the closeness to God would be peculiar and sustained, and here we would therefore expect to find the substantiation *par excellence* of the claims for miraculous performances.

H. H. Farmer, *The World and God*

pp. 107ff

The fatal mistake is to begin the consideration of miracle from the angle of a scientific or philosophic concept of natural law. Miracle being fundamentally a religious category and not a scientific or philosophic one, the proper place to begin is within the sphere of living religion itself. To define miracle as an event involving suspension of natural laws is to begin in the wrong place. We must first ask what is the significance of a miracle for religion; we must define it and evaluate it, seek to understand the indispensability of it, within that context and universe of discourse. . . . The final judgement on a religious matter must be a religious one; that is to say, it must be one such as the deeply religious man cannot help making and acting on when he is most livingly aware that God is dealing with him and he with God, as, for example, when in a critical situation he is on his knees at prayer. . . .

Miracle, like other terms, is often loosely and even flippantly used, but if we wish to keep close to the central and serious realities of genuine religion, then we must say that no man has any right to call an event a miracle who does not apprehend in some measure through it both the absolute demand and the final succour of God, and feel his spirit moved to that response of obedience to and trust in the divine purpose which is what we call faith; for unless these are present it is doubtful whether there is any of that living apprehension of God through an event or events without which there can be no revelation, and therefore no miracle, according to the use of the terms we propose.

. . . . . .

The assimilating of the idea of miracle to the idea of revelation makes clear why it is impossible ever to establish by intellectual proof that quality of an event, which makes it miraculous to the religious mind. For revelation, we have insisted, is God speaking to the individual personally, that is to say, in a way which is relevant to, and only understandable in terms of, the individual's own concrete situation; and not only is God in the nature of the case intellectually indemonstrable, but also it is impossible to take up a personal situation into a general proposition or syllogism without its concrete, historical, livingly personal quality vanishing in a cloud of abstractions. Each man's situation is entirely his own, and nobody else can ever be in it and make it his own in exactly the same sense. Hence each man's revelation and miracle must be his own also, and no amount of argument will ever suffice to convince others of the reality of his transactions with God through them. To the rationalist this indemonstrability of miracle is sufficient to put the whole matter out of court as unworthy of consideration; to the religious mind, when it understands itself and the sphere in which it moves, it is precisely this undemonstrability which is part of the certification that it is a genuinely personal dealing with the living God. . . .

Rightly understood, in fact, as already said, in the category of miracle the experience of God as personal reaches its maximum concentration. Let us make this clear by examples. . . .

Where then must we look for those experiences wherein the word miracle comes with a maximum of spontaneity and inevitability to the lips of the religious man? The answer is, in that relationship to God which we call prayer, especially as it arises out of a deep sense of need and takes the form of believing petition. An instance which came under the direct observation of the writer may perhaps be permitted.

A mother was informed by the doctors that, so far as medical science could judge, her baby could not possibly recover from sickness; whereupon she called a friend, who, like herself, was a Christian believer, and asked him to pray with her that God would restore the child. So they prayed, and within a few hours the child was on the way to a recovery which confounded all the experience of the doctors, as they were frank to admit, even including one whose whole philosophy of life tended to profound scorn of 'all that sort of thing'. Now we are concerned at the moment to discuss what such a happening may imply as to the nature of prayer, its conditions and limits, or how it may be related to our general conception of the world and of God's relationship to it. The point at the moment is that the word which came instantly to the lips of the two people who had prayed, both of whom were intelligent and cultured, was 'miracle'. They did not say 'this is providential', they said 'this is a miracle', and no other word seemed appropriate to the awed sense of having transaction with the succouring will of God in a personal situation of critical need. Perhaps, then, if we examine this instance we shall discover what essentially constitutes the religious sense of miracle when the word is used with its most pregnant and distinctive meaning.

Three things at least, would appear, from this instance, to be indispensable.

First, there is an awareness of serious crisis or need or threat of disaster in the personal life, and of helplessness to deal with it adequately and victoriously through the exercise of ordinary, unaided human powers. Second, there is a more or less conscious and explicit turning to God for assistance. Third, there is an awareness of an ad hoc response of God to the situation and to man's petitioning inadequacy in it, so that the crisis is met, the need satisfied, the danger averted, in an event, or combination of events, which would not have taken place had man not so petitioned and God so acted.

We may observe how each of these three points contributes something towards taking the experience out of the realm of the merely general and bringing it within the sharper focus of the individual and personal.

. . . . . .

p. 177

In conclusion, a concrete illustration may be given. Let us suppose, for the sake of the argument, that when the children of Israel crossed the Red Sea, what happened was that a strong wind drove back the waters just at the moment of their dire need. Two interpretations of this conjunction of events are possible. First, that it was a fortunate coincidence; the wind would have arisen in any case, and it was sheer good luck that the Israelites arrived when they did. Second, that it was a miracle; the wind would not have arisen just then, had not a transcendent factor, namely the will of God acting relevantly to that situation and in response perhaps to a prayer of need, entered in. Now the point is that from the point of view of science it is a matter of indifference which of the two interpretations is offered; neither one is called for rather than the other if the work of science is to proceed. If it were true in fact that God brought about the wind, science could still pursue its enquiries, the wind being now accomplished fact, into the question how it was related to previous meteorological conditions, and exhibited the general regularities (probably of a statistical kind) which govern the pressures and resistances of gases; for it could not become part of man's phenomenal world without manifesting those relationships and exhibiting those laws. How then could God conceivably so enter into a general meteorological situation that the outcome is different from what it would otherwise be, thus perhaps falsifying the forecasts of the weather experts attached to Pharaoh's court (forecasts, be it noted, which in the nature of the case could never be absolute certainties)? If we must form a picture, it might be along the lines suggested above, namely that God so uses His all-inclusive rapport with the ultimate entities which constitute the inner, creative, present reality of the natural order, that their various routine activities are not overriden, but used by redirecting them in relation to one another. Just as man brings about effects in nature which would not otherwise happen by redirecting its routines in relation with one another, so does God, except that God acts from the inside, so to say, by inner rapport and not by external manipulation in the gross. Such rearranging and bringing together of different series of routine events would in the nature of the case not be observable by science. In the suppositious case given, the meteorologists might explain the falsification of their prediction by saying, that a disturbance arose unexpectedly over the Indian Ocean, that the said disturbance was probably connected with air currents from the Antarctic, that those air currents derived from something else, and so on, until in principle the whole universe is theoretically involved, and thus the interest and scope and methods of science completely transcended.

John Macquarrie, 'Miracles' from *Principles of Christian Theology*, pp. 226ff

In theology therefore a miracle is understood not just as a happening that excites wonder but as an 'act' of God. Such an act may be a vehicle for revelation or for grace or for judgement or for all of these together. Thus we could say that a miracle is a providential act, in line with what has already been said about providence. While presumably all happenings can be somehow related to the divine providence, since God is present and active in the whole world process, it is clear that some happenings count for more than others, or are more important or significant than others. Even if all events belong within a continuous series, some stand out within the series as critical moments in its unfolding. . . .

However, if *everything* can be called 'miracle' the word has been generalized to the point where it has been virtually devoided of content. We have to see whether we can find a satisfactory way of describing what it is that makes a miracle stand out as some distinctive event. . . .

It is this traditional account of the distinctiveness of miracle that makes the conception very difficult for modern minds, and might even suggest to the theologian that 'miracle' is a discredited and outmoded word that ought to be banished from his vocabulary. The way of understanding miracle that appeals to breaks in the natural order and to supernatural interventions belongs to the mythological outlook and cannot commend itself in a post-mythological climate of thought.

The traditional conception of miracle is irreconcilable with our modern understanding of both science and history. Science proceeds on the assumption that whatever events occur in the world can be accounted for in terms of other events that also belong within the world, and if on some occasions we are unable to give a complete account of some happening – and presumably all our accounts fall short of completeness – the scientific conviction is that further research will bring to light further factors in the situation, but factors that will turn out to be just as immanent and this-worldly as those already known. . . .

If miracle in the sense of supernatural intervention is irreconcilable with science and history, it is also objectionable theologically. It is objectionable because it goes back to a mythological outlook and expects God to manifest himself and prove himself in some extraordinary sensible phenomena. While the early Christian writers used many arguments to establish the claims of their faith, and some of these arguments seem strange to us, most of these writers wisely avoided putting too much weight on any appeal to miracles reportedly done by Jesus. In this, they were following his own teaching and example. . . .

They (i.e. the Jews) would not be convinced because the true meaning of a miracle does not lie in some extraordinary publicly observable event, but in God's presence and self-manifestation in the event. This is not something publicly observable, nor is it something that requires some prodigy, or breach in nature, for its occurrence. What is distinctive about miracle is God's presence and self-manifestation in the event. The mythological way of thinking tried to express this distinctiveness by making the event itself something magical or supernatural, divorced from the natural sequence of events; but in doing this, it shifted attention away from the essence of miracle (the divine presence and self-manifestation) to the discredited and mistaken idea of miracle as a magic sign. Actually, if we look at stories of miracles and see how these stories have developed, we can sometimes see how some natural event which was indeed a miracle, a vehicle for God's action, gets transformed into a supernatural event as the story is embroidered by legends. The inflation of the natural event into the spectacular sign is the way by which the mythological mentality seeks to express the distinctiveness and significance of the event for religious faith. . . .

Miracle, like providence and revelation, has the character of ambiguity. From one point of view, the event is seen as a perfectly ordinary event; from another point of view, it is an event that opens up Being and becomes a vehicle for Being's revelation or grace or judgement or address. There is no public, universally observable character that attests a miracle as such. But does this mean then that the event is a miracle only in someone's subjective apprehension of it? And is the designation of the event as 'miracle' just an arbitrary label stuck upon it by someone who happens to have been deeply impressed by it? The same kind of questions arise here as arose earlier in our discussion of revelation. We shall try to answer them by examining an actual miracle.

The example chosen is the crossing of the Red Sea by the people of Israel, a miracle that impressed itself so deeply upon the mind of the people that they always looked back to it as God's great providential act on their behalf and indeed as the very foundation of their existence as a community. As is well known, the account as we now have it is put together from various sources. Scholars differ over the details of how these sources are to be disentangled, but the broad outlines are clear enough. According to the older version, we can visualize an incident which can be understood as perfectly 'natural' in the sense that it does not involve any happenings that would contradict our ordinary experience of natural phenomena. In this account, the Israelites were already encamped by the shore, and the Egyptians were in pursuit. The combination of a strong wind with a low tide enabled the Israelites to get across. The Egyptians tried to follow, but their chariots got stuck in the sand and they were caught by the incoming tide. The later version transforms the story into a 'supernatural' event by introducing magical elements. Moses stretches his rod over the sea, the waters divide and stand like walls on both sides. The Israelites go through, and the Egyptians foolishly attempt to follow and are overwhelmed by the water as it falls back down upon them.

The first version of the story, as has been said, describes what can be regarded as an ordinary natural event, and anyone who is determined to regard it as this and nothing more would say that the whole thing was just a lucky coincidence for the Israelites and that only their superstitious outlook led them to see it as God's act of deliverance. The second version may be regarded as the mythological way of trying to express the wonder which Israel had experienced in face of the event, and the meaning which they attached to it as an act of God. By representing the event as supernatural – Moses waves his wand and the waters divide and stand up like walls – this version certainly succeeds in pointing to the distinctiveness of the event, but like all mythology it obscures the real significance of the event by objectifying the divine act in terms of sensible phenomena, whereas this significance is really God's grace and judgement experienced by the people in an event which, though dramatic and memorable, was nevertheless (as we may suppose) perfectly natural. . . .

Let me here introduce the notion of 'focusing' as a useful idea for explicating miracles, and an idea of which we shall have occasion to make further use later. God's presence and activity are everywhere and always; yet we experience these intensely in particular concrete happenings, in which, as it were, they have been focused. As was said before, there is little point in talking of everything as miracle. We need not, however, try to detach any event from the natural series within which it belongs in order for that event to be experienced as a focus of divine action, that is to say, as a miracle.

But we must come back to the question whether this account of miracle has not entirely subjectivized the matter and made the designation of any event as a miracle a quite arbitrary matter. Let us remind ourselves again that even if one were to claim some publicly observable characteristics in a miracle (such as a suspension of the regular operation of natural process) this would not establish a divine act, for this could not be detected by any empirical test. But even when we reject some publicly observable anomaly, or magical phenomenon, this does not mean that miracle is being understood subjectively. . . .

In the Christian faith, the supreme miracle is the incarnation. From one point of view, Jesus represented simply another human life, the life of a turbulent innovator, in the eyes of most who saw him. But to the disciples, this life was the focusing of the presence and action of God. Faith perceived the dimension which is not publicly observable, and could not be. Was this leap of faith just an arbitrary leap, or could it be reasonably defended? Certainly, it could neither be proved nor disproved by any observation or argument. But it is confirmed in the community's subsequent life of faith, where the miracle of incarnation interprets the community's existence, lends meaning to it, strengthens its being. And again, the miracle does not remain isolated but is confirmed in a whole series of 'miracles', foci of the divine presence and acting. These happen in the life and experiences of the community of faith, continually leading it into fuller being, thereby showing that they have no illusory character. The sacraments, for instance, are such foci. Talk of the 'miracle of the mass' is not just superstitious talk but points to the focusing of the divine presence in the eucharist. Another example is afforded by the lives of the saints. Men have attributed 'miracles' to them, and this may often have been in the mythological way of ascribing public marvels to them. But this need not obscure the genuine sense in which sainthood is the focusing in a human life of the divine presence. Miracle is not magic, but the focusing of holy Being's presence and action amid the events, and persons of the world, and this has the highest reality.

C. S. Lewis, *Miracles*, p. 168

And when you turn from the New Testament to modern scholars remember that you go among them as sheep among wolves. Naturalistic assumptions, beggings of the question such as that I noted on the first page of this book, will meet you on every side – even from the pens of clergymen. . . .

In using the books of such people you must therefore be continually on guard. You must develop a nose like a bloodhound for those steps in the argument which depend, not on historical and linguistic knowledge, but on the concealed assumption that miracles are impossible, improbable, or improper. And this means that you must really re-educate yourself, must work hard and consistently to eradicate from your mind the whole type of thought in which we have all been brought up. It is the type of thought which under various disguises, has been our adversary throughout this book. It is technically called *Monism*, but perhaps the unlearned reader will understand me best if I call it *Everythingism*. I mean by this the belief that 'everything' or 'the whole show' must be self existent, must be more important than every particular thing, and must contain all particular things in such a way that they cannot be really very different from one another – that they must be not merely 'at one' but one. The Everythingist . . . thinks that everything is in the long run 'merely' a precursor or development or a relic or an instance or a disguise of everything else. This philosophy I believe to be profoundly untrue.

E. and M.-L. Keller, 'Miracles in Reality' from *Miracles in Dispute*, p. 245

Whatever may be said about the manifestations of the devil applies equally to the manifestations of God. If one thinks abstractly about the former one thinks abstractly about the latter. The man who fails to notice the demonic at work in the scenes of everyday life will also fail to find the signs of God's presence in specific situations. Christians who are always waiting for special revelations or dispensations or leadings from a heavenly world often prove to be blind towards the real world. The man whose gaze is directed towards a supernatural history and who looks for miracles and 'facts of salvation' is in constant danger of losing his eye for 'normal' history. It does not occur to him to expect divine revelations on the level of profane everyday happenings (in a political event, for example), or to encounter the Absolute in his day to day comings and goings – perhaps in a street incident. Yet it was one of Jesus' main purposes to maintain precisely this, through word and deed and through the devotion of his whole life.

Paradoxically, this purpose of Jesus' was subsequently threatened by the mythologization and hallowing of his life and work, a transformation which silently took place in the language of the proclamation and later in all details of institutional religion. Contrary to its original intention, the glorifying language of the first preachers, which exalted Jesus into heaven and declared him the supernatural son of God and man of miracles, is for contemporary people a distortion of the real heart of the message rather than a clarification of it.

Does anything in the real world depend on the way in which one interprets the miracles in the Bible or more generally, the supernatural salvation history or, more generally still, God's whole activity? It is a reasonable question; for the whole 'miracle problem' could in the last resort turn out to be of complete indifference (at least for people in general) if the widely held contemporary view that this is a 'purely religious' matter, and consequently the private affair of the individual, were true; that it is an internal theological squabble, to put it in somewhat unfriendly terms, whose result is completely lacking in interest for real life. This view certainly reflects the judgement of the contemporary mind, which believes that the miracle question is finished and done with; but it is an improbable solution, because belief in miracles crops up again and again as a question and a possibility in a religious tradition which today influences the behaviour of millions.

How can this religious tradition belonging to the past (the earliest biblical writings are, after all, nearly 3,000 years old) be taken into and absorbed into the present without contemporary life being restricted by it, yet so that the essential human experiences preserved in it are not lost? That is the leading and still unanswered question which runs through the criticism and interpretation of miracles in modern times. ...

In both the Old and New Testaments miracles were *revelations*, that is to say, something was visible or experiencible in them which had been hidden before; the people involved recognized and understood something which was of the greatest importance for their whole lives. When Peter saw how the nets broke under the weight of the fish, he fell at Jesus' feet and said, 'Lord, depart from me for I am a sinful man.' Miracles were interpreted as signs, just because they contained something which had to be understood. They were signs of the presence of God in the world at that particular moment. Today many Christians decide with an effort of will to believe that miracles are word for word true, because they are in the Bible, and struggle for an 'obedient' or even a 'joyful' profession of faith in them. But they find nothing in miracles, they understand nothing from them, and certainly nothing that is of prime importance to them at that particular moment. Where today do we wonder – in the full biblical sense of the word – over the signs of the presence of God? That is an open question.

STUDY TOPICS

These extracts have raised many issues which might at first sight appear unrelated to religion (such as, what is the exact nature and status of a scientific law?) but in fact the question of miracles does have this particular characteristic of linking fields of thought. Some specific questions are raised below to pinpoint particular aspects of the discussion.

1. How do we define a 'miracle' and in what way is a miracle different from an extraordinary event?
2. What is the role of science in relation to miracles?
3. What is the status of the miracles in the Christian faith – are they essential?
4. What does a miracle 'prove'?

One fundamental aspect remains – that of basic presuppositions. Does C. S. Lewis's line about 'asking the right questions' link up with McPherson's idea that man does not believe or disbelieve miracles solely on the 'objective' evidence alone, but also because of his 'disposition to reject a particular set of beliefs as pagan superstition'? To put it another way, what sort of presuppositions are involved in saying we must see the question of the miraculous 'in its religious context' and are these presuppositions compatible with those involved in the modern scientific outlook?

BIBLIOGRAPHY

The Hibbert Journal for 1950 (no longer published) has three short essays on miracles which are quite readable (one of them is by the Mr Lunn referred to in the first extract).

For a fairly comprehensive coverage of the biblical material concerning miracles see the relevant section of Alan Richardson's *Theological Wordbook of the Bible* SCM Press 1964, pp. 152ff.

The first two chapters of H. J. Richards. *The Miracles of Jesus* (Fontana 1975) give a brief introduction to the subject. The rest of the book is Richards's attempt to 'find the spirit behind the miracle stories', and to discover them as 'deep stories rather than tall stories'.

The outstanding recent book in this field is Ernst and Marie-Louise Keller's *Miracles in Dispute* (19). This valuable collection of ideas on miracles from biblical times to the present day is full of interesting but often difficult ideas which many sixth-formers would find beyond their requirements. An exception to this would probably be the chapter on science and miracles (pp. 159ff), given some assistance from a teacher. There are also chapters on Hume and C. S. Lewis which are very helpful.

FURTHER READING

Farmer, H. H., *The World and God* (9).
Flew, A., *God and Philosophy* (10). Chapter 7 – a stout defence of Hume's argument against miracles. Well worth reading.

Holland, R. F., 'The Miraculous', Chapter 7 in *Religion and Understanding*, ed. Phillips, D. Z., Blackwell 1967.

Kaye, B. N., *The Supernatural in the New Testament*. Lutterworth Press 1977.

Lawton, J. S., *Miracles and Revelation*. Lutterworth Press 1959. A historical survey of attitudes to the miraculous.

Lewis, H. D., *Our Experience of God*. Collins 1970.

Moule, C. F. D., ed., *Miracles*. Cambridge Studies in their Philosophy and History. Mowbray 1965.

5
Scientific Presuppositions

INTRODUCTION

Concise Oxford Dictionary: 'Presupposition – thing assumed beforehand as basis of argument, etc.'

Chambers 20th Century Dictionary: 'To presuppose – to assume or take for granted; to involve as a necessary antecedent.'

It is not often realized how much our unconscious assumptions influence not only our decisions, but also the way in which we look at the world. This is particularly obvious in areas where the personal judgement of the subject is clearly involved, such as art or music. What is it, for example, which makes you like or dislike certain types of art or music? 'The sort of person I am' might be one answer – in other words, your unconscious assumptions, the way in which, in general, you have learned to look at the world without being aware of doing so.

But it is not always seen that the same can be said of areas where the personal judgement of the subject is *not* so clearly involved – such as science. A scientist, particularly a chemist or physicist, is dealing with 'things' and it might be thought that he has no personal relationship with them. But the way in which he sees them, and the way in which he imagines them to be related to each other, may be derived from his own unconscious assumptions. And this is a very important fact. Every scientist begins his work in a historically conditioned context, that is, he inherits the work of all the other scientists up to his time. He also inherits their presuppositions (see the broadcast talk of A. R. Peacocke). The really great scientists, those who have been responsible for the revolutions in scientific thought, have been those who have questioned the presuppositions on the basis of which their fellows worked.

Thus, our first question is: What are the assumptions which scientists make about the world around them? What does the scientist automatically assume about the world he is investigating? Some people have held the view that the scientist comes to his work with an entirely open mind, free from all presuppositions, and draws inescapable conclusions from the evidence (see the extracts from Coulson and Peacocke). What is suggested here is that this is wrong because it is impossible – no one has an open mind in this sense, and certainly not the scientist. The extracts quoted here deal with this rather nebulous area; it is one that isn't often written about or referred to, but it *is* important because it is so fundamental to all subsequent work. After all, you may not be able to see the foundations of a house, but it's rather important that they were built properly!

An interesting question for you to keep in mind as you read through these extracts is whether the presuppositions of the scientist about himself and the world (and the relation between the two) differ in any significant way (and if so, how) from those of the religious man or the artist or poet. What assumptions do *they* make about the world? And remember, too, that 'the scientist' and 'the artist' are both human beings; they share a common humanity, and in acting as scientist or artist they are in a sense using only part of themselves. Its perhaps too easy to categorize them; we fail then to do justice to their totality as persons.

C. A. Coulson, 'Scientific Method' from *Science and Christian Belief*, pp. 29ff

A former Master of Marlborough College in England recently described the opening sentence of a schoolboy's essay on Science and Religion. He had written: 'The difference between Science and Religion is that Science is material and Religion is immaterial.' This is an interesting sentence, reflecting a good deal of what is commonly felt about the mutual relationship of these two movements of the spirit. It is widely held, for example, that science is concerned with what is physical, religion with what is spiritual (and, of course, with nothing else!). Science deals with things that you can get hold of, and usually measure in a quantitative fashion; religion with things that you cannot get hold of, far less measure. It may be claimed that the things which are seen are temporal, and the things which are not seen are eternal. But since seeing is believing, the obvious corollary of all this is that science is relevant, religion is irrelevant; science matters, religion does not.

These widely held convictions will prove a good starting point for our present discussion. For in the last chapter I showed how there was a sense in which the development of science had rendered God obsolete. Made, as Voltaire would say, in our image, He could remain alive and active only so long as we were ignorant of true facts: the development of science would chase Him unceremoniously away. As Dr. J. Bronowski has put it: the fundamental assumption 'amounts to this, that science is to get rid of angels, blue fairies with red noses and other agents whose intervention would reduce the explanation of physical events to other than physical terms.' There is no hope for a religious belief which either clings despairingly to the past, or digs its heels hard into the ground in defence of some hedgehog position, or searches out some unappropriated territory in which a 'God of the Gaps' could be installed. We must seek some alternative mode of thought, and it must be one that will do justice to the splendour, the power, and the dynamic and progressive character of science.

There seems to me to be only one way out of our dilemma. If we cannot bring God in at the end of science, He must be there at the very start, and right through it. . . .

I propose to show that science is an essentially religious activity, and shall do so by trying to answer two questions: first, What is Science trying to do? What does it mean by truth? and then, What presuppositions, or attitudes, are involved in the practice of science as we know it in the West? In both of these questions we shall see that profound changes have taken place in our thinking during the last fifty years, so that both questions must be answered differently now from then.

Let us begin with the first question: What is science trying to do, and what is the nature of scientific truth? The old answer would have been quite simple: our task is to find out about the world, to see what it is like, to discover nature's laws and thereby to be able to control it. In Leibniz' phrase we set ourselves to solve Nature's cryptogram; and meanwhile, Nature herself looks on, impassively, yielding up her secrets as our search progresses. As for ourselves, in order to play our part, we must try to depersonalize ourselves so that we may the more effectively deal with an objective world, and be as nearly as possible uninfluenced and unimpeded by any prior view of what we ought, or would like, to find.

In almost every detail that answer is now superseded. For we have learnt that the things we thought we were describing do not have the properties we thought they had. In that enormous liberating revolution of the first twenty-five years of physics in this twentieth century, we

Scientific Presuppositions

came to realize that the very foundations of our subject were being removed from us. Physics had been built on the concept of mass and velocity, whose study is mechanics; and on the concept of an aether and its electric forces, whose study is electrodynamics; and on the concept of continuity of measurement, so that it should be possible in principle to trace the gradual changes which come over any system or systems, and so illustrate the law of cause and effect. Stage by stage every one of these convictions has been stripped off us. Einstein's relativity showed us that there was no such thing as an absolute position, or an absolute velocity: and that the same body would not appear to have the same mass to two observers who were travelling at different speeds relative to it. The experiments of Michelson and Morley showed us that there was no substantial aether through which our solar system travelled, and the electric and magnetic forces depended on how the experimenter moved. Heisenberg's famous Uncertainty Principle underlined what every psychologist knew in his heart, even if he was not very clever at expressing it in words: that no one person could ever exactly repeat the same experiment, nor could two different people ever make exactly the same measurement. Indeed, as the anatomists were showing, all our brains, though constructed on the same general pattern, were different in detail so that every one of us was bound to see things differently from his neighbour, and no truth could be exactly the same for any two people. One reason why no measurement could be repeated, with exactly identical results, was that the act of measurement, whether in psychology or physics, altered the system measured. The observer was not, and could never hope to be, independent of the thing that he observed. To ask a question of nature was to affect her, to change her, by however little: there was no prospect of ever recording a continuity of motion of any fundamental particle. Even the principle of cause and effect must be seen in statistical terms. As for the electron, that central figure in all modern physics, whose behaviour underlies the wireless set and all the complicated intricacies of the telephone exchange and the modern electronic computer, it cannot even be seen. The naked eye, so sensitive that it can respond to a total of no more than six quanta of light, will almost certainly never be able to see an electron – certainly it has not done so yet. We have moved a long way from Democritus: 'nothing exists except atoms and empty space; everything else is opinion.' For we admit unashamedly that the atom is a fiction of our own mind; and as for space, it is at our choice whether we call it straight or curved. All that happens if we reverse our choice is that the equations of motion for an atom or a star become correspondingly more complicated or more simple.

At first it may seem from all this that science has been torpedoed, and scientific truth become a chimera. But that is not true. We have come to see the scientific implications of some of those things which Kant had said in the eighteenth century; that the raw material of science is the set of experiences, observations, measurements, of the scientist; and his task is to find a pattern of relationships between these experiences. Science grows precisely in so far as the pattern of relationships is seen to extend its range: if the pattern cannot be extended, it soon ossifies and is replaced by some new and more comprehensive alternative: this is because scientists cannot bear to live with a closed subject, and instinctively demand an open one.

As for these patterns, they are mental constructs of our own, and their ultimate sanction is that they do fit together. Scientific truth means coherence in a pattern which is recognized as meaningful and sensible. It is acceptable only so long as it does 'hold together', without internal contradiction, and is able to grow, either by the prediction of new phenomena or the absorption of old ones. We could perfectly well use Kant's own words to describe all this: 'Our intellect does not draw its laws from nature, but imposes its laws upon nature.'

This insistence on concepts and the way in which their pattern mediates truth to us, should remind us that we have now brought science much closer to other disciplines than it has often been supposed to be. Every true discipline of the mind shares this common search for unifying concepts. The historian seeks for pattern in the unending cycle of events just as much as the psychologist or the artist. In a university it should hardly be necessary to labour this point. It is the pattern that we value. The facts, which are the raw material of the pattern, yet do not belong to it; they are of relatively little value by themselves. Only the pattern gives insight.

What is coming out of all this is a new relationship to facts – a relationship which, because it is common to so many and diverse disciplines – is certainly most impressive. It is becoming clear that, whether in science or history or religious experience, facts are never known fully and can never be completely correlated. As a result our models – in science, the atoms, the genes, the complexes and repressions of the mind: in religion, the nature of God and His mode of working in the world – can never be wholly satisfactory. For at very least they must suffer from one of two complaints. Either they are overdefined, leading to internal inconsistency and contradiction; or they are underdefined, leading to 'fuzziness' and imprecision. This is true both in science and in religion; a moment's reflection will soon show us the many evils that have resulted from trying to define God too closely.

Religion and science share here a common ignorance, and a common hope. Practically all Christians (though, alas, many non-Christians do not believe this, or are unwilling to admit it) know that religion is not merely facts. Facts there certainly are, for the Christian faith has its roots firmly fixed in a moment of history two thousand years ago. But the mature Christian faith has a greater growth superimposed, the relating of these facts in a meaningful coherent pattern. Precisely the same is true of science, and he who stops at the facts misses the glory.

In his famous Riddell Lectures of 1946 on 'Science, Faith and Society' Polanyi has these opening words:

> I shall re-examine here the suppositions underlying our belief in science, and propose to show that they are more extensive than is usually thought. They will appear to coextend with the entire spiritual foundations of man, and to go to the very root of his social existence. Hence, I will urge, our belief in science should be regarded as a token of much wider convictions.

It is nothing less than tragic that this is so widely misunderstood. The greater part of our schoolboy's acceptance of science and rejection of religion springs from his unexamined belief that science accepts no presuppositions, and must therefore be superior to a Christianity which is over-loaded with them. Yet this view is wholly wrong. Theodor Mommsen's famous phrase 'science without presuppositions' is a hopelessly superficial description of our discipline. Think for a moment of some of the attitudes of mind with which any scientist comes to his search: there is honesty, and integrity, and hope: there is enthusiasm, for no-one ever yet began an experiment without an element of passion: there is an identification of himself with the experiment, a partisan character about his secret hope for its conclusion which not even an adverse result can wholly extinguish: there is a humility before a created order of things, which are to be received and studied: there is a singleness of mind about the search which reveals what the scientist himself may often hesitate to confess, that he does what he does because it seems exciting and it somehow fulfils a deep part of his very being: there is co-operation with his fellows, both in the same laboratory, and across the seven seas: there is patience, akin to that which kept Mme. Curie at her self-imposed task of purifying eight tons of pitchblende to extract the few odd milligrams of radium: above all there is judgement – judgement as to what constitutes worthwhile research: judgement as to what is fit and suitable for publication. No wonder that a modern scientist – and no Christian either – has to say that 'science cannot exist without judgements of value'.

Indeed this is the case: science could not exist, and certainly is not practised, without all these qualities. They build the ethos and the tradition which every scientist must accept and to which he must conform.

If one tenth of what I have just been saying is correct then science is full of presuppositions – it is true that these may be derived from some earlier metaphysic, but they have been adopted and, like most presuppositions, their existence is frequently not recognized even by those most affected by them. In this case the presuppositions are such as to carry science, properly understood, into the realm of religion. For that common search for a common truth; that unexamined belief that facts are correlatable, i.e. stand in relation to one another and cohere in a scheme; that unprovable assumption that there is an 'order and constancy in Nature', without which the patient effort of the scientist would be only so much incoherent babbling and his publication of it in a scientific journal for all to read pure hypocrisy; all of it is a legacy from religious conviction.

Ian G. Barbour, *Issues in Science and Religion**

pp. 16–17

Why do objects fall? For Aristotle and his followers, motion is explained by the tendency of each thing to seek its own natural resting place. The 'natural place' of fire is up, and that of earth is down. Heavier objects have a stronger tendency downward so they must fall more rapidly. The *end* of the motion – in the sense both of 'terminus' and of 'purpose' – was of more interest than the intervening process. Why does an acorn grow? To become an oak. Why is there rain? To nourish crops. Causality is described by *future goals* ('final causes') and *innate tendencies* ('formal causes'), not just by the effects of past events ('efficient causes') acting on passive materials ('material causes'). The

---

* © 1966. Reprinted by permission of Prentice-Hall, Inc., Englewood Cliffs, N.J., and SCM Press.

future goal need not be consciously entertained by an entity (for example, an acorn) but is built into its structure so that by its own nature it achieves the fulfiment of the end appropriate to its kind.

Attention was directed to the *final end* and not to the detailed process of change from moment to moment. The behaviour of each creature follows from its essential nature, defined in terms of its function. If every creature realizes its potentialities, the illuminating questions to be asked concern the uses of things and what they can do. The central feature of all changes, in this view, is the transformation of *potentiality* into *actuality*. Logical connections, not simply temporal ones, must be traced. The categories of explanation are essence and potentiality, not mass and force connected by laws in space and time.

This search for purpose was in part the result of conceiving every object as having a place in a cosmic hierarchy, the creation of *a purposeful God*. Suppose one asks: why does water boil at one temperature and not some other? The contemporary scientist will perhaps relate this temperature to other facts and laws and theories of molecular structure, but will eventually reach a point when he says: this is simply a brute fact, and it is meaningless to ask why it is thus. But the medieval tradition, going back to Plato and Aristotle, insisted that there must be a reason if the world was not irrational. God's purpose in creating things, though not always discernible, constitutes the ultimate explanation of their behaviour.

pp. 138–9

The population stereotype portrays science as consisting of *precise observation*. The scientist, in this image, deals with 'pure facts' that yield 'indubitable knowledge'. In positivism, which was perhaps the dominant school in the philosophy of science a generation ago, theories were said to be summaries of data, shorthand résumés of experience, convenient ways of classifying facts. But many recent philosophers of science have challenged this empiricist emphasis on the experimental side and pointed to the crucial role of theoretical concepts in scientific progress.

For one thing, *there are no uninterpreted facts*. Even in the act of perception itself, the irreducible 'data' given are not, as Hume claimed, isolated patches of colour or other fragmentary sensations, but total patterns in which interpretation has already entered. We organize our experience in the light of particular interests, and we attend to selected features. So, too, scientific activity never consists in simply 'collecting

Scientific Presuppositions

all the facts'; significant experimentation requires a selection of relevant variables and a purposeful experimental design dependent on the questions that are considered fruitful and the problems that have been formulated. 'Observations' are always abstractions from our total experience, and they are expressed in terms of conceptual structures. The processes of measurement, as well as the language in which results are reported, are influenced by prior theories. Each stage of investigation presupposes many principles that for the moment are taken for granted. Thus all 'data' are, as Hanson* puts it, already 'theory-laden'.

pp. 176–7

In the popular stereotype, scientific inquiry is said to be objective because it is determined by the object of knowledge, not by the subject who knows. In the light of actual scientific work, however, this view of objectivity must be modified to allow for the *contribution of the scientist* as experimental agent, as creative thinker, and as personal self. The object of study cannot be known in its existence 'independent of the observer', for it is influenced by the observer in the very process of measurement. The assessment of theories is made not by the application of 'formal rules', but by the personal judgement of the scientist. We will submit that the idea of objectivity should not be discarded, but rather reformulated to include the contribution of the subject; we will reinterpret objectivity as *intersubjective testability* and *commitment to universality*.

A. R. Peacocke, from 'Truth for the Scientist', A BBC broadcast talk in the series – *Religion in its contemporary Context*, 1971

For there is a myth about science which goes something like this: there is supposed to be something which is called the scientific mind which is capable of analytical and unprejudiced contemplation of unembroidered facts. According to this myth, these experimental facts gradually form themselves into a pattern in the scientific mind – from them laws are elicited by a process called induction, with the occasional help of some inspired guesses called hypotheses, which at worst are

---

* Norwood R. Hanson, *Patterns of Discovery* (Cambridge University Press 1958), ch. 1.

dropped, or at best are allowed to mature into full-blown theories and ultimately laws. These latter then constitute truth for the scientist.

There are no uninterpreted facts, no unprejudiced observations. All observations are 'theory-laden', as it has been put. The scientist is always peering at the world through the spectacles of a theory or a hypothesis. You can't go around arbitrarily collecting facts, there are just too many, even for the biggest computers. The scientist has to take out what he needs to build his models and concepts, and the same observations can lead to quite different conclusions in different frameworks of thought. For example: some of you may know the experiment by Michelson and Morley. This showed that the speed of light was the same in whatever direction the light travelled across the surface of the earth, which they already had grounds for believing was itself in motion. At that time it was thought that light was a kind of wave in an all-pervasive medium called the ether, and that the earth's movement was through this ether. Then, just as the speed of a sea wave looks different to people on boats moving in different directions, so, if these ideas were correct, the speed of light should have been different when moving in different directions across the earth, and so across the supposed ether. It wasn't; the speed of light was always the same in different directions across the earth. Now had this experiment been performed a few centuries earlier, when Copernicus was urging, against opponents, that the earth *was* moving around the sun, this experiment would have appeared to have established that the earth was not in fact moving at all. The same facts, introduced into different frameworks, can have two quite different interpretations.

A. R. Peacocke, *Science and the Christian Experiment*, pp. 13–15

The beginner in learning science and the non-scientist who can only examine science from the outside by noting the tone and content of scientific papers and books might well be forgiven for thinking that science is an entirely impersonal activity. For scientific thinking is apparently highly abstract: for its particular purpose, it seems to be precluded from considering any common phenomenon in its wholeness. The beauty of a sunset and the graceful lines of a tree, as appreciated by an observer, the poet, or even 'l'homme sensuel moyen' are personal reactions which are excluded from the purview of science so that the elements which are observed and noted are only those capable of

Scientific Presuppositions

quantitative formulation, and which can be generalized for comparison and correlation with the same features of other parallel phenomena (sunsets, trees, etc.).

This process of abstraction from the experience which constitutes any commonly observed phenomenon also extends to the more formalized phenomena of laboratory experiments. Only certain features are recorded and noted, many variables are not recorded at all and much of the judgement which a scientist acquires by training and research experience is concerned with discerning which observations are relevant to a particular problem. How far this process of abstraction distorts, or even replaces, the picture of the world which science constructs has been much discussed. A. N. Whitehead described this process of abstraction, as represented in Locke's distinction between primary and secondary qualities, in a famous passage:

> The primary qualities are the essential qualities of substances whose spatio-temporal relationships constitute nature. The orderliness of these relationships constitutes the order of nature. . . . But the mind in apprehending also experiences sensations which, properly speaking, are qualities of the mind alone. These sensations are projected by the mind so as to clothe appropriate bodies in external nature. . . . Thus nature gets credit which should in truth be reserved for ourselves; the rose for its scent; the nightingale for his song; and the sun for his radiance. The poets are entirely mistaken. They should address their lyrics to themselves, and should turn them into odes of self-congratulation on the excellency of the human mind. Nature is a dull affair, soundless, scentless, colourless; merely the hurrying of material, endlessly, meaninglessly. (A. N. Whitehead, *Science and the Modern World* (New York, Mentor Books 1949), pp. 55–6.)

He goes on to discuss how this practical outcome of the characteristic scientific philosophy of the close of the seventeenth century has dominated even the organization of our academic studies. He continues:

> No alternative system of organizing the pursuit of scientific truth has been suggested. It is not only reigning, but it is without a rival. And yet – it is quite unbelievable. This conception of the universe is surely framed in terms of high abstractions, and the paradox only arises because we have mistaken our abstraction for concrete realities.

I am not concerned now to follow further the discussion and counter-argument which this judgement has engendered, important as it is for arriving at an understanding of the relation between the world and scientific laws and models. My present concern is to stress that scientific experiment and observation involve a process of abstraction from man's experience – a process necessary for the construction of scientific concepts, models and hypotheses, but a process of abstraction nevertheless. Awareness by acquaintance cannot be fully subsumed into knowledge by description; or, to use Polanyi's terms, 'tacit' knowing is a *Gestalt* phenomenon with its own valid form or awareness and is distinct from explicit knowledge of particulars. The content of public, scientific knowledge, is, once ascertained, of the descriptive, explicit kind and cannot, in principle, afford a comprehensive account of the fullness of our experience of the world, which is 'by acquaintance' and 'tacit' – and, least of all, of our experience of each other. The scientific method provides an analysis of the content of human experience which is partial and abstractive (in Whitehead's sense) and complementary, but not alternative to that afforded by the humanities, including theology.

The preceding section has referred to the non-personal, explicit character of scientific knowledge once it is obtained. However, the process by which statements gain general and approved currency in the scientific community, and the way in which the individual makes his discoveries are both intimately related to the scientific enterprise as an activity of persons. The co-operative character of its inquiries and the role of the free community of scientists in transmitting new paradigms, concepts, models and hypotheses, and in formulating criteria of judgement, are absolutely essential to science. This is part of the experience of every practising scientist. Scientific work would be impossible but for the existence of this community characterized by value judgements, even if these are implicitly assumed rather than explicitly enforced.

A. R. Peacocke, *Science and the Christian Experiment*, pp. 25–6

It is not generally realized how much the scientist relies on the authority of his teachers and of his predecessors for his concepts and modes of experimentation. No one individual can ever repeat all the possible experiments and carry through all the theoretical arguments which he has to accept as the basis of his own research and teaching. He relies on

Scientific Presuppositions

the authority of his teachers and predecessors for the reliability of these experiments and theories. This is indeed a publicly assessable reliability, but even subsequent tests of the reproducibility of an experiment or the confirmation of the arguments underlying a theory have frequently been undertaken by only a few investigators, and the majority of scientists rely on these latter. This is inevitable, and makes intellectual integrity in the individual a prerequisite of scientific activity. An individual's authority in any area of science can only be founded on his intellectual integrity which, if once found wanting, immediately undermines his standing, often permanently. The mechanisms whereby the contemporary scientific community exercises authority over the individual scientist in his work involves the whole process of publication of research papers and the procedures according to which other scientists check the papers before publication: and yet others can repeat the experiments and re-argue the theories in their own subsequent publications. This authority of the scientific community over the individual scientist has been well described by Polanyi.* There is constant interplay between the individual scientific research worker and his contemporary community and between the individual scientific teacher and both past and present scientific communities. The element of authority is present in both dialogues.

STUDY TOPICS

1. Try to define 'science'. What do you think scientists are trying to do?
2. Are some sciences more objective than others? Compare the work of a chemist with that of a biologist and a social scientist.
3. What are the basic assumptions on which the artist, poet, or musician do their work? What is their relation to 'reality'?
4. Do you think it is a good thing that our society is so conditioned in its way of thinking by the influence and prestige of science? What is your opinion of the movements towards less sophistication and greater simplicity in our lives?

BIBLIOGRAPHY

Ian G. Barbour, ed., *Science and Religion* (3), especially Part Two, is

* M. Polanyi, *Science, Faith and Society*, University of Chicago Press, 1964.

particularly valuable. The Coulson extract is taken from here. Coulson's view that there are parallels between the methods of science and religion is balanced by other views. Barbour's own Chapter 1, 'Science and Religion today' should also be read.

Barbour's *Issues in Science and Religion*: (2), Chapter 6, 'The Methods of Science' should be read, along with Chapter 7, section (i), 'Objectivity and Personal Involvement in Science'. The encyclopaedic treatment of the relationship between science and religion given in this book is invaluable over the whole area of the subject.

FURTHER READING

Barbour, Ian G., *Myths, Models and Paradigms*. SCM Press 1974.

Cupitt, D., *The Worlds of Science and Religion*. (Issues in Religious Studies.) Sheldon Press 1976.

Dixon, B., *What is Science For?* Torch Library 1974.

Habgood, J., *Religion and Science* (12). Especially Chapter 2.

Hookgaas, R., *Religion and the Rise of Modern Science*. Scottish Academic Press 1973.

Isaacs, A., *Introducing Science*. Penguin 1963.

Pyke, M., *The Boundaries of Science*. Penguin 1961.

Richardson, A., *Christian Apologetics*. New York, Harper 1947.

Richardson, A., *Science, History and Faith*. Oxford University Press 1950. Chapter 2.

Smart, Ninian, *Philosophers and Religious Truth* (30). The chapter on Hume.

Vick, E. H. W., *Quest – An Exploration of Some Problems in Science and Religion*. Epworth Press 1975.

Wilkes, K., *Religion and the Sciences*. Religious Education Press 1969. Especially Part 1, Sections A to C.

6
The Question of Origins

INTRODUCTION

This topic may conveniently be divided into two – Creation, or the origin of the universe, and Evolution, or the origin of life, and, in particular, man.

Most people almost instinctively feel that there is a fundamental conflict of view between religious and scientific accounts of the creation of the universe. On the one hand religion (that is, for most people in the West, Christianity) seems to state categorically that the universe was created by divine fiat in a relatively short period, whereas science, on the basis of its empirical method, more cautiously puts forward opposing alternatives – either the 'big bang' theory, all matter originating from a primeval hydrogen mass, or the 'steady state' theory, where matter is thought of as constantly being created in the overall development of the universe. Against such an acceptable method as the scientist employs, surely the religious belief in creation is shown up as nothing more than an outmoded arrogant claim to special knowledge, which cannot be upheld by the facts? So goes the popular picture.

It has to be admitted that if the religious man claims that his belief in creation is parallel or alternative to that of the scientist, then he is going to be hard-pressed to defend it rationally. But perhaps they are not really alternatives. Part of the traditional difficulty in this area has been the readiness on both sides to take the creation account in Genesis 1 as a literally interpreted, quasi-scientific description of the origins of the universe. But if higher criticism of the Bible has taught us anything, it has surely taught us this – that such a wooden literalism, ignoring the poetic, symbolic and essentially *religious* character of the Bible, is the way to disastrous misunderstanding. Supposing what the Genesis account is proposing to do is *not* to give a quasi-scientific account, but to state, in the accepted thought categories of the time, the belief that the whole universe, and most especially man, is under the providence of God and ultimately responsible to him? And, further, that the design and harmony we find in nature is his design, imposed by his Word on the primeval chaos? If this is the case, and it is accepted by most theologians, not treating the Genesis story literally, is it then necessary that there should be a conflict between science and religion in this area? I believe not. For, however the universe originated, whether by big bang or continuous creation, it could still be claimed that it belongs to God and is responsible to him. Thus the controversy rests to a large extent on a misunderstanding. This is brought out in the extract from Gilkey.

The nineteenth-century controversy over the evolution of man from the animal kingdom stands as the prime example of the conflict of science and religion. In the popular picture, the progressive, open-minded scientists opposed the dogmatic intolerant theologians, and the victory went to common sense. The situation was a good deal more complex than *that*. But it is true that the theologians who opposed Darwin (and there were some who did not) felt that his theories were attacking the basis of the biblical picture of man, created uniquely by God's Spirit in his image, with special privileges, capacities, and responsibilities which set him apart from the animal kingdom. How, they asked, could this be reconciled with Darwin's theories?

What can we say now? In the first place, evolution *can* be seen as God's way of creating, rather than as an alternative to it, although it must be recognized (as with the argument for God's existence from design in the universe) that the wastefulness, the blind alleys, and the apparent cruelty involved in the evolutionary process raise problems for belief in a loving God such as is the Christian belief. Secondly, evolutionary theory itself has changed since Darwin's time, and more emphasis is now laid on co-operation as opposed to competition between species and members of species. In addition, the nature of the environment as the background against which evolution operates has increasingly been seen to have played a formative role. Thirdly, we no longer regard it as shocking to be told that we have descended from apes, though perhaps we can understand the psychological shock which this idea gave to our Victorian forebears. Quite possibly, this is because we are convinced that to explain the origins of something does not necessarily describe its nature – anything or anyone can rise *above* its origins: this, after all, is the basic premise and driving force of evolution itself.

There remains a question, a deceptively simple one: why should there be evolution at all? If there is a directionality about the total process, does this imply purpose and a mind behind it all? Some scientists, it should be noted, speak of 'Nature', with a capital N, almost in the same terms that theologians speak of God. Is the whole thing random and purposeless, as J. Monod, the eminent molecular biologist, in his book, *Chance and Necessity*, has argued? And, in any case, is this a question that a biologist rather than a philosopher should answer? Is it just human arrogance to see human mental and spiritual capacity as the intended end-product of the evolutionary process (a vision which Teilhard de Chardin has so eloquently described)?

It is clear that questions about evolution still remain; but they are of a different type, and are no longer simply concerned with acceptance or rejection of the theory of evolution itself. We are now concerned with how that theory should be interpreted — religiously or not? That is the question.

J. Habgood, 'Nothing But Apes?' from *Religion and Science*, pp. 64–71

When people talk of conflict between science and religion, almost automatically they think first of the nineteenth century controversy over evolution. The conventional picture of those days shows scientists and theologians in sharp opposition, the scientists ruthlessly putting man in his place as one among the animals, the theologians desperately appealing to human dignity and the authority of Scripture. From the theologian's point of view, so it seemed, the collapse of the so-called scriptural account of the origin of species, the doctrine of special creation, was bad enough; what was infinitely worse was the removal of any special mystery surrounding the origin of man himself; the last piece of evidence proving the handiwork of God in nature seemed to have been destroyed.

The last-ditch mentality of both scientists and theologians undoubtedly made the controversy more bitter than it might have been; there were some who then believed, and a small minority who still do, that evolution and Christianity are incompatible. The story goes that a group of Christians was once heard to pray: 'O Lord, don't let this evolution be true; and if it is, then don't let it be generally known.' But if there were Christians who were afraid to face the facts, on the other side there were also unbelievers who deliberately used the theory of evolution as a stick to beat the faithful with, even though their own rejection of Christianity had quite different and more personal roots. Darwin lost his faith because he could no longer stomach the crude doctrines of atonement and hell which were current in his day. His theory of evolution simply confirmed him in his unbelief; it was not the cause of it. And the same is true of many of the famous Victorian doubters.

The fact is that the issues at stake in these controversies were much more subtle than can be expressed in any conventional picture of scientific enlightenment versus theological prejudice. By now in this book, we should be used to this cautionary remark. In any controversy there are those who adopt extreme and untenable positions, and make fools of themselves; this happened in generous measure in the nineteenth century. Perhaps more eminent Christians, at least in England, made fools of themselves than at any other time. But it is worth recording that there were also theologians (notably Dr Hort of Cambridge) who saw straight away the importance of Darwin's theory, and accepted it gladly; and there were scientists who, for what seemed then to be good scientific reasons, rejected it. If the majority of theologians had been less closely tied to a literal interpretation of the Bible, and if some scientists had been rather less sweeping in their claims about evolution, most of the controversy could have been avoided. Most, but not all.

The actual course of events has been described many times, and so there is no need to retell the story here. I want to concentrate instead on the larger issues. First, what was Darwin's achievement? Secondly, what, if any, were the genuine reasons for theological anxiety?

It has been said that Darwin did for biology what Newton did for physics. He provided a framework into which an immense number of biological observations could be fitted; and he gave biology a new model of what counts as an explanation. The idea of evolution had been in the air a long time before the *Origin of Species* was published in 1859. Darwin's achievement was to link it to the concept of natural selection, as the mechanism by which changes in biological make-up could be used and stabilized, and to show that this mechanism was, in a great many different examples, sufficient to account for the facts. I have deliberately used the word 'mechanism'. The theory completely avoided

The Question of Origins

talk about purpose, life forces and all the rest of the vitalistic language we met in the last chapter. Though Darwin himself did not go far in this direction, it was he who made it ultimately possible for biologists to use mathematical explanations. The modern evolutionist, with the knowledge of the mechanism of heredity which was denied Darwin, can make an assessment of the probabilities of evolutionary change, and show that evolution is mathematically feasible according to the laws of statistics. To be able to do this is to put biology almost on a level with physics, and it is in this sense that Darwin paved the way for a new type of biological explanation.

To say this is not, of course, to surrender to a mechanistic view of life. It is simply a further working-out of the principles discussed in the last chapter. But it raised, and still raises, theological problems.

The most urgent of these concerned the notion of providence. There is always a tendency among Christians to think of God's activity in the world as being confined to the processes which are not understood. The origin of life is a puzzle; the bewildering variety of animals and plants cries out for explanation; the early history of man is largely unknown; the difference between men and animals seems, from certain points of view, to form an unbridgeable gulf. These gaps in our knowledge have provided tempting opportunities for religious people to say, 'Aha, here we must talk about a special act of God.' When science then begins to close the gaps, the result has too often been religious bewilderment and alarm, the feeling that God has been shown to be unnecessary. Even if it is still claimed that He is necessary in some ultimate sense, the feeling remains that He has been pushed one step further away from any real concern with the affairs of the world.

Darwin's theory at first produced precisely this feeling. If evolution was a process which went inexorably on its way and could account for the variety of living creatures by the operation of a mechanistic law, in what sense was it still possible to believe in God's providence or to think of Him as the Creator? Worse still, one of the most popular arguments for the existence of God had been the apparent design in nature which could only be explained by believing in a Designer. The theory of evolution seemed to shatter this argument; the wonderful adaptation of living things to their environment and to each other, so far from being evidence of a Master Mind, was accounted for by the fact that only those creatures which adapted themselves successfully managed to survive.

It was not long before theologians began to counter these feelings by talking about evolution as God's way of creating. All science had done was to reveal the processes through which God was at work. God works through natural laws, not in spite of them; therefore no amount of explanation in terms of natural laws can make anything less truly the handiwork of God. Indeed there were soon seen to be theological advantages in Darwin's theories as against the doctrine of special creation. The latter implies that God has only created at certain moments and in certain places; whereas evolution presupposes that God is continually active, and that there is never a moment in which it makes sense to think of Him as absent.

Even the argument for God's existence from the apparent design in nature, was shown not to have been so fatally wounded as was feared at first. The real basis of the argument is not that this or that animal fits perfectly into its environment, but that nature is rational, that it makes some sort of sense. And this is something which men must believe before they can even begin to be scientists, and therefore it is a belief which no amount of scientific discovery can possibly destroy. In fact, the more science makes sense of things, the more firmly ought we to believe that the reality behind nature is a mind not unlike our own.

Important though they are, such arguments do not have the same direct appeal as the older ones; and even if they are accepted, there remain some awkward questions. A God who works through natural laws feels much more remote than a God whose special acts of creation and whose interventions are obvious for all to see. And there is a difficulty, too, about the *kind* of laws through which evolution is said to operate. Is it fitting that God should create through an apparently blind process dependent on chance – a process which demands a life and death struggle between His creatures?

I do not believe these questions can yet be answered entirely satisfactorily, but their awkwardness has been eased considerably since Victorian theologians puzzled over them. As so often happens, the easement has come through the advance of science itself. Many biologists are now beginning to stress that evolution is far less mechanical a process than it seemed to be in the first flush of discovery. In the days when physicists thought primarily in terms of little hard billiard ball-like atoms and mechanical forces between them, it was natural for biologists to wish for the same simplicity; hence we find accounts of evolution which treat animals merely as if they were physical objects in competition with each other. In a later stage of evolutionary theory all the emphasis was on the evolution of germ cells

The Question of Origins

or genetic materials, as if the body which grew from those cells were comparatively irrelevant. But this is altogether too narrow a view. In recent years it has been realized that whether an animal survives or not depends on its behaviour as well as on its physical make-up. C. H. Waddington even writes about animals 'choosing their environments' and gives this an important place in his account of evolution. To put it in more general terms, the role of consciousness cannot be irrelevant in evolution, otherwise conscious creatures would never have evolved; and they undoubtedly have, or you would not be reading this book. But if consciousness plays a real part in the process, and if the end products are conscious creatures capable of understanding their own development, in what sense can the whole process be called blind?

There have been attempts to rewrite the story of evolution, stressing this conscious side of it. One of the most popular of them, *The Phenomenon of Man* by Teilhard de Chardin, described itself as the story of the evolution of consciousness written from within. By taking the fact of consciousness seriously, he claimed to be able to show that the process, far from being blind, is profoundly meaningful; it reaches its climax in the emergence of consciousness in man, and in his possibilities of response to God. Some scientists have been scathing about this account; but at least the point has been made that a religious view of evolution can be more than a set of platitudes, and can draw attention to facts which are largely ignored in other accounts. Whatever the final verdict on Teilhard de Chardin, he has shown that to talk about evolution merely in terms of 'blind chance' begs just as many questions as to talk about it as an act of God.

But what of the method of evolution? Here again, we can note that modern biologists talk less about the 'struggle for existence' and 'nature red in tooth and claw' than did their forefathers. Animals and plants do not merely compete with and kill one another; they also depend on one another and co-operate with one another. Is it more natural to talk about a cow struggling against the grass in the fight for life, or about a cow depending on grass? Surely both kinds of language have their uses when we want to make different points about the cow-grass relationship; the former when we want to describe the forces which control the spread of grass, the latter when we are thinking about the internal economy of cows. Both kinds can be misleading when we read our own feelings into them and try to make out that the universe is either a charnel-house or an immense and beautiful harmony.

We are not in a position to say whether God could or ought to have devised a different method of bringing us all into existence. All we know is that the universe seems to be a mixture between good and evil, beauty and pain, and that suffering is at least one of the instruments used in the process of creation. The only people who need be disturbed by this are those who believe that our sole source of values and the sole basis for any sort of religion is nature itself. This explains why some of the most persistent objectors to the theory of evolution have not been Christians, but various kinds of post-Christian moralists, like Bernard Shaw, who wanted to retain Christian values without Christian doctrine. Christians themselves, on the other hand, have always believed in the love of God because He has revealed Himself as Love in Jesus Christ, not because they have found that on the whole the universe points to the value of love, rather than *vice versa*. Furthermore, they should hardly be suprised to find suffering being used creatively in God's world, when the central symbol of their faith is the Cross.

I do not pretend that these thoughts clear up all the difficulties. It is part of the main thesis of this book that there is always a tension between the scientific and the religious ways of looking at things. But a great deal of the tension, where evolution is concerned, seems to have had two unnecessary causes. First, the theory was put forward at a time when Christians were still hoping to find evidence of God's activity in the gaps in scientific knowledge; and Darwin's closure of this particular gap seemed like the last straw. Secondly, the language used by evolutionary enthusiasts, and the tendency to read all sorts of moral implications into the facts of nature, seemed to suggest that the universe was a cruel and heartless place, unworthy to be called the creation of a loving God.

There were, however, still further grounds for theological anxiety – and more valid ones. The evolutionary account of man's origin seemed to be in direct conflict with certain Christian doctrines. According to Darwin, man is one among the animals; according to theology, man is unique, fundamentally different from animals in possessing a soul. Even if we believe, as most Christians now do, that the stories of Adam and Eve are profound myths and not literal history, some difficulties remain. The doctrines of the Fall and of the uniqueness of man are not just forced upon Christians because they happen to be there in Genesis 1–3. They are essential pieces of Christian theology, interlocking with a complex, integrated system, and cannot be removed without putting the whole structure in jeopardy. It seems, at first sight, as if theology must here come into a head-on collision with the findings of science.

The Question of Origins

I believe, however, that a better description of what has happened is that theology has here learnt from science, and learnt to its great profit. To admit this is not to sell the theological pass to the scientists, or to allow that in theological matters science must always have the last word. It is simply to recognize that one of the important ways in which God leads us to the truth is through science; and although theologians claim to be able to say some true and valuable things about God and man, they cannot and should not claim to be able to say everything. There are times when they must discover the meaning of their own doctrines with the help of others.

The doctrines of the Fall and of the uniqueness of man *look* as if they were statements about the origins and early history of man, as if they were saying that at some time in the dim, distant past God created a special kind of creature, new things called souls began to exist, and at some point in time the first of these went wrong. It is by no means certain that in the beginnings of Christian theology these doctrines were bound up with these particular historical claims. But by the nineteenth century, and for centuries before that, an overwhelming majority of theologians thought they were. What science did was to help them to think again.

This rethinking has led many modern theologians to see that these doctrines are not speculative pieces of history at all, but statements about the nature of man as he is now. Man is unique because he alone of all creatures desires to enter into relationship with God. The story of how he came to be unique is for science to trace, so far as it can; to understand the story cannot diminish the importance of the fact. Man is fallen, theologians say, because although he desires to enter into relationship with God, he cannot do it. He is divided against himself. The psychological roots of this division are for science to trace, so far as it can; but again, to expose them cannot diminish the importance of the fact. Theology is telling us about these present facts of experience from its own distinctive point of view, because it claims to have a decisive clue to the understanding of man, given to it in the unique man, Jesus Christ. That a scientific understanding of the same facts may also be possible, simply illustrates the truth that there are many different ways of understanding things, and that in this field, just as much as in the fields of atomic physics or astronomy, we have to look suspiciously at the assumption that only science can tell us about 'reality'.

Enough has been said, I hope, to show that the theory of evolution has made a profound difference to theology, as great as that made by

Newton's theory of gravitation two hundred years earlier. But it would be a mistake to interpret the religious implications of either of these discoveries just in terms of scientific advance and theological retreat. In both periods theologians had good cause for anxiety; but anxiety is not the same as defeat in battle. The theologians who tried to come to terms with these discoveries made many mistakes, and probably still do. They grasped, however, the important truth that theological doctrines are not, any more than scientific theories are, definitive blueprints of reality. Theology must learn from science, as well as from its own sources, and it is no dishonour or disaster when in the light of science old doctrines are understood in new ways.

L. B. Gilkey, 'What the Idea of Creation is About' from *Maker of Heaven and Earth,* as quoted in *Science and Religion,* ed. Ian G. Barbour, pp. 172–81

The best way to understand what is the subject matter of the doctrine of creation is to distinguish between certain basic kinds of questions that men ask. People ask many kinds of questions about the origin of things, and these are often radically different from each other in meaning and intention. Consequently the answers to these questions can be in quite distinct realms of discourse. It is therefore in terms of the differences in the kinds of questions men ask that we can most easily see the distinction between scientific, philosophical and theological answers, and can most easily apprehend the different kinds and levels of truth that each one seeks.

First of all there is the scientific question about origins. Here we are inquiring about 'causes' or developments preceding a 'state of affairs' in nature that we may now know something about. We are pushing our inquiry further back in time by asking about the factors which brought about the state where our last inquiry left us. Thus we can in scientific knowledge move back beyond the formation of the seas and the mountains to the cooling of the earth, back from there to the whirling gases which formed the earth, and back beyond there to the nebular hypothesis, and so on. The questions of origins here ask merely about the character of the preceding 'state of affairs', about the circumstances among finite things that brought about our present situation, about the unknown finite 'causes' that produced the known effects. Scientific hypotheses and statements are thus by definition *about* relations between finite things in space and time. They assume that the process of

The Question of Origins

events in space and time is already going on, and they ask about their character and the laws of their interrelationships. They cannot and do not wish to ask questions about the origins of the whole system of finite things. Therefore, while science may be able to push its inquiry back *toward* an 'ultimate origin of things', if there be one, clearly it can never find or even inquire about such an ultimate origin. For the question of an *ultimate* origin asks, if it asks anything at all, about the cause of every finite state of affairs, including each preceding one. It is the question of the origin of the whole system of finite relations, and thus can never be found by an inquiry that restricts itself to the relations within that system. In science there is nothing that corresponds to or can conceivably conflict with either a metaphysical understanding of origins or with the theological doctrine of creation.

Another kind of question people ask about 'origins' is more strictly philosophical or metaphysical in character. It goes something like this: 'In or behind the changing things that make up existence as we find it (trees, rocks, stars, people, ideas, sensations, etc.) is there any sort of thing (or substance or principle) which is always there, which always has been there, and so from which all these things can be said (by analogy) 'to come'? Is there any basic, fundamental, permanent substance, being or set of principles which underlies them and so which gives them all the reality they possess? Is there a Really Real at the origin of things, and if so what is it?'

This is the question which tantalized the early Greek and Indian philosophers and so incited the great tradition of speculative philosophy. It is the question of what it means for anything 'to be', of what must be there if something is to exist at all, and so the question of that upon which changing existences ultimately depend – it is the 'ontological' question of 'being' or 'existence'. And the answers have been fascinatingly various in the history of thought: there are the water, air, and fire principles of the earliest Greek thinkers; there are the Boundless, the Unmoving Being, and the atoms of more sophisticated thinkers; the Ideas of Plato, the One of Plotinus, the transcendent, unnamable Brahman of Hinduism – and so on to the *Natura Naturans* of Spinoza, the Monads of Leibnitz, the elaborate categorial factors of Whitehead, and the 'Nature' of contemporary naturalistic philosophy. In each case, in order to find the 'origin' or foundation of experienced existence, the mind asks about an underlying level of reality beyond and yet within sensible experience. This is the metaphysical question of origins.

The Question of Origins

Now as one can easily see, this is a very different sort of question from the scientific question we noted above. Here we are not asking about the finite 'causes' out of which a given state of affairs arose. And the reason is that the metaphysical question would apply with equal cogency to that preceding set of circumstances. In fact, as philosophy quickly realized, our question is not really concerned with what happened 'beforehand' at all. Rather we are asking: 'Assuming *all* the various "states of affairs" that have characterized the universe of finite things, on what fundamental structure of relationships or substance or being do they depend for their existence and reality? What is the source and "origin" of their total being?' Thus even substantial changes in the answers to scientific questions about origins need not have a fundamental effect on metaphysical viewpoints. A man can remain a positivist, a naturalist, an idealist, a pluralist, or monist, whatever the present status of the nebular hypothesis or the idea of evolution.

Finally there is another kind of question that involves the issue of 'origins'. This is a much more burning, personal sort of question than the scientific or metaphysical ones, which are rightly motivated by a serene curiosity about the universe we live in. Here we ask an ultimate question with a distinctly personal reference. We are raising the question of 'origins' because we are asking about the ultimate security, the meaning and the destiny of our own existence. It is the metaphysical question of being in an 'existential' form, a question about the ultimate origins of our *own* being, and so a question in which we ourselves are deeply involved. For when we ask about the security and meaning of our own life, we are not asking about something else (a nebula, or even a first substance) outside of us; our question is about ourselves as we are caught within the mighty forces that impinge on us, determine our life, and mete out to us our fate. Consequently, we can never back off from these issues and gaze at them objectively. Rather they come to us in the midst of our involvement within them. Thus we experience them not as spectators but as participants – and so the problems of security, meaning and destiny, partly engulfing us, become something we can never completely conquer and reduce to intelligible size. They are, as Marcel points out, 'mysteries' and not 'problems' – something we must think about, but not something we can control, dissect, measure, test, or even contemplate objectively and define clearly. They elude our easy intellectual grasp because they grasp us.

This kind of question comes to us all at certain times. We are aware of them especially when our security has been somehow rudely shaken, as in a sudden brush with death on the highway, and we realize the arbitrary and precarious hold each of us has on existence and life. We suddenly sense our own creaturely dependence on things and events beyond our control, or we feel with a shudder our own life span slipping away from us – and, wondering how long we will be here, we ask if there is any thing that is truly dependable and secure, not to be removed by anything, upon which our own existence depends. Or this kind of question can come when we can find no apparent purpose or meaning making coherent our existence amidst the baffling events of life, and we wonder why we are here. Then we ask (with Pascal) 'Who has put me here?' What is the meaning behind my own being at this concrete moment and place? Have I merely been hurled into existence at random by blind forces of parentage and environment as the planets were hurled off into space by the whirling sun? Is there no Creator who has placed me here and given my concrete life a purpose, a destiny, and a ground for hope? Or again, we may ask: 'What ultimately determines my life – who or what is in charge here? I see my life determined by powerful, often meaningless, and surely blind forces: outside of me there are floods, wars, conquests, and economic cycles; within me are hereditary weaknesses, neuroses, fatal flaws, and the corrosion of the years. Are these, then, the Lords of my existence? Am I dependent solely on them, and on my own strength to defeat or control them, in order to find a purpose and direction in all I do? Am I merely a cork tossed about on mighty waves, since so clearly I am not able to be captain of my own destiny? Is there no sovereign Lord of all, who is Creator and Ruler over all these powers that rule over me?'

Such questions about the ground of our contingent being, about a transcendent purpose for our short life, and about the Lords of our destiny, are a part of the life of us all. Here we ask why *we* exist, and on what power that existence depends. This is not a speculative question for us, but a deeply personal question about the meaning and security of *our* existence. Such questions, therefore, do not spring from intellectual curiosity so much as they come from anxiety about the mystery of the existence in which our whole being is involved. And they must be answered somehow, if any human being is to live free of insecurity and frustration. Sometimes they are answered superficially in terms of immediate securities and small 'meanings' – such as a new car, a paid-up mortgage and an insurance policy. But when these little supports are shaken by some shattering natural, psychological or historical event, the ultimate questions of the origin, the meaning and destiny of life itself, rush powerfully to the fore and seem to blot out all our other questions. We live in such a time today.

Two things should be said further about questions of this sort. First of all, they are peculiarly 'religious' in character. That is, they ask about the ultimate ground and meaning of our existence, they search for a faithful and healing answer to our deepest problems, and they are answered in terms of affirmation and trust, rather than in terms of proof and demonstration. Let us look at this last point for a moment; we shall return to it often again. As we have pointed out, these questions represent 'mysteries' and not 'problems'. What brings these questions on us pell-mell is not usually an intellectual problem which arouses our curiosity and calls for an intellectual solution. Rather they rush up within us because we find ourselves in some personal crisis that has created inner anxiety and a sense of utter lostness. It is our anxiety, our frustration, our futility, our guilt – not our curiosity – that must be assuaged and satisfied. In such a situation an intellectual solution, or even demonstration, may be quite irrelevant. An academic proof of God's existence will not help a man who is overcome with futility or guilt. His problem is not ignorance or unclarity of mind, so much as it is turbulence and anxiety of spirit. What he needs, therefore, is not a demonstrated concept of deity in his mind, so much as an experienced encounter with Almighty God. For only in such an encounter, and the living relation that flows from it, can a man find the courage and conviction, the purpose and inner strength to accept and to conquer the 'mysteries' of existence. Certainly our answers to these questions must satisfy the mind with regard to validity. But because they stem from transforming experiences that are deeper than proof and demonstration, real answers to existential questions primarily tend to promote confidence and serenity in facing life, rather than intellectual satisfaction at resolving a 'curiosity' problem. When, therefore, an answer to these questions is received, we speak more meaningfully of faith and trust than we do of knowledge or complete understanding; and so we call these 'religious' questions and answers.

Secondly, although these religious questions are centred upon immediate problems of meaning in our contemporary personal or group life, nevertheless inevitably they too imply the question of ultimate origins. The question of the meaning and destiny of our present life can only be answered if we can have confidence in the fundamental goodness of life as promising fulfilment; and such confidence in the promise of life is possible only if we have some basis for trust in the

The Question of Origins

source of all being. The religious question of the meaning of our being drives us to the religious question of the origin of all being in God. To the anxious question: Why are we, and on what do we ultimately depend? the Christian faith gives the answer: We are creatures of God dependent utterly upon His sovereign power and love. Thus in asking the religious question 'Who created the world?' men are not so curious about how or when the universe came to be as they are deeply concerned about the goodness and meaning of their life, and so about the character of the ultimate source and ruler of their life. The religious affirmation that God created the world is, therefore, fundamentally concerned to give a positive answer to the baffling mystery of the meaning of our life here and now as finite, transient creatures. For it asserts above all that our present existence is in the hands of the One Almighty Lord whom we know as love. The theological idea of creation is first of all an answer to the religious question of the meaning and destiny of man's historical life.

Now if there is anything upon which contemporary theology agrees, it is that the biblical belief in creation derives from an answer to this 'religious' question, rather than from an answer either to a scientific or a metaphysical question. The Israelites, who expressed this doctrine in psalms, history, and prophecy, were not prompted by a scientific curiosity about the exact series of events, or the set of relations and circumstances which accompanied the origin of the world. Nor were they concerned with the speculative question of an underlying substance which would explain the world of changing things. They were overwhelmingly interested in the mystery of the purpose and meaning of their history as a people, and so with the nature of the Ruler of all history. Correspondingly, they sought, in calling God 'Creator', to affirm the total sovereignty and the almighty power of the God who had revealed Himself as the author of Israel's destiny and the executor of Israel's fulfilment. They, and the Christians who followed them, confessed God to be the Creator and Ruler of all things, because each had received a vivid answer to fundamental religious questions. Who has put us here; who has fashioned us and for what purpose; who is the ultimate power over our existence; and who claims us as the Lord and Ruler of our life and destiny?

Their doctrine of creation, then, is an affirmation of faith that despite the mystery and anxiety of their creaturely dependence and temporality, they, as biblical people, have found God revealed to them as the Almighty Power who created them and all that seemed to threaten them, and created them for such a purpose that they might through Him have confidence and trust in life and in its meaning.'

The Christian doctrine of creation, therefore, expresses in theoretical language those positive religious affirmations which biblical faith in God makes in response to the mystery of the meaning and destiny of our creaturely finitude. These affirmations are: (1) That the world has come to be from the transcendent holiness and power of God, who because He is the ultimate origin is the ultimate Ruler of all created things. (2) That because of God's creative and ruling power our finite life and the events in which we live have, despite their bewildering mystery and their frequently tragic character, a meaning, a purpose, and a destiny beyond any immediate and apparent futility. (3) That man's life, and therefore *my* life, is not my own to 'do with' merely as I please, but is claimed for – because it is upheld and guided by – a power and a will beyond my will. This is what the Christian means when he says, 'I believe in God the Father Almighty, Maker of heaven and earth.' This is what the idea of *creatio ex nihilo* is essentially 'about'.

I. G. Barbour, 'Theological Issues in Evolution' from *Issues in Science and Religion*,* pp. 88–98

1. *God and Nature: The Challenge to Design*

The prevalent version of the argument from design was particularly vulnerable, for it had started from the observed *adaptation of organic structures to useful functions*. But such adaptation could be accounted for by natural selection without invoking any preconceived plan. Usefulness was an effect and not a cause; it was the end product of an impersonal process. The species in existence are present simply because they have survived while thousands of others lost out in the struggle for existence. Instead of marvelling that a fish has an eye that can see under water, we should have reason to be surprised only if this were *not* the case. Moreover, some of the facts that had always created difficulties for the advocates of design – such as useless rudimentary organs and traces of long-vanished limbs – could now be readily explained.

In some of his writings Darwin expressed the view that the *laws* by which life evolved were created by God, though the particular species resulting were the product of *chance* rather than design:

---

* © 1966. Reprinted by permission of Prentice-Hall, Inc., Englewood Cliffs, N. J., and SCM Press.

The Question of Origins

> There seems no more design in the variability of organic beings and in the action of natural science than in the course which the wind blows. (Everything in nature is the result of fixed laws).... On the other hand, I cannot anyhow be contented to view this wonderful universe, and especially the nature of man, and to conclude that everything is the result of brute force. I am inclined to look at everything as resulting from designed laws, with the details, whether good or bad, left to the working out of what we may call chance. (Darwin, *Life and Letters*, Vol. I, p. 279; Vol. II, p. 105.)

Chance seemed to be the antithesis of design. Darwin assumed that organic change is the product of a very large number of random spontaneous variations occurring entirely independently of each other, so the final result is accidental and unpremeditated. But the element of lawfulness, which received greater emphasis than the idea of chance, was also understood in a way which denied design. To earlier generations, scientific laws expressed the wisdom and constancy of God and were instruments of his purposes. Now they were increasingly taken as the autonomous and mechanical operation of impersonal forces. Law as well as chance appeared to be blind and purposeless.

Darwin at one point indicated that lawfulness does not exclude the concept of *God as primary cause*; he even spoke of natural laws as the 'secondary means' by which God created. He came close to recognizing that the scientist studies the domain of secondary causes and cannot ask why nature works as it does. But the following passage suggests that his own epistemology was undermined by the admission of the lowly origins of man's mind, so that in his later years he took a more agnostic position. He maintains:

> ... the impossibility of conceiving this immense and wonderful universe, including man with his capacity for looking far backwards and far into futurity, as the result of blind chance or necessity. When thus reflecting I feel compelled to look to a First Cause having an intelligent mind in some degree analogous to that of man: and I deserve to be called a Theist.... But then arises the doubt, can the mind of man, which has, as I fully believe, been developed from a mind as low as that possessed by the lowest animals, be trusted when it draws such grand conclusions. (Darwin, *Life and Letters*, Vol. I, p. 282.)

Neither in the typical formulations of the design argument, such as

Paley's nor in the rejection of it by Darwin and others of his time, was the nature of divine causality discussed. Usually God's activity had simply been assumed to be like that of a workman; and evolution made this simple 'maker' analogy untenable.

One way out of this dilemma was to *broaden the concept of design* by applying it not to specific organs or organisms but to the evolutionary process as a whole. Asa Gray, Harvard botanist and leading interpreter of scientific opinion to the American public, maintained that the over-all history of nature could be understood in purposeful terms, despite the occurrence of waste and struggle. 'Emergence is design by wholesale, the direction of the process by which mind and moral personality arose, which are not explainable by matter in random motion.' Gray defended the idea of a Creator working through evolution to produce a gradually unfolding design; he also argued that God providentially supplies the new variations in the right direction. Other scientists held that God does not intervene, but has built design into the very structure of the process through which higher forms of life and eventually man could come into being. The anthropologist Eiseley has recently written:

> Darwin did not destroy the argument from design. He destroyed only the watchmaker and the watch.... Darwin had delivered a death blow to a simple, a naively simple, form of the design argument, but as Huxley himself came to realize, it is still possible to argue for directivity in the process of life. (*Darwin's Century*, p. 198. Copyright © 1958 by Loiren C. Eiseley. Doubleday and Victor Gollancz.)

2. Man and Nature: The Challenge to Human Dignity

In the Western tradition, *man was set apart* from all other creatures. Man alone was a rational being; human reason was considered totally different in kind from whatever intelligence animals have. Man alone possessed an immortal soul, which defined his true being and his relationship to God. Man's distinctiveness put him in many respects 'outside' nature, despite his sharing with other creatures a common dependence on God and a common finitude and temporality. This uniqueness of status now appeared to be denied by the theory of evolution. Distinctions between human and animal characteristics were indeed minimized by Darwin and his followers. Surviving primitive tribes, as Darwin portrayed them, almost closed the gap between man and animal. Huxley claimed that there is less difference between man and the highest apes than between higher and lower apes. Man himself, absorbed into nature, seemed to be the product of accidental variations and the struggle for survival, a child of blind chance and law.

Man's moral sense had always been considered one of his most distinctive capacities, but Darwin claimed that it too had originated by selection. In the early history of mankind a tribe whose members had strong social instincts, such as fidelity and self-sacrifice for the common good, would have had an advantage over other tribes. If morality conferred survival value, standards of conscience would have tended to rise. In the extinction of savage races in conflict with more civilized ones Darwin saw further evidence of built-in ethical advance. In a similar fashion he traced each of man's emotional and intellectual characteristics back to origins in the earlier stages of human and subhuman development.

There were other biologists, however, who gave greater emphasis to the *distinctive characteristics of man*. A. R. Wallace, who had formulated the principle of natural selection independently of Darwin, recognized that the presence of the human brain radically altered the character of evolution; with the development of intellect, bodily specialization and changes in physical organs were outmoded. Wallace also recognized that the gap in intellect between man and ape was far greater than Darwin had acknowledged; nor could 'primitive' tribes fill the gap, for their inherent mental capacities are actually as great as those of civilized peoples. Again, he saw the distinctiveness of language as symbolic communication, where Darwin had seen little difference between animal signals and human speech. At each of these points, subsequent investigation has tended to vindicate Wallace's contributions.

In his later writing, Wallace went further and claimed that natural selection cannot account for *man's higher faculties*. He pointed out that the brain size in very primitive tribes, which is comparable to that in highly civilized groups, actually provides a mental capacity far beyond the simple needs of their aboriginal patterns of life, for which a much smaller brain would have sufficed. 'Natural selection could only have endowed savage man with a brain a little superior to that of an ape, whereas he actually possesses one very little inferior to that of a philosopher.' C. A. R. Wallace, *Contributions to the Theory of Natural Selection*, 2nd edn (New York, Macmillan Co. 1871), p. 356.) And how can one explain musical, artistic, or ethical capacities that contribute nothing to survival? Wallace felt that such 'latent powers' possessed in advance of the need to employ them indicate that 'some higher intelligence may have directed the process by which the human race was developed'. More recent opinion has not supported Wallace's idea of 'latent powers', but it has tended to agree with him in holding that man's evolution involved distinctive processes which Darwin's purely biological framework ignored.

It is perhaps understandable that Darwin overemphasized *the continuity of man and animal*. The earlier tradition had portrayed such an absolute discontinuity that to establish man's rootedness in nature Darwin looked for all the similarities he could find, overlooking the differences. The tremendous scope of the theory of evolution had been amply demonstrated, and it was easy to assume that all human phenomena could be exhaustively interpreted in essentially biological terms. It is also understandable that there were both scientists and theologians who, in reaction to such claims, insisted that natural selection could not account for man. Today we can see that in the long history of the world, man's emergence marks a genuinely new chapter – one not disconnected from previous chapters, and yet involving factors not previously present. Something radically different takes place when culture rather than the genes becomes the principal means by which the past is transmitted to the future, and when conscious choice alters man's development.

Moreover, both opponents and proponents of evolution often seem to have made the implicit assumption that *man's descent determines his nature*. Much of the emotion accompanying the rejection of the idea that 'we have apes in our family tree' can be traced to this notion that source fixes meaning. Belief in evolution was equated with belief that man is 'nothing but an animal'. Man's origins were too readily taken by both sides to be the chief clue to his significance; a subhuman past somehow came to imply a less than fully human present. This is a genetic or temporal form of 'reductionism', which finds the significance of an entity not in its smallest parts, as with eighteenth-century materialism, but in its most primitive beginning; it is a philosophical assumption equally destructive to the dignity of man, and equally unwarranted as a conclusion from the data.

3. Methods in Science: The Challenge of Evolutionary Ethics

If Darwin and his defenders believed that the theory of evolution had undermined the argument from design and the traditional status of man, it might be expected that their attitudes toward the future would have been pessimistic. But amid the optimism of the late nineteenth century the total evolutionary picture seemed to convey a hopeful message. In the climate of the Victorian era the idea of *evolutionary progress* became a secular substitute for providence; blind fate was transformed into beneficent cosmic process, which was taken to guarantee the final fruition of history and even the perfectibility of man. Faith in progress replaced the doctrines of creation and providence as assurance that the universe is not really purposeless. Neither uniform law nor accidental chance is any threat if it leads to inevitable advance and if nature is a coherent and intelligible system. The Harvard philosopher John Fiske wrote that man was reinstated because evolution 'shows us distinctly, for the first time, how the creation and perfection of man is the goal toward which nature's work has been tending from the first'. The Enlightenment faith in social progress had been expanded to confidence in a progressive universe.

Was this concept of progress a conclusion reached *by the methods of science*? Darwin himself was evidently aware of the ambiguity at this point. He recognized that in speaking of 'the fittest to survive', a biologist is not rendering a moral judgement, but only referring to physical endurance. The 'improvement' of a species means only an advantage in competition in a given environment; it might appear to be 'retrogression' in a different environment or when viewed against the whole pattern of organic development. If Darwin and Spencer nevertheless often used 'progress' in a way that implied a value judgement, they did so, says J. C. Greene,

> ... because in their heart of hearts they believed that the processes of nature operated, however slowly and sporadically, to produce ever higher forms of existence. As naturalists they tried to define 'improvement', 'fitness', 'highness', and the like in biological terms, but their use of the terms was subtly coloured by the indomitable optimism of their age. The nineteenth century believed in progress, but it was not very careful to define what it meant by progress. (*The Death of Adam.* © 1959 by the Iowa State University Press, p. 301.)

The problem of *the relation of ethical norms to evolution* becomes acute if man's free and conscious choice guides his own future evolution. In some passages Darwin implied that anything man does is an expression of natural selection, and that if progress is inherent in the process no human decision can hinder it. In other passages, he urged man to choose deliberately the pattern which the rest of nature exemplifies. He warned that future progress would be hindered by sentimental policies which protect weaker individuals, such as the sick or maimed, who would be eliminated under more competitive conditions. 'There should be open competition for all men; and the most able should not be prevented by laws or customs from succeeding best and rearing the largest number of offspring.' But Darwin was not altogether consistent, for there was 'deep in his character a warm humanitarianism and a strong hold-over of the Christian ethic in which he had been trained'. (Greene, ibid., p. 81.) He recognized a 'higher morality' which would encourage respect and love toward all men, including the weak; but such a morality would lessen the competitive struggle and thus undermine what he had taken to be the source of progress. He also pointed out that even among animals brute strength is often not the most important factor in survival.

The belief that *competition promotes progress* fitted in well, however, with the predominantly individualistic social philosophy common in this period. Biological and political ideas merged in what has been called 'social Darwinism'. Even before he read Darwin, Herbert Spencer had tried to show that *laissez faire* private enterprise was in keeping with the stern disciplines of nature that produce biological improvement. He found in the evolutionary struggle as Darwin described it a justification for his claim that economic competition unhampered by government regulation fosters human welfare. The survival of the fittest was to be the instrument for the evolution of society also; here, too, rugged individualism would bring beneficial results. Competition between groups and the conflict of races had been valuable historically, 'a continuous over-running of the less powerful or less adapted by the more powerful or more adapted, a driving of inferior varieties into undesirable habitats, and occasionally, an extermination of inferior varieties'. But Spencer, like Darwin, faced difficulties in his attempt to derive ethical norms from evolution. Having made biological survival his criterion of progress, Spencer could provide no satisfactory basis for rejecting an appeal to arms, such as that of Prussian militarism which would try to prove a nation's fitness on the battlefield.

T. H. Huxley, taking issue with both Darwin and Spencer, held that valid *ethical norms cannot be derived from evolution*. Standards appropriate for human conduct simply cannot be obtained from examining natural selection or copying the law of the jungle; 'Let us understand, once for all, that the ethical progress of society depends not on imitating the cosmic process, still less in running away from it, but in combating it.' (*Evolution and Ethics* (New York, Appleton, 1896), p. 83.) Huxley asserted:

> The practice of that which is ethically best – what we call goodness or virtue – involves a course of conduct which in all respects is opposed to that which leads to success in the cosmic struggle for existence. In place of ruthless self-assertion, it demands self-restraint; in place of thrusting aside or treading down all competitors, it requires that the individual shall not merely respect, but shall help his fellows; its influence is directed, not so much to the survival of the fittest, as to the fitting of as many as possible to survive. It repudiates the gladiatorial theory of existence. (Ibid., p. 81.)

Having rejected both 'evolutionary ethics' and revealed religion, Huxley fell back on a sort of moral intuitionism as the source of ethical norms – though the goals he actually defended seem principally to reflect his religious upbringing and surrounding culture. We will find this discussion of the relation between evolution, progress, and ethics continuing vigorously today, accompanied by a more careful analysis of the methodological distinctions between scientific and ethical questions.

4. Methods in Theology: The Challenge to Scripture

Long before Darwin, *biblical literalism* had been cast in doubt by scientific knowledge – from Copernican astronomy to the new geology. Moreover, the scholarly analysis of biblical texts – the historical and literary research known as 'higher criticism' – had already on completely different grounds begun to call the inerrancy of scripture into question. It appears surprising therefore that part of the popular outcry against evolution centred on the challenge to biblical authority. One reason was that, for the first time, central biblical beliefs – the purposefulness of the world, the dignity of man and the drama of man's creation and fall – seemed to be threatened. Many Christians knew only one way to defend these religious convictions, namely to reassert the doctrine of biblical infallibility that had been typical of the 'scholastic' period of Protestant orthodoxy.

Besides, some of the leading scientists had linked evolution with their own *atheistic viewpoints*, and conservative churchmen opposed both indiscriminately. Such a liaison between a scientific theory and a sweeping attack on religion had occurred previously among the French sceptics, but it was a less familiar phenomenon in England and

America. Darwin himself was cautious in his criticism of religion, but some of his defenders – most notably Huxley – went on the offensive against Christianity in the name of the freedom of science. Again, a number of assumptions that had been part of the *intellectual milieu* of the West for centuries were closely associated with particular biblical passages, as we have seen; familiar patterns of thought were defended by appeals to scripture. For example, the traditional view of man's status seemed to many people inseparable from the biblical account of Adam's creation in a unique act of God.

For the biblical literalists, then, there could be *no compromise with evolution*. Genesis describes the once-for-all creation of species in their present form, and if Darwin maintained that species change he was simply mistaken. Philip Gosse proposed that God had put all those fossils in a plausibly misleading pattern in order to test man's faith. From the ages of Adam's descendants, Archbishop Ussher had calculated that creation must have occurred in 4004 B.C. Others pointed out that evolution is 'only a theory, not a fact', and that 'it has not been proved' – remarks that are valid but show an inadequate understanding of the character of scientific inquiry, for no scientific theory can ever be proved with certainty to be true or immune to future modification. There was abundant opportunity for appeal to prejudice – or to sentiment, as when Wilberforce asked Huxley whether he traced his descent from an ape on his grandfather's side or his grandmother's.

But there were many others whose view of scripture *allowed the acceptance of evolution*. The majority of Protestant authors distinguished between the religious ideas of Genesis and the ancient cosmology in which these ideas were expressed. They interpreted the biblical account as a symbolic and poetic rendition of affirmations about the dependence of the world on God – affirmations they found not incompatible with the picture of evolution as God's way of creating. The modernists went further; for them the Bible was a purely human document, a record of man's religious insight. The evolutionary view of nature moulded the modernist understanding of God; the divine was now an immanent force at work within the process, an indwelling spirit manifest in the creative advance of life to ever higher levels. Catholic thought avoided the extremes of both literalism and modernism. Though Rome was at first reluctant to accept evolution, a position was gradually defined which acknowledged man's physical derivation from animal ancestry but preserved his uniqueness as a spiritual being.

STUDY TOPICS

1. Trace the development of Darwin's thought in relation to the events of his life. What were the weaknesses of the evolutionary theory as he presented it?
2. Is it reasonable to consider evolution as presently explained, as another way of looking at God the creator? Can it be described as His way of creating?
3. What is the significance of suffering, evil, and a lack of design in the makeup of the universe as we know it?
4. How significant is the development of mind, consciousness, and spiritual capacity in evolutionary terms? Would it be reasonable to speak of a directionality (or directedness) in evolution?
5. What is the meaning of 'progress'?

BIBLIOGRAPHY

Ian G. Barbour, ed., *Science and Religion*, (3), Part Three, 'Evolution and Creation', a group of selections from important writers, is especially relevant to this chapter.

J. Habgood, *Religion and Science*, (12). Chapter 8, 'Nothing but apes', is quoted in this chapter, but the whole book is eminently clear and readable, and is an excellent introduction to the whole question of the relations of science and religion.

Ian G. Barbour, *Issues in Science and Religion*, (2). Chapters 4 and 12 are particularly relevant to this theme, and deal very comprehensively with the whole topic.

FURTHER READING

Flew, A., and MacKinnon, D., 'Creation', Chapter 9 in *New Essays in Philosophical Theology*, ed., Flew, A., and MacIntyre, A. (11).
John, Laurie, *Cosmology Now*. BBC 1973.
Monod, J., *Chance and Necessity*. Collins 1972.

Taylor, J. V., *The Go-Between God*, SCM Press 1972. A discussion of the Holy Spirit and the Christian Mission, with an interesting sidelight on evolution and its implications.

Teilhard de Chardin, P., *The Phenomenon of Man*. Collins Fontana 1959.

7
Modern Biology and Theology

INTRODUCTION

It is probably true that one of the fastest growing areas of study, especially in the educational world, is biology. It is also having an increasing impact upon our daily lives. We must ask here certain basic questions about it. They come under three headings:

1

What can we say about the area of study which biology 'maps out' for itself? What do we mean by 'life'? What distinguishes it from 'non-life'?

Clearly, the very basis of all philosophical thought is that we ourselves are thinking, sentient beings with feelings, affections, will, and experiences; without this simple fact there could presumably be no coherent thought at all. How significant is it that we who are involved in the business of being and living from the inside, so to speak, as actors, are able, and indeed consciously desire, to look at life and livingness from the outside also, as spectators? Thus, the fact of the existence of the science of biology has implications for the significance of man.

2

What are the implications of present biological research for the future of man, insofar as they can be drawn from present trends?

The extracts from Gordon Rattray Taylor's book *The Biological Time-Bomb*, may seem to some readers a little far-fetched, but one has only to consider the enormous advances in other branches of science in the twentieth century to realize that we are likely to underestimate the potentialities. There are very serious questions about the nature of being human, the nature of individuality and personhood, and the nature of relationships with other people raised here, which the extracts make clear.

3

Connected with these questions is the whole area of ethical

decision. More and more enormously important questions of social and individual morality are being raised by biological research and its technological application − contraception, abortion, euthanasia, population problems, eugenics, and organ transplantation to mention only a few.

We cannot go into these questions in any detail here, but we cannot avoid mentioning them: they are implicit in the subject and in the nature of man. The reader must work out for himself the ethical implications of this branch of modern science.

G. Rattray Taylor, *The Biological Time-Bomb*

Where are the Biologists Taking Us? pp. 9–16

Two hundred years ago the French Encyclopaedist Diderot, in an ironical vision of the future which he called *The Dream of d'Alembert* described how one day human embryos would be artificially cultivated and their hereditary endowment predetermined. His hero saw 'a warm room with the floor covered with little pots, and on each of these pots a label: soldiers, magistrates, philosophers, poets, potted courtesans, potted kings. . . .'

Today his vision no longer seems entirely fanciful, and some biologists believe that, before the end of the century at latest, it may be realized. Other writers − among them Shaw and Wells − have dreamed of the control of growth, of tampering with memory and of the extension of the human life span to many centuries. None of these seems any longer to be so impossible of achievement. Indeed, some may be alarmingly close.

All these are biological advances. We are now, though we only dimly begin to realize the fact, in the opening stages of the 'biological revolution' − a twentieth-century revolution which will affect human life far more profoundly than the great 'mechanical revolution' of the nineteenth century or the 'technological revolution' through which we are now passing.

For too long the public has maintained a false stereotype about biology: it was the science of classification, of botanizing and studying bees. Biologists were dry-as-dust creatures who studied the migrations of birds or dissected frogs to see how they tick. In contrast the physicist was seen as much more involved in reality. His tinkerings with sparks and wires produced, in due course, radio and television, not to mention the telephone. His interest in atoms seemed a little recondite at first, but, sure enough, in due course, it produced the atom bomb and nuclear energy, and that is practical enough for anyone. But the biologist was different – biology was 'natural history', a subject for young ladies and elderly clergymen.

This stereotype is about to be shattered. The biologists have got up their sleeves discoveries which have just as universal and earth-shaking an effect as those of the chemists and physicists. Attentive readers of the scientific journals have noticed, during the past five years or so, the appearance of a series of warning statements by eminent biologists, some made verbally at meetings or symposia, others in special articles or letters – warnings about the direction in which biology is heading. . . .

The difficulty which a writer faces in writing about such developments is that a general statement conveys only a feeble impression of the potentialities of the advance, whereas a concrete one appears hopelessly sensational and even repellent. Thus if I say that grafting techniques may make body parts completely interchangeable I suggest little more than a medical advance. On the other hand, if I say that one day someone might say to you, indicating another person, 'I want you to meet my uncle and niece; they were in a car smash but fortunately the surgeon was able to get one complete body out of the undamaged bits,' I am more likely to evoke incredulity than alarm.

I suspect that the immediate reaction of many people to such forecasts is that, if not downright impossible, they lie so far in the future as to be of no practical importance to people now living. Nothing could be farther from the truth, I regret to say. While some of the possibilities hinted at by biologists, such as the attainment of personal immortality, may lie a century or more in the future, it is certain that much of what they are doing will begin to bear fruit in the lifetime of those now living. For instance, the growing ability to control mental states is *already* facing us with problems such as the inability of young people to make a mature use of LSD. But this is not a once-for-all phenomenon. The hallucinogens are merely one of the first of an indefinitely long series of advances in the direction of mental control, and the present generation will certainly live to see many comparable problems as well as others less definable.

Again, the discovery of oral contraceptives is merely the *beginning* of a new world of expertise in the control of the reproductive process, and the controversies which have raged about the use of such pills will soon be lost in the thunder of even more desperate battles.

No one can say for sure when anything will be discovered, but it is fair to assume that at least *some* of the matters on which biologists all over the world are working will yield breakthroughs in the next five or ten years. For instance, there is an imminent prospect of being able to control the process by which the body rejects grafts of tissue from other organisms; this will make a wide range of transplantation operations possible. The heart transplantations which make news stories today should be viewed simply as the earliest advances in a long campaign. To look on such developments as complete and final is to repeat the complacency of the man who dismissed the automobile with the comment, 'Very clever, but it will never replace the horse.'

The fact is, we are all short on imagination. How many people, looking at a black bakelite telephone or brown bakelite switch-cover, thirty years ago, envisaged the world of brilliantly coloured plastics, both rigid and flexible, which we know today? Equally, it takes uncommon imagination to see in the hard-won and often unsatisfying biological achievements of today the fantastic possibilities which will be taken for granted by the generation of tomorrow. And I don't mean the day *after* tomorrow. Many of the possibilities discussed in this book, incredible as they may seem to some, will become realities only too soon.

It is, therefore, not merely interesting but socially important to try to evaluate them without delay.

But why do these barely credible developments threaten to burst upon us precisely now? What has been going on in the laboratories of the biologists that they have started to spew forth problems all much at the same time?

The Biological Breakthrough

Every science has a natural curve of development. At first it is burdened with erroneous pre-scientific beliefs and poses its problems wrongly; progress is slow. A slow gathering of carefully observed facts is the indispensable preliminary to the forming of generalizations. Then as insight is obtained, first in one subsection, then in another, progress becomes more rapid. The various fields begin to coalesce and illuminate one another.

Physics and chemistry, being simpler and more uniform, entered on their growth sooner than biology. The word 'biology' was only coined at the beginning of the nineteenth century, when people began to see it as a discipline distinct from medicine, larger than 'natural history'. Before this time there had been no real awareness that a science of living things might constitute a coherent discipline. Work was predominantly observational and classificatory until the first great insights came in the first half of the nineteenth century; the cell theory of Schwann and Schleiden, which provided a common denominator for all forms of life, and the theory of evolution propounded by Chambers and Matthew (for which Darwin was soon to propose a suitable mechanism). Soon after came Mendel's work, neglected at the time, which opened up the study of heredity.

Progress also depends upon the availability of suitable tools. Until the achromatic microscope was devised early in the nineteenth century, the study of the cell was impossible, while the study of structures within the cell, such as the chromosomes, was dependent upon the apochromatic oil-immersion microscopes which did not become available until near the end of the century.

The fantastic quickening in the pace of biological research in the past few years is due, above all other factors, to the provision of new and extraordinarily powerful tools for the study of living things. Probably the chief among these is the electron microscope, which can magnify as much as a million times and reveal structures quite beyond the power of the light microscopes to resolve. Seeing is believing, and a picture conveys in one instant information about shape, size, number, relative arrangement and other parameters, each of which might have to be deduced separately from tedious experiments, were no pictures available. It was not until after the last war that these instruments became commercially available.

Also important are various remarkably subtle and powerful methods of separating out the various components in a complex biological mixture. Not only the various parts of the cells of which all creatures are composed, but even various types and sizes of molecules can be sorted out, and often identified, by devices such as the ultracentrifuge, which exposes liquids to forces 100,000 times as great as gravity, or methods like electrophoresis which sifts molecules with electric force. Automation of many laboratory processes has also speeded work. In most biological laboratories today one will find machines which work all night as well as all day, tirelessly making measurement after measurement and recording them – or even calculating results from them. Because biology deals with such complex and delicate material, often present in vanishingly small quantities, it could not go far without techniques like these.

Modern Biology and Theology

Still more, however, the breakthrough has been made possible by the growing sophistication of chemistry, which has proved able to explain the incredibly complex sequences of reactions within the cells of the body, as well as those which may take place in the blood, lymph and elsewhere, making biochemistry almost a separate discipline. We may, indeed, be moving into an era in which physics rather than chemistry will be needed to provide the necessary data to explain what happens at the cell surface, how muscles contract and how nerves conduct. Biophysics grinds even smaller than biochemistry.

Whatever the reason, it is fair to say that biology has moved into a phase of accelerated development to which it is not too much of an exaggeration to apply the word 'breakthrough'.

In so doing, it has also moved — as physics did earlier — into an era of million dollar machines and large multi-disciplinary teams of specialists: cytologists, crystallographers, biochemists, neurologists, molecular biologists and a dozen more.

The approach is no longer merely observational: instead the biologist makes hypotheses and devises experiments to test them. His measurements are made with the utmost precision and his approach is often statistical. The distinction between biology and medicine is rapidly becoming more acute.

However, blanket statements of this sort obscure the fact that biology is a group of disciplines, some of which are in a far more developed stage than others.

Biology, it can be said, seeks to answer seven distinct questions, and the pattern of this book is dictated by that fact, since each of these lines of development is advancing at a different rate. The questions can be briefly stated thus:

1. How did life of any kind originate?
2. What accounts for the variety of life forms (species)?
3. What is the nature of ageing and the cause of natural death?
4. How do living creatures function: what biochemical mechanisms do they depend on? (Including: how do they resist infection?)
5. How is the behaviour of living creatures controlled? (Including: how does the brain work?)
6. How do living creatures replace themselves? (How does conception occur and what determines hereditary similarity?)
7. How do living creatures grow and develop? (Including: how does the egg develop within the womb?)

The nineteenth century saw one of these questions substantially answered – No. 2. What accounts for the variety of the species? Recently we have seen the effective solution of another, No. 6. The details of fertilization and the mechanism of heredity are understood in considerable detail, even though there are some obscure points remaining to be cleared up. There has also been substantial progress on No. 4. the vast group of topics which we call physiology. Many of the social and ethical questions which are beginning to face us arise from progress in these two fields.

The problems which lie in the middle distance are those which derive from fields 3, 5 and 7: ageing and death, growth and development, hormones and the brain. Beyond them lies the ultimate question of the origin of life. But even here biologists begin to glimpse an answer.

I shall examine these fields in turn, starting with those which are already beginning to affect us and going on to the remoter or more speculative possibilities. Leaving aside the question of evolution, which caused such a furore in the last century, as a bomb which has already gone off, we are left with six sensitive areas – six bombs with smouldering fuses of varying lengths.

Who Am I?, pp. 87–90

This line of development (the combining of men and machines in a single body) fills many people with a deep sense of alarm, because it raises the question of personal identity. The question 'Who am I?' probably occurs to all of us at some point in life, and usually quite young. It may be said to mark a person's emergence as an individual. Philosophers of the personalist school, such as Martin Buber, or Husserl, not to mention existentialists such as Sartre, have devoted much attention to this basically unanswerable question. In so far as an answer can be given, today it generally takes the line: 'You are an unique individual, unlike any other in the universe, and your name, X, denotes that precise aggregation of qualities which you possess and no others.' Our sense of personal uniqueness would suffer a severe blow if we learned that, in some universe parallel to our own but inaccessible to us, every individual on earth had his precise counterpart or twin. Even though the inhabitants of this other world could not communicate with us, so that their existence could never affect us directly, we should find it hard not to think from time to time: how would my double behave in this situation? Or perhaps: I am determined to differentiate myself from him by doing something different from what he would do in this situation.

Consequently, if we acquire prosthetic organs which are identical with those carried by other people, we may feel the less unique, the less ourselves. It has been claimed that we shall also feel some dilution of ourselves when we carry a kidney or other organ donated by another. Probably, as the situation becomes commoner, this response will become weaker or fade away. Man seems to have a considerable power of assimilating machinery to himself: it has often been observed that people come to regard their cars as extensions of themselves, and even modify their kinaesthetic responses to include it. A man who has driven a car for some time 'feels' where the limits of his car lie and can steer it through a narrow gap almost as well as he could steer his body: when he takes over a new car, for some days it 'feels strange' and his awareness of its limits and capabilities is lost.

Indeed, there is a sense in which even our bodies are only machines which we drive, and the limits of our identity are coterminous with the brain. An amputee, however much he regrets the handicap, does not feel that he is to any degree dehumanized as a person. But other people may. Many people feel a certain horror in meeting an amputee and an unjustifiable sense that he is somehow less than human. So cyborgs are likely to arouse these unconsciously motivated fears. And when Dr Comfort asks 'Could even a disembodied brain be more "sinister" than a similar head attached to a paralysed patient in an iron lung?' the answer may well be 'yes'.

The question 'Who am I?' comes second only to the question 'Who are you?' As some psychologists have recently emphasized, we all feel deep anxieties when we encounter another human being in any kind of interpersonal relationship. Do they represent a threat to us, physically, emotionally, in terms of status, or in any other way? Shall I be able to meet their demands – for, if not, I suffer in my own self-respect as well as in their eyes. If they represent a threat, or even a challenge, at any of these levels, shall I be able to cope with it?

It is because of this group of basic reactions, deeply built into all of us, that many people fear the robot, the zombie and the computer. They have no experience in dealing with their demands, which are by definition to some extent different from genuinely human demands; what is worse, they are uncertain even what these demands are. Anyone who has had to deal with insane, or even highly neurotic, individuals will know the sense of fear and helplessness which assails one, as one realizes that all the normal human techniques for influencing others – persuasion, threat, reward, punishment etc. – have no effect or even quite the wrong effect. The same kind of feeling in a much milder form is felt when we first try to control some unfamiliar machinery and it does something we don't expect.

But if we fear the intelligent machine, it is quite natural to fear even more the object which looks like a human being but turns out not to be one. This, I am sure, is the source of revulsion many people feel at the prospect of man-machine hybrids. The idea of a computer which bursts into tears and demands affection is a little harassing, since we don't know how to comfort it, but we can relieve ourselves of the responsibility by remembering that it is 'only a machine'. Much harder to cope with, I suppose, is an android, which we treat with the circumspection due to a human being, expecting a similar degree of consideration in return, only to find that it is unaffected by human emotions, insensible to the pain or misery which it may cause, planning its actions in wholly logical terms of material advantage.

If the robot is equipped with a simulacrum of human emotions – and experiments to this end are already under way – the overt situation may be improved, since they are less likely to act 'inhumanly' and so to cause unintended suffering. But the psychological situation is worsened, for the fear remains that at some point the programming will prove inadequate; and the damage done, we anticipate, will be all the worse if we have been put off our guard and have lowered our defences.

The situation will be something like having a dog of uncertain temper, normally friendly but occasionally liable to snap even at its master. Only if years of experience prove that unpredictable reactions are rare in robots will they become fully acceptable. For a time, we must expect to see headlines in our newspapers which echo the personal disasters which we manage to tolerate today: ROBOT'S ERROR STARTS FIRE, or BERSERK ANDROID SLAYS FOUR, and even WEDDING STOPPED: BRIDE EXPOSED AS 'NOT FULLY HUMAN'.

But when the robot and the human being become indistinguishable, we are driven back to less logical fears, and the question 'Who are you?' may become unanswerable, just as it does should we encounter an alien intelligence or a being from another planet. And when that other proves to be stronger, more intelligent and equipped with a far wider range of sensory and effector organs, our fear is bound to be intensified.

In conclusion, I believe one should stress the real danger of the human race becoming divided into two classes: the haves (who have the advantages of modern prosthetics) and the have-nots (who struggle along with nothing but what nature provides). Frantic efforts will be made by the have-nots to cross the divide, but in the nature of things the effort will rarely be successful, and the gap will steadily widen and become harder to cross. Criminal methods will often be employed. Perhaps renegade surgeons, blackmailed or deprived of their will by drugs, will be used to rob privileged haves of their prosthetic devices and to implant them in the unprivileged have-nots. In some countries, no doubt, the state will decide who is to be promoted to the privileged class, and there may be degrees of privilege. Manual workers will have exoskeletons, athletes will have spare hearts, and computer programmers spare heads. Only the head of the state will have all the advantages. Outstanding workers may be rewarded by a licence to acquire an additional prosthesis, and laggards punished by removal and downgrading. In other countries, costly prosthetic devices may be leased, so that one can enjoy a wider range of experience for a time. The leasing of under-water swimming equipment today provides an exact analogy. These speculations should not be dismissed too quickly as merely fanciful.

Life and Death, pp. 114–17

The fact is, the age old distinction between 'dead' and 'alive' has broken down. And while we have people who are technically alive – if 'alive' is defined in terms of the heart beating – we also have people who are technically dead, since their heart has stopped, but who are not lost to life since they can be revived. Surgeons now draw a distinction between 'clinical death' and 'biological death'. Not very well chosen terms: reversible death and irreversible death would express the distinction more clearly and precisely.

Many doctors think that brain function is a better criterion of death than heart function, and that death should be diagnosed on the basis of EEG (electro-encephalograph) tracings of the brain's electrical activity. As the Boston neuro-surgeon Dr Hannibal Hamlin puts it: 'Although the heart has been enthroned through the ages as the sacred chalice of life's blood, the human spirit is the product of man's brain, not his heart.' But in legal practice generally, as also by custom, the stopping of the heart is taken to be the sign of death.

The French, renowned for their icy logic, have already tackled this issue. In May 1966, by a unanimous decision, the French National Academy of Medicine decided that a man whose heart is still beating may be ruled dead. The Academy's decision, which was based on the report of a special commission set up four months previously, has the effect of permitting doctors to remove living organs for transplantation purposes from people who have no hope of survival. And it recommended that the demise should be confirmed by the electroencephalograph: if the brain shows no activity for 48 hours, the brain, and the patient, are assumed to be dead.

These attempts at a redefinition of death, however useful in the case of mortally injured persons, give the doctor no help in the case of the 'vegetable' type of patient, part of whose brain, at least, is still functioning. Neither do they help the doctor in the case of the slowly dying patient, whose end can be protracted unmercifully with modern techniques. Such a patient can be forcibly brought back from the brink of the grave a number of times before death claims him.

We must face the unpleasant fact that death protracted by such methods is usually visibly more painful than if the patient had been denied the treatment. Charles F. Zukosi III, surgeon at the Veteran's Administration Hospital in Nashville, Tennessee, observes: 'This is an agonal type of death. We can carry the prolongation of so-called life too far.' And as another doctor has urged, 'Let them die with dignity.'

Apart from the situation of the patient, the prolongation of death puts a massive strain on relatives. The patient's family not only suffer cruelly, but may have to pay as much as $250 a day for the use of the equipment, in the absence of a national health service. There is, also, in the present conditions of equipment shortage, a dilemma for the surgeon. 'When do you pull the plug out and make this expensive equipment available to someone else who might live?' asks Dr Robert S. Schwab of Harvard.

Of course the problem is not an entirely new one: few doctors with terminal cancer patients who may be in great pain and whose death is a matter of days feel themselves obliged to throw in major medical resources to prolong their suffering. Many doctors solve this ethical problem by permitting themselves inaction while forbidding themselves any positive action. Thus they would not give a patient a drug in order to hasten his death but would feel free to withhold medication, should the patient develop a respiratory infection (as often happens) on top of his mortal illness. To many this will seem ethically unconvincing, even if it provides a useful rule of thumb in practice. And it makes little sense in terms of the new mechanical devices: once it has been decided to apply the respirator, one can never 'pull the plug out' since that is a positive action.

The ethical problem here is perhaps the most pregnant so far raised by the new biology, and has given rise to a Papal pronouncement, which was given before an audience of clinicians, surgeons and scientists on 24 November 1957. The main point was summarized by the Most Rev. Fulton J. Sheen, The Roman Catholic Auxiliary Bishop of New York, in 1964, in these terms: 'Life may be prolonged by either ordinary or extraordinary means, such as a battery of tubes and devices in a terminal cancer patient. No one is obliged to use such extraordinary means, and there would be no moral difficulty in asking that they be removed.' Though helpful, such a definition leaves a doubt as to what qualifies as 'extraordinary'. The extraordinary means of today become the ordinary means of tomorrow.

On the other hand, Dr Immanuel Jacobovits, Chief Rabbi of the British Commonwealth, says that Judaism 'emphatically denies' the right of the doctor to let his patient die in peace, since it derives its sanction from the biblical 'thou shalt surely cause him to be healed'. But he qualifies this admirably clear statement by adding that Jewish law does not require the physician to prolong the patient's misery by *artificial* means. 'Artificial' remains undefined.

Apart from the religious aspect, even those who take a wholly pragmatic view will want to be sure that the doctor's new power of life and death is not abused, and that every case is considered on its merits. In Britain in 1967 a television producer, attending a hospital for a check-up, found an instruction had been issued to the hospital staff concerning the use of resuscitation equipment. Whole categories of people, notably those over a certain age, were automatically excluded from resuscitation treatment. He subsequently made a television programme which became front page news. This kind of publicity, which activates fears and prejudices, is liable to make the introduction of a 'die with dignity' policy even harder than it is at present, but it gives us a foretaste of the kind of controversy which will become more and more common in future and demonstrates the importance of establishing acceptable ground rules.

Even the rather straightforward-seeming decision to disconnect the machine when the brain's electrical signals have ceased can lead to misunderstanding and alarm. At Massachusetts General Hospital, for instance, it is a rule of thumb that if the brain trace has been flat for 24 hours and does not respond to stimuli, such as loud noises, and if the patient has no heart-beat and respiration of his own, he can be pronounced dead and the equipment disconnected.

But when one of the world's leading heart-lung surgeons, Dr Clarence Crafoord of Sweden, made a similar suggestion in May 1966, there was a public outcry: people seem to have thought he meant that the machines maintaining the patients should be switched off so that their organs could be used for transplanting purposes. He was, of course, referring only to the hopeless cases, but the incident suggests that some measure of public education may be necessary.

More than a century ago, Arthur Hugh Clough wrote, with bitter irony:

> Thou shalt not kill; but needst not strive
> Officiously to keep alive.

He intended to satirize the way men were left to die of malnutrition and lack of medical care. Today, his words have taken on a more literal meaning. Dr Donald Gould, former editor of *World Medicine* and currently editor of the *New Scientist*, declares: 'The pattern of advance of medical technology suggests that before too long we may have to decree that the various pumps, potions and prostheses which can keep a man alive beyond his natural span would be withdrawn when he reaches some statutory age.'

I. G. Barbour, 'Conclusions: On Man and Nature' from *Issues in Science and Religion*,* pp. 357–64

In the previous chapter we outlined four types of solution of the problem of human freedom: *reductionistic* views (stressing either determinism or indeterminacy at the atomic level); *dualistic* views; *'two-language'* views; and finally a *metaphysics of levels* – which we only began to develop – that interprets the self as the total person in its unified pattern of higher-level activities. We may now apply these same classifications to the problems of this chapter and draw some conclusions about the implications of the biological and cybernetic data for the Christian understanding of man. We group together similar types of answer to the main topics discussed: (a) emergence versus reduction (b) teleology versus mechanism and (c) mind versus body.

1. Dualistic Views

In common, these interpretations assert that there are in the world radically contrasting kinds of entity which follow principles unrelated to each other. (a) In *vitalism* the ontological gap lies between life and

---

* © 1966. Reprinted by permission of Prentice-Hall, Inc., Englewood Cliffs, N.J., and SCM Press.

matter. In most versions of *emergence* there are said to be no laws connecting phenomena of higher and lower levels. (b) *Teleology* and mechanism are taken to be mutually exclusive; the operation of purposes is understood to require a gap in the chain of physical causes, in which factors of another kind can enter. (c) *Mind-body dualism* represents mind as a distinctive entity interacting with matter in the brain. On this assumption, a computer, since it is a physical system, can have no truly mental characteristics; the dualist emphazises the limitations of 'artificial intelligence.' We have suggested, however, that these various 'gaps' and dichotomies (living-nonliving, mind-brain, and so forth) are difficult to maintain in the face of recent scientific evidence (such as DNA, brain physiology, and computer technology).

2. Reductionistic Views

Here it is believed that the behaviour of any system can be exhaustively explained in physico-chemical terms. (a) *Mechanists* and extreme *reductionists* hold that all biological theories are in principle deducible from the laws of physics and chemistry. This position is often coupled with a metaphysics of materialism. (b) 'Purpose' is equated with a particular type of mechanism, of which the *cybernetic model* (the target-seeking missile) is taken as typical. Higher-order 'purposive behaviour' is understood to be distinguished therefrom only in its complexity. (c) In *epiphenomenalism* causal efficiency is assigned only to physical events; in *behaviourism* all 'mental' concepts must be translated into statements about observable behaviour. If one anticipates that computers will be able to duplicate all types of human behaviour, and if one admits only behaviourist criteria, one concludes that there is no significant difference between man and machine. Man, in short, is a complex mechanism whose operation is predictable from physical laws. We have suggested that this view is unsatisfactory even within science.

3. 'Two Language' Views

Every language is selective and serves distinctive functions; conceptual schemes that seem to be mutually exclusive should be taken as alternative modes of analysis. The concern here is methodological rather than metaphysical. (a) Multi-level analysis is often fruitful in science, and a variety of types of models and symbol-systems can be employed concurrently. The biologist uses distinctive higher-level theories involving concepts that cannot be defined in lower-level terms, but he also seeks inter-level laws. Even where reduction is possible there is no reason to assume that the phenomena to which the higher-level concepts refer are less real than phenomena at lower levels. (b) *Teleological* and *mechanical explanations* are not mutually exclusive. Purpose and mechanism are two ways of regarding the same system; patterns in events can be analysed in terms of either 'goals' or 'causes'. (c) *'Mental'* and *'physical' languages* are two ways of regarding man – from within and from without, in 'actor-language' and 'spectator-language' respectively. In each of these cases we found much to commend this approach, which acknowledges that science is abstractive and that concepts must be employed in interpretative contexts. It provides a ready solution to other issues which will arise in the remaining chapters. Moreover, there is no problem here (as there is in any metaphysical dualism) as to how two dissimilar substances or principles could interact; it is man's language, not reality itself, which is dual. But we were driven beyond this position by our commitment to 'critical realism' and by our understanding of the unity of man. In other words, one must ask about the activities within man's total being which give rise to these diverse languages.

4. *A Metaphysics of Levels*

We suggested that 'levels of analysis' reflect 'levels of organisation' and 'levels of activity' in nature. (These terms seem preferable to 'levels of being' which has a more static connotation and might seem to refer to separate entities or objects.) The important point is that 'levels' like 'languages' are not mutually exclusive. Since any representation of a level is admittedly an abstraction, this approach differs from that of 'alternative languages' only in its insistence on ontological reference. (a) *Organicism* in biology stresses the presence of system-laws and the distinctive activities of *wholes*, as well as hierarchies of organizing relations in unified systems. Although the laws of these higher levels cannot be derived from studying lower-level phenomena among the separate parts, the activity of the whole is always dependent on that of the parts. (b) *Purpose* is found at various levels, which differ both in the way the future is represented in the present and in the kinds of flexibility of response displayed in goal-seeking. But we need not deny that there are some features common to these various levels of purpose, nor that there are causal factors at work in all of them. (c) *Parallelism* takes the mental and the physical to be two aspects of one set of events. Whereas the advocates of metaphysical dualism and 'alternative languages' find the extension of mental concepts beyond the human sphere problematical (even for the animal kingdom), advocates of psychophysical parallelism ascribe low levels of mentality at low levels of organization – in organisms or in computers. Recognition of both the diversity of activities at various levels and the continuity between levels enables us to avoid the ontological discontinuity of dualism as well as the one-level metaphysics to which reductionism usually leads. The analogy of a 'spectrum' suggests not only the value of interpreting the lower in terms of the higher, and the higher in terms of the lower, but also the need for distinctive categories at various levels.

Such an interpretation of levels can contribute to a *view of man* which takes both the scientific and the biblical understanding into account. It can allow for DNA and neurons, but also for personality and selfhood, the highest levels in man, to which both the religious tradition and human experience testify. Yet this many-levelled complexity must be seen within the total unity of man, to which biological science and biblical theology alike bear witness. Any general conclusions about the nature of man are, of course, beyond the compass of this book; they would require a discussion of the findings of the social sciences, an exploration of the many facets of the biblical understanding of human nature, and a comparison of religious and psychological concepts (such as sin and guilt, love and self-fulfilment). We will, however, consider briefly the relation of the *biblical view of man* to the biological evidence.

The Old Testament sees man *rooted in nature*, sharing the finitude, creatureliness and death of all living things. 'You are dust and to dust you shall return.' (Genesis 3.19; cf. Isaiah 31.3; 40.6; Job 14.1–17.)

Man and beasts are equally perishable. Yet man is distinguished from the animal world by his special relationship to God. Man alone is *a responsible self* who can be addressed by God. Man, as a free purposeful agent who can respond to the demands of righteousness and justice, is made 'in the image of God'. Man's 'breath' or 'spirit' is not a separate entity but the animating principle of the total person, the vitality of the whole individual in his biological, mental, and emotional life. Biblical scholars are agreed that 'there is no dichotomy or division into body and soul, for these various functions are not considered as distinct notions'. (Vriezen, *An Outline of Old Testament Theology* (Blackwell 1958), p. 203.) 'Opposition between body and soul is not to be found in the Old Testament: man is a psychophysical being.' (Jacob, *Theology of the Old Testament* (Hodder & Stoughton 1958), p. 157.) 'Biblical man, from the standpoint of a psychological approach to his nature, is a *unitary* being. He is body, spirit, self, feeling, mind and heart.' (Baab, *The Theology of the Old Testament* (Nashville, Abingdon Press 1959), p. 68.) 'Characteristic of the Old Testament, the idea of human nature implies a unity not a dualism. There is no contrast between the body and the soul such as the terms instinctively suggest to us.' (Robinson, *Religious Ideas of the Old Testament* (Duckworth 1913), p. 83.)

The biblical view of *the unity of man* is also evident in the fact that when belief in a future life finally developed, it was expressed in terms of the *resurrection of the total person*, not the immortality of the soul ... Cullmann has shown that in the New Testament the future life is seen as a gift from God 'in the last days' and not an innate attribute of man. 'The Jewish and Christian interpretations of creation exclude the whole Greek dualism of body and soul.' (Cullmann, *Immortality of the Soul or Resurrection of the Dead?* (Epworth 1958).) Even Paul, who was strongly influenced by Greek thought, speaks of the dead as 'sleeping' until the day of judgement when they will be restored – not as physical bodies nor as disembodied souls, but in what he calls 'the spiritual body' (1 Corinthians 15). Such views of the future life may be problematical for modern man, but they do testify that our faith must be in God and not in our own souls, and that man's whole being is the object of God's saving purpose.

Paul's contrast of 'flesh' and 'spirit' (e.g. Romans 8) at first seems to support a dualistic view of man, but more careful analysis shows that this is not the case. He never portrays a body which is inherently evil and a soul which is inherently good. Sin is in the will, which governs man's whole being: 'spiritual' sins such as arrogance and ingratitude are prominent in Paul's account. Similarly, the power of the Holy Spirit transforms man's *total* life, the inner and the outer man.

. . . . . .

Among the contemporary options, a *dualism* that assigns *the body* to science and *the soul* to religion might seem to allow man to participate in both realms. The soul would be an immaterial entity inaccessible to science, which in turn would be confined to the study of man's body. But such a dichotomy may be challenged on other grounds besides biblical exegesis. If mind is integral to the soul as the rational principle in man, we are faced with all the problems of a mind-body dualism. Again, we know that genes, environmental influences, and chemical changes can drastically influence human personality in its psychomatic unity. Thus one must either say that chemicals can alter the soul, or else postulate that the soul is an unchanging entity untouched by personality changes, and thus apparently unrelated to personal existence as we know it.

The idea of man as a *many levelled unity* seems to us more consonant with both the biblical and scientific viewpoints. The highest level of man's total being may be represented by the concept of *the self*, conceived not as a separate entity but as the individual in his unified activity of thinking, willing, feeling, and acting. The self is described not in terms of static substances but of dynamic activites at various levels of organization and functioning. It is this integral being whose whole life is of concern to God. Whereas the soul is usually imagined as a self-contained individual unit, which is only incidentally and externally related to anything else, a selfhood that is social in character is portrayed in the biblical view. A person is constituted by his relationships – he is who he is precisely as father, husband, citizen, and servant of God. The dominant image of person-in-community emphasizes this corporate dimension of selfhood without absorbing the individual into the collective. It was noted earlier that selfhood as we know it, including language and symbolic thought, would be impossible without society. We will find that many biologists today recognize man's nature as a social being, and assert that human evolution is now cultural rather than biological.

The presence in man of *levels of activity not found among other creatures* has been widely acknowledged by biologists, as will be seen in the next chapter. In the capacity for abstract thought and symbolic language there is a radical distinction between man and animal. Self-conscious awareness, critical self-reflection, and creative imagination are found nowhere else in nature. In memory of the past, anticipation of the future, and envisagement of ideal potentialities he transcends his immediate environment. He is unique in his search for truth, concern for moral values, and acknowledgement of universal obligations – and, above all, in his relationship to God. As we take up the problem of evolution, we will consider further the issue of man's relation to nature, as understood by both biology and biblical theology.

We will find also that *the uniqueness of each individual* can be defended on purely biological grounds. Each human being represents a novel genetic combination not duplicated elsewhere in the universe, and his life history is an unrepeatable set of events; it [has been] suggested that such uniqueness is compatible with the existence of lawful regularities. Moreover our account has surely not exhausted the mystery of self-consciousness whereby each of us is aware of himself as a unique centre of experience. Even if I matched someone else identically in every empirical description, I would never confuse myself with him; this distinctiveness is reflected in the logical peculiarities of the first-person language. The biblical conviction of the uniqueness of each person derives, of course, from other considerations, especially the idea of God's love for each man as an irreplaceable individual. The sacredness of personality and the fundamental equality of man are rooted in the value of every person in God's sight. The belief that each man is a special creation of God must be seen today as an assertion of individuality, novelty, and dependence on God, rather than as a denial of genetic and evolutionary continuity.

T. Dobzhansky, 'Self-Awareness and Death-Awareness' from *The Biology of Ultimate Concern*, pp. 63–9

There is no more succinct, and at the same time accurate, statement of the distinctive quality of human nature than that of Dostoievsky: 'Man needs the unfathomable and the infinite just as much as he does the small planet which he inhabits.' Gardner Murphy gives a more biological but a negative formulation: 'The human nervous system possesses, then, curious and profound hungers for many objects which are neither meat nor drink, neither satisfiers of oxygen need, nor of sex need, nor of material need, nor any other more obvious visceral demand.' What is 'curious' about these needs is their origin in biological evolution. We know that biological evolution is utilitarian; evolutionary changes occur in response to environmental challenges, and natural selection makes the changes favour the perpetuation of the species in which they occur. The changes serve to maintain or to advance the adaptedness of the organism to its environments, i.e. the ability to survive and to leave progeny in these environments. The hungers for 'the unfathomable and the infinite' do not seem, however, to promote adaptation; they are, in fact, liable to damage the prospects of survival of those in whom they are especially strongly developed. And yet it is indisputable that the potentiality to experience such hungers is biologically, genetically, implanted in human nature. The proof is that these hungers occur only in man; even the cleverest animal cannot imagine the infinite and, therefore, cannot hunger for it.

It has been pointed out above that useless and even harmful qualities may sometimes become established in evolution, provided that they are components of organic systems which are adaptively useful as wholes. One can hardly imagine anything so preposterous biologically as the painfulness and hazardousness of human childbirth. This flagrantly maladaptive quality is, however, a part of the complex, including also such things as erect posture, larger heads and brains, long infancy and childhood during which the individual acquires the cultural heritage of the group to which he belongs, human family organization, etc. The complexity calls for caution in attempts to arrive at evolutionary interpretations. It is a misconception to assume that every trait and quality of the organism must have a biological adaptive value by itself, taken in isolation from the rest of the living system. We must be reminded that what survives or dies, reproduces or remains childless, is a living individual, not a separate part of the body or an isolated gene. Of course, the performance of some one organ or a function may under certain conditions decide an individual's fate. The adaptive value, the Darwinian fitness, of a class of individuals is, however, a matter of a balance of advantages and disadvantages, strengths and weaknesses, abilities and failings.

A biologist cannot help being puzzled by the scant attention devoted to and by the meagre success achieved in psychology in the task of providing meaningful accounts of the differences in mental ability between man and animals. There is to be sure, no shortage of words used to describe man's supposedly unique attributes. Man is said to be a being who lives by reason rather than by instinct; man is aware or conscious of his self; he has a mind, an ego and a superego; he is capable of insight, abstraction, symbol formation, symbolic thinking, and of using symbolic language. The dominant trend in academic psychology, which at least until recently was in the United States behaviourist psychology, rejects these words and the concepts for which they stand. These words are deemed to be too vague, imprecise and unprofitable as operational tools in psychological research. Many recent textbooks of psychology simply do not mention these slippery words at all. The trouble is, however, that pretending that the problem of the nature of the difference between the human mind and the rudiments of mind found in animals does not exist is no help in bringing nearer a solution of this problem. When those who insist on using exclusively the most rigorous mechanistic approaches in science (sometimes nicknamed 'hard' science) refuse to handle a problem, it falls by default to the exponents of 'softer' varieties.

. . . . . .

With some notable exceptions, psychoanalytically oriented writers have devoted little attention to the evolutionary origins of the human psyche. In the classical Freudian triad of id-ego-superego, the first member is derived from biologically determined impulses of man's animal nature, while the latter two are more or less distinctively human. 'Where id was, there shall ego be,' is Freud's pithy formulation. Menaker and Menaker present a biologically more coherent view. In their words, 'When consciousness evolved as the highest expression of the evolution of nervous control, it was inevitable that an integrating principle evolve in conjunction with it. Man could not have experienced awareness without having evolved a way of organizing, integrating, co-ordinating the "different awarenesses", otherwise his psychological state would be chaotic.' This organizer is the ego, which 'is that psychological capacity through which consciousness is organized and integrated, through which the person is set in function both physically and mentally, and through which adaptive thought and behaviour is achieved'.

Existentialists affirm that it is man and man alone who truly 'exists'. This 'existence' is what sets him apart from all other forms of life. The existentialists are perhaps on the right path towards identification of man's basic biopsychological singularity. However, because man experiences, strictly speaking, only his own individual consciousness or self-awareness, it is difficult to prove rigorously the existence or the nonexistence of some elements of awareness in animals other than man. However, to an evolutionist the most satisfactory statement, incomplete though it is, is that given by Fromm. In his words:

> Man has intelligence, like other animals, which permits him to use thought processes for the attainment of immediate, practical aims; but man has another mental quality which the animal lacks. He is aware of himself, of his past and of his future, which is death; of his smallness and powerlessness; he is aware of others as others — as friends, enemies, or as strangers. Man transcends all other life because he is, for the first time, life aware of itself. Man is in nature, subject to its dictates and accidents, yet he transcends nature because he lacks the unawareness which makes the animal a part of nature — as one with it. (E. Fromm, *The Heart of Man*. New York, Harper & Row 1964; Routledge 1965.)

Self-awareness is, then, one of the fundamental, possibly the most fundamental, characteristics of the human species. This characteristic is an evolutionary novelty; the biological species from which mankind has descended had only rudiments of self-awareness, or perhaps lacked it altogether. Self-awareness has, however, brought in its train sombre companions – fear, anxiety, and death-awareness. Menaker and Menaker have stated this discerningly:

> In the animal world from which we emerged, anxiety – or shall we say, fear – serves a survival function and appears as a warning of impending danger to be reacted to with the full panoply of automatic instinctual equipment which is available for the individual's survival. Human evolution poses a new problem, although it is motivated by the same survival need. It is obvious that the great human evolutionary acquisition, awareness, must add a special dimension to fear. (E. and W. Menaker, *Ego in Evolution*. New York, Grove Press 1965.)

Man is burdened with death-awareness. A being who knows that he will die arose from ancestors who did not know.

Hugh Montefiore, 'Medical Engineering' from *Can Man Survive?*, pp. 188ff

Most of us are very concerned about our bodies. 'No man', we read in Ephesians, 'has ever hated his own flesh, but nourishes it and cherishes it even as Christ also the Church.' For the most part we would agree. When we get ill, we want to get well again, and only fanatics like Christian Scientists refuse the benefits of medical knowledge and surgical skill.

My subject is medical engineering. The advances of knowledge and technology are perhaps more striking in the medical field than in any other; or rather, here they affect us most. Medicine has made and will continue to make tremendous strides through developing different forms of medication. Then there are all sorts of medical engineering – electrical, mechanical, chemical, biological, even genetic. Many of our medical inventions are amazing. It would be fascinating to describe and consider such inventions as the Amauroscope – a Mexican development that uses photo-cells to feed electrical signals to a blind person's brain, allowing him to distinguish hazy patterns of light and shade – or the use of pin-pricks on a blind man's skin to produce patterns of sensation, rather like a 625-line television set, which enable him as it were to 'see' with his skin. Or one might consider the 'pod', the invention of Israeli scientists, which is a remotely controlled capsule designed to zip through the larger tracts of the body (such as the major blood vessels) at a speed of one foot per second, by lashing its tail in response to a rapidly changing magnetic field arranged outside the body. Or one could describe the artificial hand which works by tapping the muscles of the other hand – I have seen a picture of such an artificial hand actually using a telephone receiver. Tokyo University is developing artificial fingers that can be programmed by computers to carry out quite complicated tasks, such as using chopsticks. Or take the exo-skeleton. Just step inside this hydraulically powered skeleton, and a weight of 1,500 lb will seem no heavier than 60 lb!

And so one could go on and on, with heart pacemakers, with artificial kidneys and hearts and lungs and even artificial glands gradually releasing their secretions over the years, with transplants and metal bone joints and even heart valves from pigs. All I have time for is to raise with you three different kinds of medical advance, and to ask what kind of questions they pose for Christian beliefs and for Christian behaviour, and what kind of modification of medical practice may become necessary if we think out their implications in Christian terms.

The three sets of medical problems that I want to take are these: drugs, transplants and the process of ageing.

First, drugs. There has recently been issued by the Office of Health Economics, a body set up by the Association of the British Pharmaceutical Industry, a report called 'Medicines in the 1990s'. Not all pharmacologists would agree with its predictions; but it can scarcely be doubted that the future will see a tremendous increase in the amount of medication taken. Many of us here today must have had many occasions to be grateful for the tablets we have been given; whether they be antibiotics against infection, or anti-histamines against allergies, or pills against depression, or perhaps tablets to make us sleep. Even though we've been ill, we've been able to cope. It is sometimes said that if the young are addicted to pot, then the middle-aged are addicted to barbiturates, but both parts of such a statement are gross exaggerations. Perhaps some of us do take too many pills, perhaps too many of us cannot get on without our tablets, but on the whole medication has been a huge blessing to a huge number of people.

But where should it stop? One forecast said that by 1990 every individual will be taking psychotropic (or mood-changing) drugs continuously or at intervals. Another forecast suggests that by then psychotropic drugs to blunt curiosity and initiative will be available. It is suggested that by 1990 the social use of drugs will have been accepted as legitimate. Today tea, coffee, alcohol and tobacco are, I suppose, the only social drugs which society as a whole allows. We regard these, if properly used, not only as socially acceptable but as legitimate ways of enhancing our enjoyment of life. We already know that tobacco and alcohol, although socially acceptable, can lead to terrible disasters; on the one hand to cancer and chronic bronchitis, and on the other hand to addiction and personal deterioration. It is thought that other drugs will be introduced which may take their place. It is forecast that drugs will be introduced that can improve our dexterity, or counter stress and fatigue, or enhance or modify the way in which we perceive the world around us. Drugs will also be used, it is said, for purely cosmetic purposes.

Now medication of this kind raises tremendous ethical issues. Is it right to take drugs which can remove all sense of stress? Let me put this in a stark form. Jesus in Gethsemane, we are told, was so stressed that he sweated blood. If he had one of these predicted drugs he would not have felt any feelings of stress at all. Would this have really been better? Does God create us all for happiness, and so is it right to try and remove all that conflicts with feelings of happiness? Or is it true, in a strange way, that through the experience of struggle and doubt and anxiety and pain we can gain a maturity of character that is denied to us in any other way? I am not of course suggesting that we ought to look for occasions of stress and hardship: I am suggesting that we should not seek to avoid them because, when and if they come, unpleasant though they be, they are means whereby we can develop our full maturity of character. Drugs which make life more pleasant, whether in terms of pure pleasure or in terms of release from stress, tend to remove us from reality. Drugs which modify our perception of life around us once again interfere with our encounter with reality. I would like to suggest to you that while medicine in general is a great blessing, those drugs which can remove us from reality end by dehumanizing us and prevent us from gaining our true maturity of character.

The second category of medical practice that I want to put before you concerns transplants. There are of course many parts of the human body that can be transplanted – and in some cases parts of other animals too. There are human skin transplants, kidney transplants, liver transplants, even heart transplants. (There have been for many years successful corneal transplants.) As most of you will know, the difficulty in grafting tissue is not the technical problem of the surgeons in carrying out the transplants, but the defence mechanism of the body itself which has evolved a most effective means of killing off all its intruders – so much so that, contrary to what most people believe, there is as yet no question of a totally successful heart transplant. The most that can be achieved is the slowing down and the control of 'rejection' by the body of the transplanted tissue. There are various theories about how the body defences can be overcome, and probably in the future some means of overcoming these defences will be achieved; but as yet there are only theories.

Now the question of heart and liver and kidney transplants raises a number of serious problems. The first of these concerns resources. Liver transplants and kidney transplants are carried out in Cambridge at Addenbrookes Hospital. No doubt if they were not, there would be resources released to give more intensive medical care than is at present available for other kinds of serious illness. Which is the more urgent? At least it is a question that Christians should ask. Or again, on what scale are transplants envisaged? There are over 15,000 deaths a year in this country among people with chronic heart diseases between the ages of 20 and 54 alone; even if there were sufficient hearts donated, think of the cost in terms of manpower and resources. Even now, to take kidney transplants, I am told that many of these with fresh kidneys, unless these come from a blood relative, die within a year. Are the resources well spent on such operations? These questions must be asked, and I do not pretend to know the answers. And this leads me to the more important question – what right have we to continue to live on borrowed organs? Transplants may suggest that this life is the only one; as though death were always a disaster. But on a Christian view this life, although vitally important, is but the prelude to the larger life that lies ahead of us all.

This brings me to my last point – ageing. I came across a case (not here), where a man had been admitted to a local hospital; and his wife, who loved him dearly, found that he was being kept alive artificially with a hopeless prognosis. So she gave instructions that the artificial life-savers be discontinued, and he died. The hospital made her sign a piece of paper before they were prepared to carry out her wishes. Surely she was right. Man is made in the image of God, and to live artificially as a cabbage is not to live in God's image; and in any case it is ahead of us that our future destiny lies. Life is not to be artificially retained at the cost of all human dignity, whether in a geriatric ward of a hospital or as a patient kept alive with a hopeless prognosis.

This leads us to the process of ageing. At present it is a secret. No one knows the cause of ageing. But although we may be able to live a few years longer than our ancestors, it is very rare even to make a century. Although we put a stop to disease, the cells of the body still grow old and die. Perhaps there is a kind of clock built into our cells; perhaps they deteriorate because they don't reproduce themselves quite accurately enough: they may suffer from a kind of faulty copying. Perhaps the trouble is not in the cells but in the molecules, as though the material itself, and not just the way it is organized, breaks down in the end. We don't know. But I expect we shall. If we could, should we reverse the process of ageing? Should we all remain – well, just at what age would you like to remain? 15? 21? 31? 61? It is certainly odd that just as we reach our highest potential in the 60s we start to decline so rapidly that people have to *retire* at their peak. This again seems to raise the most momentous theological questions. Is life an experience we should go through because out of this experience there can emerge a mature human being capable of going on to the next stage of development beyond this life? Or are we justified in stopping our development at any particular stage just as we like? Would it be better to remain in the flesh, or would it be far better, as St Paul said, to depart and be with Christ?

Drugs, transplants and ageing are only three parts of medical science. They raise the questions: what is man? what is his nature? what is his destiny? And let me remind you of our Christian insights. They are these. Man is here to develop his human maturity. Man's greatest endowment is that he is made in God's image, able to think and be responsible and to respond to people. Nothing must interfere with that. And Jesus Christ is the perfect man, at every point obedient to the will of his heavenly Father. And man's destiny is to share with Christ in the life of God and to enjoy him for ever.

STUDY TOPICS

1. Is man totally explainable in physico-chemical terms?
2. What would be the religious implications of the discovery of intelligent life on other worlds?
3. Can computers think?
4. What does the theologian have to say on 'spare-part' surgery?

BIBLIOGRAPHY

In addition to books recommended in the other sections concerned with modern science, G. Rattray Taylor, *The Biological Time-Bomb* (31) is very readable and stimulating.

Alister Hardy's set of two Gifford lectures, *The Living Stream* and *The Divine Flame* (Collins 1965) asks: Does biology give grounds for belief in a purpose in the evolutionary pattern?

Aldous Huxley's *Brave New World* (Chatto and Windus 1932, Penguin 1955) and *Brave New World Revisited* (Chatto and Windus 1959) consider the possible implications of biological research for society.

J. H. Hick, *Biology and the Soul* (Cambridge University Press 1972) should also be read.

FURTHER READING

Barbour, Ian G., *Issues in Science and Religion* (2).
Habgood, J., *Religion and Science* (12). Chapters 7, 12.
Monod, Jacques, *Chance and Necessity* (Collins 1972), especially the last three chapters. Advanced.
Montefiore, H., *Can Man Survive?* (26). Especially Part 1, 'The Question Mark: The End of Homo Sapiens?'

8
Modern Physics and Theology

INTRODUCTION

Our modern life is dominated by science, usually in the form of technology. We are not so concerned, usually, with the scientific theory lying behind the practice; but if we are to be concerned with the truth of things, or perhaps the truth behind things, then we must be concerned with the theoretical side of science, and not just remain content with accepting the good (or bad) things which scientific technology offers us. But the situation is complex, not only from the scientific side, where scientific thought is, like any other, in a state of constant change, as new developments take place and new explanations are put forward, but also from the theological side. Some theologians are of the opinion that theology has something to learn from the findings of science, while some refuse to admit this, suggesting that the two enterprises are quite separate, and ruling out of court any 'natural theology' of this kind (see section on 'Revelation'). The first extract, from Barbour's *Science and Religion*, sets the scene for us and gives us an overview of the various movements in theological thought which have influenced the relationship between science and religion in recent years.

Then accepting that it is at least worthwhile to attempt to find out what science has been saying about the world in which we find ourselves, we turn to what Harold K. Schilling calls 'post-modern physics' (attempting thereby to mark out the radically new discoveries of the twentieth century and its mind-stretching suggestions about the mysteries of matter). We ask what the main implications of modern physics might be. Clearly this is an extremely difficult task, but the subject is so important that some attempt has to be made.

We consider a number of fields where science may have implications for theology and/or philosophy, since it is clearly necessary to limit ourselves. They are:

the subatomic world, the question of time, the vast regions of the cosmos, the directionality of the total process.

One such field is the contribution science can make to the 'where-are-we-going' question. Does the history of the universe in general and the world in particular have an 'upward trend' or a 'direction' of development? God may be 'working his purpose out', but can we, with our very limited perspective, discern what it is? Since we can only see a small part of the totality of things and we are part of the thing under consideration (i.e. the universe), does this not affect our judgement and perception? Does the fact that the universe appears to be within the limits of time imply an element of purpose in its construction? If God created the universe did he create time as well? Time is a very complicated concept. (Before reading what Schilling has to say, it might be a useful exercise to attempt a definition of it.) What does it mean to a scientist to talk of immortality?

Schilling also provides food for thought on the question 'what is fundamental reality?' The old view of 'matter' as essentially substantial has now been superseded by the concept of 'matter-energy'. This raises the old question of 'is the most fundamental structure of Being, in a philosophical sense, non-material?' Perhaps the idealist philosophers were on the right track after all, although Barbour rejects this idea.

Another major field is the problem of man's relationship to the world about him. Does he control it or is it only given to him for a time as a steward who will one day have to account for his actions? This question has significant implications for technology and industry and those concerned with the world's environment ('the global village'). (See H. Montefiore's book *Can Man Survive?*) It is tempting to try to deal with nature piecemeal rather than to take it as a whole. This is also true on the larger scale of the universe. Both theology and philosophy have to come to terms with the 'givenness' of the universe (the fact that it *is*) as a whole rather than attempt to deal with its constituent parts.

It will become particularly clear here that as in all the other sections of this book, our purpose is to raise questions in the student's mind, and not to pretend that it is possible to frame answers which will be permanently acceptable. Theories change, viewpoints alter, and theologians and scientists themselves differ from time to time about the nature of their work and its significance. But the questions have got to be raised and discussed with as much knowledge and concern for the truth as possible on both sides. What is attempted here is a charting of some of the paths, along with suggestions as to what further areas might profitably be explored by the student.

Ian G. Barbour, *Science and Religion,** pp. 8–24

II *Three Ways of Isolating Science and Religion*

We have seen that in past centuries scientific and religious questions were often confused. On the one hand, literalists treated the Bible as a textbook in science. On the other, well-meaning scientists and theologians invoked the 'God of the gaps' to explain the scientifically unknown, while naturalists and modernists tried to base theology on the findings of science. It is not surprising that twentieth-century thinkers wanted to preserve the integrity of both science and religion, and took great pains to put up *No Trespassing* signs between them. . . . I shall summarize three movements which have contributed to this separation:

1. The neo-orthodox emphasis on *the distinctiveness of revelation*,
2. The existentialist insistence on *personal involvement* in religious questions,
3. The claim of analytical philosophers that scientific and religious languages *serve unrelated functions* in human life.

1. THE DISTINCTIVENESS OF GOD'S SELF-REVELATION

The dominant movement in Protestant thought between the two world wars was *neo-orthodoxy*, which sought to recover the Reformation emphasis on the centrality of Christ and the primacy of revelation, while fully accepting the results of modern biblical scholarship and scientific research. According to Karl Barth and his followers, God can be known *only as he has revealed himself* in Christ and is acknowledged in faith. No argument from the world, no attempted 'natural theology' can reach the transcendent God who in his freedom has disclosed himself in history – and not, except very ambiguously, in nature. . . . Religious faith depends entirely on divine initiative, not on human discovery of the kind by which science advances. The scientist is free to carry out his

* Edited by Ian G. Barbour. Copyright © 1968 by Ian G. Barbour. By permission of Harper & Row, Publishers, Inc., and SCM Press.

Modern Physics and Theology

work without interference from the theologian, and *vice versa*, since their methods and their subject matter are totally dissimilar. . . .

As an example of the neo-orthodox separation of religious from scientific questions, consider the presentation of the *doctrine of creation* given by Langdon Gilkey. . . . He asserts that the religious meaning of creation is on a totally different level from all scientific theories about cosmic or biological evolution. Science deals with finite causal relations within the temporal process. Religion deals with the meaning of our personal existence and the status and significance of the whole world process. Thus the doctrine of creation is not really about temporal origins in the past, but about the *basic relationship between God and the world in the present*. In Genesis these religious insights were expressed as a myth of primeval beginnings, employing the imagery of a prescientific cosmology. But the two main *religious* affirmations, which we can still accept, are about the fundamental character of God and the world: God is sovereign, transcendent and purposeful. . . . The world is orderly and essentially good. . . .

These assertions about God and the world are said to be the distinctive *theological* content of the idea of creation. The religious meaning can be separated from the ancient cosmology in which it was expressed. . . .

2. RELIGIOUS INVOLVEMENT vs. SCIENTIFIC OBJECTIVITY

Another movement which has contributed to the sharp separation of the spheres of science and religion in the twentieth century is *existentialism*. Here the contrast is based on the dichotomy between the realm of *personal selfhood*, which can be known only in subjective involvement, and the realm of *impersonal objects*, which is known in the objective detachment of the scientist. Common to all existentialist writings – whether atheistic or theistic – is the conviction that we can know authentic human existence only by being personally involved as unique individuals making free decisions. The meaning of man's life is found only in commitment and action, never in the spectatorial, rationalistic attitude of the scientist searching for abstract general concepts or universal laws. . . .

Rudolf Bultmann's version of Christian existentialism has had considerable influence since the Second World War. He maintains that God's activity cannot be described in the language of space and time as if it were on the same plane as natural occurrences. Moreover, he asserts, nature is known today to be a completely closed system of cause-and-effect laws. The Bible sometimes uses 'objective' language to speak of God's acts, but we can retain the original experiential meaning of such passages by translating them into *the language of man's self-understanding*, his hopes and fears, choices and actions. One must ask of any biblical assertion: What does it say about my personal existence and my relationship to God? The Christian message always refers to *new possibilities for my life* – decision, rebirth, the realization of my true being; it never refers to observable occurrences in the external world apart from my involvement. Religious faith brings a new self-understanding amid the anxieties and hopes of personal life – without conflicting with the scientific assumption that the world is law-abiding.

The doctrine of creation, as Bultmann interprets it, is not a statement about the origin of the universe, but a personal confession that '*the Lord is my Creator*'. It is not a description of purported past actions of God in space and time, but an acknowledgement of present dependence on God and a confession 'that I understand myself to be a creature which owes its existence to God'. . . . There is no 'God of the Gaps' here, because God acts in the realm of selfhood, not in the realm of nature. . . .

3. SCIENCE AND RELIGION AS UNRELATED LANGUAGES

In addition to the neo-orthodox emphasis on revelation and the existentialist emphasis on personal involvement, a third development has contributed to the sharp differentiation of science from religion: the school of *linguistic analysis* which is predominant among philosophers in England and America today. A generation ago, many philosophers endorsed logical positivism, which looked on scientific statements as the norm for all discourse and dismissed any statement not subject to empirical verification as 'meaningless'. Since World War II, however, it has been increasingly recognized that differing types of language serve differing functions not reducible to each other. Each area of discourse – artistic, moral, scientific, religious and so forth – reflects a distinctive interest and fulfils a distinctive purpose in human life. Science and religion are both legitimate enterprises, but they do totally different jobs.

Scientific language, according to these philosophers, is used primarily for prediction and control. A theory is a useful tool for summarizing data, correlating regularities in observable phenomena, and producing technological applications. Science asks carefully delimited questions of a specific and technical kind. Its conclusions must be testable by observations. We must not expect it to do jobs for which it was not designed, such as providing an overall world view, a philosophy of life, a metaphysical system, or a set of ethical norms. The scientist is no wiser than anyone else when he steps out of his laboratory and speculates beyond his strictly scientific work. . . .

The distinctive function of *religious language*, linguistic philosophers tell us, is to recommend a way of life, to elicit a set of attitudes, to acknowledge and encourage allegiance to particular moral principles. Religious statements also propose a characteristic self understanding, expressing and engendering certain attitudes toward human existence as well as commitments to patterns of action. Other statements express and evoke worship, and are used in the context of the worshipping community; or they may grow out of and perhaps lead to personal religious experience. Much of the recent philosophical discussion has dwelt on such functions of religious language as ethical dedication, self-commitment, and existential life-orientation. . . .

In summary, the combined effect of these three movements – neo-orthodoxy, existentialism, and language analysis – has been *to isolate science and religion* from each other. The distinctive features of religion – namely revelation, personal involvement, and endorsement of a way of life – are held to be absent from science. There can be no significant dialogue if there are no common interests and no points of contact between the fields. . . . All three movements discourage the construction of any general picture of reality and abandon the search for inclusive metaphysical categories. Science and religion are left each to its own specialized job, and each to accomplish its own purpose in its own way. There can be no conflict between them; but neither can there be fruitful communication.

III Some Areas of Recent Dialogue

1. METHODOLOGICAL PARALLELS

The contrast between the methods of the two fields has been questioned from both sides. Let us first note some recent *challenges to the positivist interpretation of science*. It has been pointed out that the actual practice of scientists is a much more human enterprise than the logician's idealized account had recognized. . . .

Both positivists and existentialists had accepted a dichotomy between the realm of personal involvement and the realm of objective detachment. By contrast, Polanyi devotes a major volume to *the personal role of the knower in science*. The scientists, he suggests, must exercise personal judgement in the assessment of evidence — for example, in the decision whether an unexplained discrepancy disproves a theory or can be set aside as an anomaly or attributed to chance variation. . . .

In this contribution to the present volume, C. A. Coulson holds that *the methods of science and religion have much in common*. On the one hand, science has its presuppositions, such as the orderliness and intelligibility of the universe; moreover the moral attitudes required by science are similar to the virtues enjoyed by religion, including humility, co-operation, universality, and integrity. Science advances by creative imagination, not by any mere collecting of facts. Conversely, religious inquiry should involve critical reflection on experience not unlike that which goes on in science. . . .

2. EVOLUTIONARY THEOLOGIES

Turning now from dialogue about method to dialogue about content, we find evolution prominent among the scientific discoveries in whose theological implications there is renewed interest. Consider first some of the themes of Whitehead's *process philosophy* which are reflected in Charles Birch's recent book (*Nature and God*, SCM Press) and his article reprinted here: very similar ideas were expressed by the Jesuit palaeontologist, Teilhard de Chardin:

(a) *Nature as a dynamic process.* The world is a process of becoming, always changing and developing, radically temporal in character. It is an incomplete cosmos still coming into being. Birch criticizes the prevalent deterministic and mechanistic view of nature, and affirms the presence of chance and indeterminacy. There is novelty, spontaneity, and risk in the history of nature. . . .

(b) *Continuity of the levels of reality.* Teilhard states that each level (matter, life, thought, society) has its roots in earlier levels and represents the flowering of what was potentially present all along. The higher is already in the lower in rudimentary form. There is no sharp line between the non living and the living; life is incipient in matter. Teilhard attaches great importance to the 'within of things' which finally developed into consciousness. In a similar vein, Birch (following Whitehead) considers even low-level organisms as centres of experience, though he attributes consciousness only to higher animals. He looks on 'matter' and 'mind' not as two entities or substances, but as different patterns of events in systems having many levels of organization: among simple organisms the patterns of 'mentality' are almost negligible. But in principle man is continuous with the rest of nature (rather than essentially discontinuous, as neo-orthodoxy and existentialism assume). . . .

(c) *The directionality of evolution.* Birch interprets the past as a slow development towards increasing freedom and awareness, but it has been a costly trial-and-error experiment. Evolution, he suggests, resembles a long and risky travail, not a simple and direct ascent. It involves both chance and order; it is a creative process, whereby the improbable becomes probable but not inevitable. Teilhard also mentions 'chance' and the 'groping' progress of evolution, but makes out a clearer directionality towards complexity and consciousness – a 'favoured axis' as he calls it in the article reprinted here. The universe is 'personalizing', and in its further social development personality will be enhanced and not submerged.

In contrast to neo-orthodoxy, Birch holds that these characteristics of the evolutionary process *are relevant to our understanding of God's relation to the world.* He is not proposing a natural theology; he is asking how the God known in the experience of forgiveness and grace is to be understood as Creator, and he proposes that the theologian must take evolutionary ideas about man and nature into account. He argues that creation is a slow and incomplete process, and that God respects the freedom of his creatures. He calls this 'a God of persuasion rather than coercion' who shares in the suffering of the world. Costly love, of which the cross is the supreme expression, is woven into the fabric of all existence. . . .

In Whiteheadian thought, the idea of creation takes the form of *continuing creativity.* Every event is looked on as the outcome of three factors: lawful past causes, God's influence, and the emerging entity's own action towards the future. Human experience is used as the clue for understanding the experience of all entities, though Whitehead recognizes that for low levels of existence the opportunity for novelty is vanishingly small. . . . Thus God acts along with other causes; we can never extricate his action from the complex of natural processes through which he works. Yet God makes a difference in events – not just in our attitude toward events as the existentialists and language analysts propose. God continues to be a source of order and novelty, but this function is not associated with a primeval beginning; it occurs throughout time, which may be infinite and without 'beginning'.

H. K. Schilling, *The New Consciousness in Science and Religion*

Directionality of Total Process, pp. 138–40

Nature is still in process of becoming. Indeed it seems to be a process more than a 'thing' or system of 'things'. That which exists is forever pregnant with possibilities for more complex existence. At any stage of its development physical reality is like a rose bud I once dreamed about, ready to unfold into a flower; then each petal somehow unfolded as though it were itself a bud becoming a new flower, and the first flower in this way became a multiple flower, and so on and on. What we have here is a vision of effluence, not of external sameness but of ever-increasing variety; from the simple to the complex and luxuriant, and from the inanimate to the organism that is self-conscious. This is why it is *creative* effluence.

For many men this vision of nature's remarkably innovating and ever-enriching effluence has led to a sense of a preferred direction, or even 'purpose' in the universe. Though science itself must eschew ideas of conscious purpose in subhuman nature, it nevertheless seems clear to numerous scientists that there *is* something systematic in the flow of its major events, a definite trend in the long-range sequence of emergences; namely, from a few levels of depths to many, from relatively undifferentiated uniformity to great qualitative variety and diversity, from the inert to the dynamically self-replicating, from insensitivity to high degrees of responsiveness to environment, from atomistic individualism to social existence and community. This trend would seem to be precisely the kind that would prevail if deliberate benevolent purpose were operative, for it follows an evident pattern of development, towards a richer, more unified and more meaningful existence. In this sense, and in terms of the 'highest' values we cherish today, the evolutionary trend must be regarded as 'upward', and it has persisted long enough – several billions of years – to justify the tentative conclusion that it is a permanent, basic feature of the universe. The many transient, short-range departures from it, that have often been 'downward', impoverishing or even destructive, have not cancelled out the unmistakable long-range 'gains'.

Without a truly cosmic perspective we are likely to get a distorted understanding of history. For there is a certain amount of tyranny in very short ranges of history, such as human history, which, as we have seen, is extremely short relative to cosmic history. It imposes foreshortened temporal perspectives that are debilitating and distorting in their effect upon human consciousness. A very short time view confines the imagination, dulls the sensitivities to, and inhibits the discernment of, long-range patterns of historical change. In the exceedingly restricted field of view that human history provides, major catastrophes, such as wars with their Hiroshimas, and Buchenwalds, always *seem* utterly devastating, seemingly negating any advances that may have preceded them and destroying any hope of genuine permanent advancement in the future. Worse than that, short-term history provides no way of checking on the accuracy of the 'momentary' impression of the state of affairs; and, of course, from a cosmic perspective human history can of itself provide no more than momentary impressions. To use an analogy from photography, short-range history yields only exceedingly short-exposure snapshots of the human scene, and these can tell us almost nothing of the direction of its movements. From a genuine 'snapshot' of a train one cannot tell whether it is standing still or moving forward or backward, whatever it may actually be doing at the time. Only a time exposure or a series of successive snapshots (as in moving pictures) allows one to conclude anything about the motion of the train. Only extended time, not local time, allows us to discern genuine trends and to distinguish between temporary losses or gains and long-range ones.

The more one thinks about this, the more conscious one becomes of a rather formidable mystery in the overall scheme of things, the *mystery of the 'upward' pressure of nature's creative effluence.*

Time's Relational Character, pp. 120–5

Temporality is so fundamental and obvious an aspect of human existence that the concept of time seems quite indispensable to any satisfactory description or interpretation of the world. There is, however, something so tantalizing, elusive, and baffling – and truly mysterious – about it that it has been the subject of much philosophic debate for ages, during which time no unanimity of opinion has been achieved as to its fundamental nature or its basic significance for the cosmos. In some cultures it is regarded as essentially cyclical, in others as linear; in some as bounded, in others as unbounded – without beginning or end.

There are, of course, various kinds of time, e.g. psychological, historical, physical time. Physical scientists deal with the kind they can measure with clocks, i.e. in terms of the uniformities of motion of, say, the earth or pendulums or atomic oscillators. This temporality is especially significant for our purposes, because it refers to that dimension of the actual world without which it seems impossible adequately to conceive or describe the phenomena of motion, change and becoming. This is physical time.

One of its features disclosed by post-modern science is that it is rather different from the way Newton conceived it to be, as set forth in his *Principia*: 'Absolute, true, and mathematical time, of itself, and from its own nature, flows equably and without regard to anything external, and by another name is called duration.' As discerned today it is not absolute but relational. Moreover, it has a unique relationship to space, which is also relational; and together they constitute an indissectable continuum, space-time, of which each is a component complementary to the other.

To say, from the viewpoint of physical science, that there is no separate or independent space or time but only the reality space-time is not to make a primarily philosophical assertion but rather a strictly scientific one, since it refers fundamentally not to metaphysical abstractions but to concrete things and events. What it says is that in general the timing of events calls for the use not only of clocks to measure time but also of rods to measure distance. One reason for this is that observed physical events always occur at a distance, near or far, from an observer. Since signals are transmitted not instantaneously but with finite velocities (e.g. with the speed of sound or light), the distances from the observed events and the observer must be taken into account. For example, to measure the time when a space ship is lost sight of behind the moon, one cannot simply tick off its disappearance and reappearance with some sort of stop watch but must allow for the time it takes the signals to traverse the distances from the moon to the observer. Thus space measurements become integrally a part of the measurement of time intervals, and *vice versa*.

Unfortunately – or fortunately – when such situations are analysed rigorously they are found to be much more complex than these simple considerations suggest. Thus if several observers were to measure a given time interval between two events they would in general get different results, depending upon their various positions and motions relative to the events. It turns out that the simplest way of resolving such perplexing complexities is that of Einstein's theory, in which time and space are regarded as constituting one integrated reality, space-time.

From this point of view the only way different observers can get the same result is for them to measure the combined 'space-time interval' between the events, rather than only the supposedly separate time and distance intervals. And that 'space-time interval' can be computed by a formula combining those separated intervals.

The Physical Content of Time, pp. 120–5

Not only, however, have our post-modern instruments and ideas opened our eyes to the world of extended time, but to the internal depths of local or momentary time. Moments of time once regarded as negligible in duration, and empty of content, are now seen to be temporal worlds of vast depth and dynamism. Certainly not long ago a second seemed to be a very small bit of time. Now it seems very large indeed, and we know it to be packed with huge amounts of activity (temporal reality), for instance in electronic computers that achieve in one second what large teams of human computers could achieve formerly in months or years. Consider also the incredibly many natural micro-events that normally occur within atoms in a small part of a second. Talk about millionths and even billionths of seconds is now commonplace, and we have a feeling of familiarity for the vast content that may be found within such short moments.

. . . . . .

Returning to extended, rather than local time, there is another sense in which post-modern science has given us a feeling for its depth, and this is related to the spatial immensity of the stellar universe. The fact that many stars are now known to be as far away as billions of light years has great significance for our consciousness of time. Were an informed latter-day (post-modern) psalmist to look at the nocturnal heavens, he would be aware of much more than were his ancient Hebrew predecessors. Not only would he see, as did they, the grandeur, beauty, and radiance of the celestial spectacle, its stately, uniform march across the sky, and its repetitive features from day to day and year to year, but he would be aware of seeing spread out before him a tremendous panorama of time and change – in a momentary view of much of cosmic history in its physical aspects. Of course, in his reflections upon the sight he would call upon the knowledge that has come to him by means of his remarkable instruments. What this would tell him is that when he looks *now* at the stars he sees them not as they are *now* but as they were when long ago they emitted the light that enters his eyes or instruments *now*. Seeing a star ten light-years away is seeing it as of ten years ago; seeing one a billion light-years distant is seeing it as of a billion years ago. Whether or not these stars are still there *now* the observer does not know, but he does know that they were there respectively ten and a billion years ago. What he sees for the most part, therefore, is exceedingly ancient history. This is indeed seeing time in depth – in this case, the depth of its long range extension. Here is direct evidence, and direct consciousness, of the immensity of the temporal extent of cosmic existence in its physical aspects. Here in one present *now* we become aware of the reality of a long sequence of myriads of *nows* scattered over the vast expanse of the past.

Awareness of the 'Nature' of Physical Reality, pp. 24–8

Clearly . . . our next subject must be man's radically new understanding of the basic nature of reality – here taken to be that which impresses itself upon the human consciousness coercively, which exists whether it is perceived or not and is not therefore merely imagined. Our question is: What is the fundamental character of reality so conceived? What has man learned recently about its basic structures, dimensions, and attributes? More especially, in this section we shall be concerned with that segment of reality which we come to know verifiably through the natural and social sciences, and which I shall designate as *physical reality*. And I begin with that component of it which is commonly called *matter*.

It would be virtually impossible to exaggerate how truly revolutionary man's contemporary scientific conception of matter is. Almost everything once said about it is now being denied. To illustrate, matter was assumed to consist of atoms that are unchangeable, indestructible, without internal 'parts' and to consist of primordial substances whose 'properties' are inherent and in no sense derivative, and in terms of which all the objective characteristics of the world may be explained. To ask what something *is* was to ask what it is made of fundamentally. Table salt, for example, was said to be that particular form of matter whose molecules consist of an atom of sodium and one of chlorine; and the atom of sodium *is* simply a bit of the cosmic stuff called sodium, and the atom of chlorine a bit of that called chlorine. Nothing more could or needed to be said, because nothing more simple or fundamental was known or, according to current thought, conceivable.

Now, however, we feel differently about all this, for matter has shown itself to have a remarkable hierarchical structure with levels and depths ... and atoms are by no means its most fundamental units. We now know that atoms are exceedingly complex, and dynamic rather than static, with both particle and wave properties. Contrary to earlier views, they do have internal structure and consist of much smaller entities, such as electrons, protons, neutrons, and still others, among which occur very strange happenings. Were we to ask what these subatomic entities are 'made of' we would be told that this sort of question has become inappropriate these days, since it represents a way of thinking that is no longer useful. As science has explored the micro-world within the atom it has not found there anything to which the traditional notion of substance might be applied usefully.

On the other hand these explorations have led to the remarkable insight that the most fundamental realities of matter, and more generally of physical reality, are relationships, processes, and events rather than bits of substance. From this point of view, to say what an electron or neutron *is* is to say what it is by virtue of its behaviour, and not of its material content. Thus, to be specific, an electron is conceived of as that micro-entity which behaves in certain specifiable ways in the presence of other entities; and similarly a proton or neutron is defined by a uniquely different behaviour pattern. It follows that its properties must be regarded not as intrinsic essences but as consequent characteristics deriving from relationships disclosed in its behaviour. Thus man has become keenly conscious that fundamentally *matter is relational*, much more like a delicate fabric of dynamic inter-relationships than an edifice of hard building blocks.

It is relationality that confers upon matter the exceedingly interesting qualities we shall look at next. For one thing, the nature of matter's internal relationships is such that the so-called 'elementary particles' as well as other 'parts' are *gregarious*, i.e. they display a tendency to aggregate or unite into larger and more complex structures. Thus protons and neutrons tend to join, producing atomic nuclei; these with electrons form atoms; atoms with atoms make molecules; molecules congregate producing matter in bulk, i.e. large objects, from crystals to rocks to mountains, plants, galaxies. There is then in our universe much coming together and sticking together – gregariousness.

Next, aside from mere joining together, there is also much building together, of the kind which in temporal perspective is seen to be *historically developmental and evolutionary*. According to the post-modern vision there has been an evolution not only of the biological species and of the geological features of the earth but also of inanimate matter itself. Long ago there existed only its elementary particles, or at most its simplest kind of atoms, those of hydrogen. The many species of other atoms and of molecules came on the scene later, and the combinations of molecules, such as crystals and rocks, rivers and oceans, planets and galaxies, still later. In other words, to begin with there were no complex structures of matter, and later there were. The dynamism of its relationality is such that matter displays remarkable developmental drives, so that matter itself may be said to be constructive and developmental – it builds.

Another important aspect of this relationality has come to light through the momentous discovery that matter is *transmutable* into energy and *vice versa*, and that therefore neither matter nor energy may be regarded as the completely autonomous eternal reality it was once thought to be. The two traditional conservation laws, one for matter and one for energy, have become one, for *matter-energy*, proclaiming that it is the single compound reality, matter-energy, that is conserved. How much of the matter-energy may in a given situation show up as matter or as energy will depend on the physical relationships prevailing at the time. It would seem that neither matter nor energy is 'the basic stuff' of physical reality. It is matter-energy that plays that fundamental role. Matter and energy are simply two different states of matter-energy, very much as water and ice are different states of the one substance, H_2O. Actually, then, what has been said thus far about the nature of matter applies as truly – and more fundamentally – to matter-energy. Matter itself is relational, gregarious, and developmental because this is the case for the more inclusive reality, matter-energy – and indeed for physical reality in general. Certainly the complex structures we have considered are structures not only of matter but of matter-energy.

Matter-energy also *creates* – *de novo or ex nihilo*. Not only does it build new structures out of older parts (when, for example, it builds molecules out of existing atoms or subsequently builds material structures out of those molecules), but it actually creates entities of a quite different kind, such as have no pre-existing parts in the usual sense. These are the qualities that characterize the new structures as wholes and emerge as products of their systemic wholeness and holistic (whole-istic) drives. Thus when material objects (matter in bulk) appeared on the scene there emerged with them a vast array of formerly non-existent qualities, such as solidity, fluidity, malleability, elasticity, temperature, colour, electrical conductivity, and magnetic polarity. These are physical realities as truly as the material objects whose attributes they are, though not of the kind that have 'parts'. Nor did they exist on earth prior to the genesis of matter in bulk or of complex physical systems, for individual molecules do not have such qualities. There is no such thing as a hot or cold molecule, or a malleable one, or an electrically conducting one; there never was. Such attributes are exhibited by systemic wholes only, not by individual parts or constituents.

Nature as a Source of Insight for Faith, pp. 223–5

To get down to specifics, I suggest that today the insights embodied in the following affirmations constitute powerful reasons for confidently accepting life and the world as basically meaningful and *for good*. They point to aspects of reality that are truly faith-generating for many men in our time. With these truths in their minds and hearts they can face the future, confident that the ground of being is *for* them, *not against* them. These insights are not, of course, specifically Christian, but this simply means that they are universally acknowledged aspects of the way of things. The first is that *the observable events of the world are understandable to a large extent in terms of cause-and-effect relationships (laws of nature) among its constituent entities*. Second, *much of nature*, including man and his social structures, *is not only explicable but predictable and manageable to a large extent*. It can be changed by man to improve himself and his environment for good, and thus to make life more abundant. Third, *nature itself exhibits patterns of change for good*, aside from those man imposes upon it. There are at least two of these: the universal long-range process of evolution and the shorter-range processes that bring new life out of wreckage in particular situations. Fourth, *nature is creatively and innovatively effluent, so that much change is brought about through the emergence from time to time of genuine novelty*. Fifth, *the morality of nature* is characterized to a remarkable degree by constructive, *symbiotic co-operation and mutual aid*. It was formerly thought that evolution of the biological species was achieved mainly in blood and gore, by sabre-tooth and claw, i.e. by survival of the fittest in destructive competition. More recently, however, biology has been accumulating evidence that this has been greatly exaggerated. All of these propositions refer, I submit, to faith-generating aspects of reality; and today we not only *think* them, but *intuit* and *feel* them as well.

These pattern-aspects of nature are widely held to signify that nature is hospitable to human inquiry and control, rather than forbidding or inimical; that it is dependable and comprehensible in large measure, not haphazard or rationally opaque; and that it is both transformable and itself dynamically creative, rather than intractable and statically sterile. To recognize and say this is to express a powerful faith, a faith that removes much of the fear and dread of nature that dominated men for so long a time. If anything is to be feared, this faith says, it is our ignorance of nature, our high-handed interventions in it, and the evil uses to which we may put our knowledge of it. As far as nature itself is concerned, the more we learn about it, the less we need fear it, and the more we can trust it and enter with joyous expectancy into its life and further development. In his relations with nature man has therefore much solid ground to stand on; he can be sure it will yield to his desire to transform it for better and will support him as he commits himself to living the good life – though he realizes that this support is by no means unequivocal or completely at his command.

This, then is the aspect of faith that comes out of man's natural experience and the insights of science. Often this is regarded as a faith in its own right, called the 'scientific' or 'humanistic' faith. I can see no objection to this. It certainly is a potent faith, and it is not in principle inimical to biblical faith. It becomes so only if it claims ultimacy for itself, by denying what biblical faith affirms, that the range of reality extends beyond nature and man and that *the ultimate Source, Guide and Goal of nature, in all its scientifically discernible levels, and aspects, is creating and redeeming God. Without this latter* (sixth) *affirmation, faith remains secular* and rests, legitimately as such, only on nature and man taken as gods. With it, faith becomes religious and rests upon the ultimate creative principle or reality that transcends nature and man, and is taken as God. As biblical faith sees it, this sixth interpretative affirmation, about God acting creatively in nature, does not in any way contradict the factual affirmation – embodied in the first five and made by secular faith – that nature is self-consistent (though not self-sufficient), creatively effluent causal system, the operation of which can be understood (scientifically) in terms of the laws of nature. Indeed, biblical faith in its contemporary interpretive modes regards all six affirmations, and still others like them, to be mutually consistent and quite necessary to an adequate expression of the faith in our time.

I. G. Barbour, *Issues in Science & Religion**

The Heisenberg Principle and the Wave-Particle Dualism, pp. 279ff

Instead of exact values for predictions, quantum theory can give only probabilities, but the magnitude of the resulting uncertainty varies greatly. It can be shown from the postulates of quantum theory, and has been confirmed experimentally, that certain pairs of variables are related to each other in a peculiar way; the more accurately one of the quantities is known, the less accurately the other quantity is predictable. For example, the more accurately the position of an electron is measured in an experimental arrangement, the greater is the uncertainty in any prediction of its velocity. This is the famous *Heisenberg Uncertainty Principle* or *Principle of Indeterminacy*.

. . . . . .

The Principle of Complementarity

The wave-particle dualism of electrons in the above experiment (described by Barbour) is a feature of other entities also. Light in some situations (for example, interference effects) behaves as a wave, in others (for example, photoelectric effects) as a particle. Bohr used the word 'complementarity' to refer to such sharply contrasting concepts, of which he writes:

> However far the phenomena transcend the scope of classical physical explanation, the account of all evidence must be expressed in classical terms. The argument is simply that by the word 'experiment' we refer to a situation where we can tell others what we have done. . . . This implies the impossibility of any sharp separation between the behaviour of atomic objects and the interaction with the measuring instruments which serve to define the conditions under which the phenomena appear. Any attempt of subdividing the phenomena will demand a change in the experimental arrangement, introducing new possibilities of interaction between objects and measuring instruments which in principle cannot be controlled. Consequently, evidence obtained within a single picture must be regarded as *complementary* in the sense that only the totality of the phenomena exhausts the possible information about the objects! (Niels Bohr,

---

* © 1966. Reprinted by permission of Prentice-Hall, Inc., Englewood Cliffs, N.J., and SCM Press.

Atomic Physics and Human Knowledge, (New York, Wiley 1958), p. 39.)

Bohr's rather complex argument can be separated into the following points:

1. We cannot avoid the use of conventional concepts in describing the *experiment*, which employs apparatus and observations in space and time.

2. No sharp line can be drawn between the *process of observation* and what is observed; thus conventional concepts inevitably enter our attempts to picture what is going on in the atomic world. Moreover, the process of observation influences what is observed, so we cannot form a picture of the atom-in-itself apart from the total experimental situation. No clear line can be drawn between subject and object; various lines can be drawn for purposes of analysis, yielding alternative representations. We are actors rather than spectators, and we freely choose the experimental arrangement we will employ.

3. Familiar concepts, such as wave and particle, are inescapable and useful in referring to the atomic world, but we have to *use different models* in different experimental situations. Their alternate use is 'complementary' rather than contradictory, since they do not occur in the same experimental situation.

4. We cannot make from conventional concepts a unified image of the atomic world, because of *the limitations of such concepts* when applied in a new range of dimensions.

Conclusions: On Implications of Physics, pp. 314–16

We have suggested that modern physics has important implications for epistemology, but that its implications for metaphysics are more modest. Let us summarize first its *epistemological significance*. A recurrent theme has been the involvement of the observer in the results of observation. Another striking featue is the symbolic nature of the concepts used and the absence of visualizable models. A theory is no longer taken to be a literal representation, as in naive realism. Because the connection between theory and experiment is very indirect, it is understandable that some physicists, stressing the theoretical and mathematical side, have found encouragement for philosophical idealism; whereas others, stressing the empirical side, have concluded that theories are only useful fictions for co-ordinating observations. The limitations of theoretical concepts are dramatized in the Complementary Principle. We maintained, however, that the principle does not lead to positivism, and that its application to problems outside physics sometimes hinders the search for coherent interpretations. The principle is nevertheless a valuable reminder of the partial character of human knowledge and the inadequacy of our models. In the critical realism which we have defended, theories are acknowledged to be highly abstract and symbolic, but are taken to be attempts to represent the structure of nature.

Concerning metaphysical implications, we have taken issue with some of the more far-reaching claims made for quantum physics. We rejected arguments for idealism based on the role of the observer, the prominence of mathematics, and the new view of matter. Probability-waves may be less 'substantial' than billiard-ball atoms, but the new atom is no more 'mental' or 'spiritual' than the old. If science is indeed selective and its concepts limited, it would be as dubious to attempt to build a metaphysics of idealism on modern physics as it was to build a metaphysics of materialism on classical physics. We also maintained that the attempt to found a concept of human freedom on atomic indeterminacy is as guilty of reductionism as was the earlier denial of freedom on the basis of classical physics. Such metaphysical claims for quantum theory seem unwarranted.

Yet we submit that contemporary physics does contribute to *a new view of nature*. One should not expect that the metaphysical categories in which such a view is expressed will be direct conclusions from the scientific data of any one field, but rather that such categories will be relevant to the coherent interpretation of theories from various fields of inquiry. Among the ideas put forward tentatively in this chapter is the thesis that *'the whole is more than the sum of its parts'*. As against reductionism, which seeks to explain the activity of complex entities in terms of the laws of their components, we have maintained that higher organizational levels involve distinctive patterns of behaviour. The Pauli Exclusion Principle which links physics to chemistry – but which cannot be derived from the laws of single particles – was offered as an illustration of this thesis.

It was also proposed that *alternative potentialities* exist for individual events. We urged, in accordance with critical realism, that the Heisenberg Principle is an indication of objective indeterminacy in nature rather than the subjective uncertainty of human ignorance. In both quantum physics and relativity, *time* is a more constitutive aspect of reality than in the classical representation. It was suggested, however, that human freedom must be approached through the distinctive experience of the self in decision, for which no model taken from physics is satisfactory. Freedom and indeterminacy thus occur at very different levels, but both exhibit the novelty and openness of the world. On this reading, physics makes only a modest contribution to an inclusive view of reality; but this is perhaps all that should be expected from a field that studies inanimate objects at the lower levels of existence. It is at least clear that physics can no longer be the chief witness called on behalf of reductionism or determinism.

STUDY TOPICS

1. Are theology and science, considered as endeavours of the human mind, entirely parallel and distinct from each other?
2. If one theologian says that the purpose of God is visible in the universe, is he saying something about the universe, or merely something about the particular interpretation which some people put on the universe? Does the scientist have anything distinctive to offer here?
3. Man is involved in his own experiments, the scientist is part of the process of observation. Does this have any significance for the status of scientific knowledge?
4. What is meant by the word 'time'? What do you understand by the expression 'eternal life' – is it in any way self-contradictory?

BIBLIOGRAPHY

The range of books on this subject is, of course, enormous, and the reader merely has to scan the shelves of his local public library for his appetite to be whetted. But certain recommendations should obviously be made. The list here given mentions merely those books which have been found particularly helpful.

Basic books from which extracts have been drawn are: Ian G. Barbour, *Issues in Science and Religion* (2), Ian G. Barbour, ed., *Science and Religion* (3), and Harold K. Schilling, *The New Consciousness in Science and Religion* (29). These three books are of fundamental importance for the subject under discussion.

FURTHER READING

Coleman, J. A., *Relativity for the Layman*, New York, Mentor Books 1958, Macmillan 1959. A very readable attempt to grapple with the problems (mostly of mental adjustment) implied in Relativity theory. Very successful and enjoyable.
Gilkey, L. B., *Religion and the Scientific Future*. SCM Press 1970.
Habgood, J., *Religion and Science* (12).
Hoyle, F., *Astronomy Today*. Heinemann 1975. Lavishly illustrated.
Isaacs, A., *Introducing Science*. Penguin 1963. A good introduction, with an interesting section on the boundaries of knowledge.
Pyke, M., *The Boundaries of Science*. Penguin 1963. Stimulatingly written.

The following books in the Life Science Library, published by Time-Life Books, are beautifully produced and carefully edited, and form a splendid introduction to the current state of knowledge, expressed in an easily assimilable way:
Goudsmit, R., and Claiborne, S. A., *Time*. 1968.
Lapp, R. E., *Matter*. 1965.
Mark, H. F., *Giant Molecules*. 1967.
Pfeiffer, J. E., *The Cell*. 1965.
Rudolf, M., and Mueller, C. G., *Light and Vision*. 1968.
Wilson, M., *Energy*. 1963.
Wilson, J. R., *The Mind*. 1966.

Bibliography of Sources

(1) Baillie, D. M., *The Idea of Revelation in Recent Thought.* Columbia University Press 1956.

(2) Barbour, Ian G., *Issues in Science and Religion.* SCM Press 1966.

(3) Barbour, Ian G. ed., *Science and Religion.* SCM Press 1968.

(4) Barth, Karl, *Against the Stream.* SCM Press 1954.

(5) Brown, Colin, *Philosophy and the Christian Faith.* Tyndale Press 1973.

(6) Coulson, C. A., *Science and Christian Belief.* Oxford University Press 1955.

(7) Dobzhansky, T., *The Biology of Ultimate Concern.* Collins Fontana 1971.

(8) Donovan, Peter, *Religious Language.* Sheldon Press 1976.

(9) Farmer, H. H., *The World and God.* Nisbet 1935 and Collins Fontana 1963.

(10) Flew, A., *God and Philosophy.* Hutchinson 1974.

(11) Flew, A. G. N., and MacIntyre, A., *New Essays in Philosophical Theology.* SCM Press 1969.

(12) Habgood, J., *Religion and Science.* Hodder and Stoughton 1972.

(13) Hebblethwaite, Brian, *Evil, Suffering, and Religion.* Sheldon Press 1976.

(14) Hick, J. H., *Evil and the God of Love.* Collins Fontana 1968.

(15) Hick, J. H., *Philosophy of Religion.* Prentice-Hall 1973.

(16) Hull, John M., *Sense and Nonsense about God* (CEM Senior Study Series). SCM Press 1974.

(17) James, William, *The Varieties of Religious Experience.* Collins Fontana 1974.

(18) Jurgens, W. A., *The Faith of the Early Fathers.* Liturgical Press 1970.

(19) Keller, E. and M.-L., *Miracles in Dispute.* SCM Press 1969.

(20) Lewis, C. S., *Miracles*. Collins Fontana 1974.
(21) Lewis, H. D., *Teach Yourself the Philosophy of Religion*. English Universities Press 1965.
(22) Mackie, J. L., 'Evil and Omnipotence' (*Mind*, April 1955).
(23) Macquarrie, John, *Principles of Christian Theology*. SCM Press 1966.
(24) McPherson, Thomas, *Philosophy and Religious Belief*. Hutchinson 1974
(25) Mitchell, B., ed., *Philosophy of Religion*. Oxford University Press 1971.
(26) Montefiore, H., *Can Man Survive?* Collins Fontana 1971.
(27) Peacocke, A. R., *Science and the Christian Experiment*. Oxford University Press 1955.
(28) Russell, B., *Why I am not a Christian*. Unwin Books.
(29) Schilling, H. K., *The New Consciousness in Science and Religion*. SCM Press 1973.
(30) Smart, N., *Philosophers and Religious Truth*. SCM 1969.
(31) Taylor, G. R., *The Biological Time-Bomb*. Thames and Hudson Ltd 1968.
(32) Vidler, A. R., ed., *Soundings*. Cambridge University Press 1966.
(33) Wollheim, R., ed., *Hume on Religion*. Fontana Library of Theology & Philosophy 1966.

Index of Authors

Where appropriate the original source (with editor) precedes the author's extract. Numbers in brackets indicate sources; see Bibliography, pp. 229–30.

BAILLIE, D. M.
The Idea of Revelation in Recent Thought (1)
    The Good News   44
    The Mighty Acts of God, Event and Interpretation   45

BARBOUR, I. G.
Issues in Science and Religion (2)
    Scientific Presuppositions   146
    Theological Issues in Evolution   169
    Conclusions: On Man and Nature   192
    The Heisenberg Principle and the Wave-Particle Dualism   224
    The Principle of Complementarity   224
    Conclusions: On Implications of Physics   225
Science and Religion (ed. Barbour, I. G.) (3)
    Three Ways of Isolating Science and Religion   209

BARTH, K.
Against the Stream (4)
    The Christian Understanding of Revelation   47

BRAITHWAITE, R. B.
Philosophy of Religion (ed. Mitchell, B.) (25)
    An Empiricist's View of the Nature of Religious Belief   25

BROWN, C.
Philosophy and the Christian Faith (5)
    Natural Theology   40
    Revelation and History   63

COULSON, C. A.
Science and Christian Belief (6)
    Scientific Method   141

Index of Authors

DOBZHANSKY, T.
The Biology of Ultimate Concern (7)
   Self Awareness and Death Awareness   198

DONOVAN, P.
Religious Language (8)
   Ian Ramsey on Religious Language   15
   The Bible as Authoritative Religious Language   28
   Getting at the Truth in Religion   31
   On Not Having the Last Word   32

FARMER, H. H.
The World and God (9)
   Miracles   128

FLEW, A.
God and Philosophy (10)
   Religious Experience   55

New Essays in Philosophical Theology
(ed. Flew, A. G. N. and MacIntyre, A.) (11)
   Theology and Falsification – The Gardener   8
   Theology and Falsification – The Problem of Evil   90

GILKEY, L.
Science and Religion (ed. Barbour, I. G.) (3)
   What the Idea of Creation is About   163

HABGOOD, J.
Religion and Science (12)
   Nothing but Apes?   156

HEBBLETHWAITE, B.
Evil, Suffering and Religion (13)
   Coping with evil and explaining evil   99
   Heaven and Hell   100

HICK, J. H.
Evil and the God of Love (14)
   Augustine   95

Index of Authors

Irenaeus	96
The Traditional Freewill Defence	96

Philosophy of Religion (15)

The Doctrine of Analogy (Aquinas)	9
Religious Statements as Symbolic (Paul Tillich)	13
The Road	34
The Propositional View of Revelation and Faith	67
A 'Non-Propositional' View of Revelation and Faith	69
A Corresponding View of the Bible and Theological Thinking	71
Grounds for Disbelief in God	87

HULL, John M.
Sense and Nonsense about God (16)

Nonsense: Meaning: God	3
Some More Replies	19
The Uses of Language	23

HUME, D.
Hume on Religion (ed. Wollheim, R.) (33)

Dialogues Concerning Natural Religion	85
An Enquiry Concerning Human Understanding	109

JAMES, W.
The Varieties of Religious Experience (17)

Mysticism	54

KELLER, E. & M.-L.
Miracles in Dispute (19)

Miracles in Reality	136

LEWIS, C. S.
Miracles (20) — 135

LEWIS, H. D.
Teach Yourself the Philosophy of Religion (21)

The Problem of Evil	86
Some Outstanding Problems	125

MACKIE, J. L.
Mind (April, 1955). (22)

Evil and Omnipotence	95

Index of Authors

MACQUARRIE, J.
Principles of Christian Theology (23)
    A General Description of Revelation   73
    Revelation and the Modes of Thinking and Knowing   76
    A Further Scrutiny of Revelation   80
    Natural Evil   97
    Miracles   131

McPHERSON, T.
Philosophy and Religious Belief (24)
    Miracles   121

MITCHELL, B.
New Essays in Philosophical Theology
(ed. Flew, A. G. N. and MacIntyre, A.) (11)
    The Stranger   33

MONTEFIORE, H.
Can Man Survive? (26)
    Medical Engineering   201

NOWELL-SMITH, P.
New Essays in Philosophical Theology
(ed. Flew, A. G. N. and MacIntyre, A.) (11)
    Miracles   106

ORIGEN
The Faith of the Early Fathers (ed. Jurgens, W. A.) (18)
    De Principiis   39

PEACOCKE, A. R.
Truth for the Scientist (Broadcast Talk)   148
Science and the Christian Experiment (27)
    Scientific Presuppositions   149

RUSSELL, B.
Why I am not a Christian (28)
    Has Religion Made Useful Contributions to Civilisation?   86

SCHILLING, H. K.
The New Consciousness in Science and Religion (29)
    The Problem of Evil   91
    Directionality of Total Process   215

Index of Authors

Time's Relational Character	216
The Physical Content of Time	218
Awareness of the 'Nature' of Physical Reality	219
Nature as a Source of Insight for Faith	222

SMART, N.
Philosophers and Religious Truth (30)

F. R. Tennant and the Problem of Evil	93
Hume on Miracles	112

ST CYRIL OF JERUSALEM
The Faith of the Early Fathers (ed. Jurgens, W. A.) (18)

Catechetical Lectures	40

TAYLOR, G. R.
The Biological Time-Bomb (31)

Where are the Biologists Taking Us?	181
The Biological Breakthrough	183
Who Am I?	186
Life and Death	189

WOODS, G. F.
Soundings (ed. Vidler, A. R.) (32)

The Idea of the Transcendent	11